A Certain Difficulty of Being

A Certain Difficulty of Being

Essays on the Quebec Novel

ANTHONY PURDY

McGill-Queen's University Press
Montreal & Kingston · London · Buffalo

For my mother, Muriel Purdy
In memory of my father, George Purdy

©McGill-Queen's University Press 1990
ISBN 0-7735-0770-1

Legal deposit second quarter 1990
Bibliothèque nationale du Québec

Printed in Canada on acid-free paper

Canadian Cataloguing in Publication Data

Purdy, Anthony George, 1949–
A certain difficulty of being: essays on
the Quebec novel
Includes index.
Bibliography: p.
ISBN 0-7735-0770-1
1. Canadian fiction (French)—Quebec (Province)—
History and criticism. 2. Canadian fiction (French)—
20th century —History and criticism.
I. Title.
PS8199.5.Q8P87 1990 C843´.509714 C90-090129-2

The typeface used in the text is ITC Garamond®
Light with old style figures from the Adobe
Garamond Expert Collection® set by the
Instructional Communications Centre
at McGill University.

Contents

Acknowledgments

This book has been published with the help of a grant from the Canadian Federation for the Humanities, using funds provided by the Social Sciences and Humanities Research Council of Canada. I wish to thank the federation and the members of its publications committee for their support and the two anonymous readers who reported on the manuscript for their comments, suggestions, and encouragement.

Parts of chapter 1 and chapter 3 were originally conceived for papers given in French at conferences organized, respectively, by the Research Institute for Comparative Literature at the University of Alberta in November 1987 and by the Modern Language Association of America in San Francisco in December of the same year. An early version of chapter 4 appeared in *Dalhousie French Studies;* it has since been enlarged and considerably revised. A French version of chapter 2 was published in *Voix et images,* as was some of the material used in chapter 5. The essays printed here rework and expand upon the original material and introduce significant modifications in the arguments. As for my ideas on Aquin as an essayist, which account for a part of chapter 5, I made earlier attempts to formulate them in an article in *The French Review* as well as in the introduction to *Writing Quebec: Selected Essays by Hubert Aquin,* published by the University of Alberta Press. If they are rehearsed again in this volume, it is in a different context and for a different purpose.

The book has grown into what it is over a number of years of

reading and teaching the Quebec novel. My greatest debt is undoubtedly to my students at the University of Alberta who, between 1981
and 1986, participated in various ways in the thinking through of most
of the problems I raise here. This is very much the book of the
course. A sabbatical leave granted by the University of Alberta in
1987–88 allowed me to finally get down to the writing.

Foreword

Peter Brooks, in an illuminating discussion of plots and the ordering of stories, describes narrative as an unpacking of metaphor, an acting out of its implications (Brooks 1984, 26). In the pages which follow I also shall be engaged in unpacking a central metaphor – that of the Quebec novel's "difficulty of being." In a different way in each chapter, I shall trace the various discontinuities, ambiguities, and conflicts which surface upon close examination of how specific novels go about the process of "making sense," of grappling with the problems of pattern, shape, and form in a world which, for the most part, has lost its sense of divine order and finds itself adrift on the tide of human history. (I hope it goes without saying that I am using the expression *difficulty of being* neither pejoratively nor polemically, in much the same way as the sadly missed André Belleau used terms such as "conflict of codes" and "marginalization," insisting they carried no negative connotations for him.[1])

The subtitle of this book is "Essays on the Quebec Novel." I use the term essay deliberately, in Holdheim's sense of cognition in progress; rather than a finished product to be served up by the author and digested by the reader, the essay represents a process of getting to know. In this sense, the hermeneutic enterprise is to be seen as an exploration or, in Holdheim's somewhat intimidating phrase, "interpretation potentiated by its own self-reflection – an ongoing elucidation of the way understanding actually comes about" (Holdheim 1984,

11–12). Which is why the reader will find here no single methodology or all-embracing system. In affirming the primacy of text over method, these essays seek not to confirm or invalidate a theory but to understand how these particular novels – in their individuality, their differences, and their changing socio-historical contexts – function, how they achieve or fail to achieve what they set out to do. This does not mean that the essays eschew theory but, simply, that, while they draw on a fairly wide range of theoretical writings with which they attempt to engage and, whenever necessary, take issue, they reflect no systematic attempt to formulate a unified position either on narrative in general or on the Quebec novel in particular. Thus, while each essay strives to situate its method in relation to other possible approaches, this is always a function of specific problems encountered in reading a particular text. The point of view may, as Saussure so aptly reminds us, create the object of study, but it is itself suggested by the material to be explained.

In keeping with recent tendencies in narratology, the essays take their bearings from insights gleaned from earlier, more formalist studies in order to go elsewhere. In this they are functional, contextual, and pragmatic; they situate narrative meaning (or, to use an expression favoured by both Ross Chambers and Gerald Prince,[2] narrative point) within the circuit of communication or exchange in which narrative occurs and which narrative in turn produces or modifies. Why, the essays ask, are the narrators of these novels telling the stories they tell and why do they not always succeed in what they apparently set out to do?

Such an approach necessarily involves an examination of the principle of "end-determination," of what Peter Brooks calls the *anticipation of retrospection*,[3] that is, the shaping of narrative by its ending or closure, which informs an entire modern narratological tradition from the Russian Formalists through to Kermode, Barthes, and Genette.[4] For while, as David Miller argues in an interesting book on the nineteenth-century novel, the assumption that "everything in a narrative exists in view of the hidden necessity determined by its final configuration of event and meaning" is powerful and illuminating, it does have its limitations: "Once the ending is enshrined as an all-embracing cause in which the elements of a narrative find their ultimate justification, it is difficult for analysis to assert anything short of total coherence. One is barred even from suspecting possible discontinuities between closure and the narrative movement preceding it, not to mention possible contradictions and ambiguities within closure itself" (Miller 1981, xiii). The danger, of course, is that once the principle of end-determination is enunciated, it tends to spread insidiously to critical practice and to the act of reading itself, as theory produces its own closure, generating pseudo-problems and pre-programmed "readings," and colouring methodological distinctions with a Manichaean hue. The remedy, as Miller suggests, lies in close attention to the texts themselves: "Since the trouble is specifically textual, there can be no shortcut through the detailed process of reading the texts" (xiv). Only in this way can we hope to avoid the radical oversimplifications and reductions which have been the bane of theory-directed criticism.

In chapter 1, then, I look at the kinds of discourse developed about the novel in some nineteenth-century novel prefaces. More particularly, I try to trace a topos of generic denegation – "This is not a novel" – and to relate that topos to a more general conflict of codes within the literary institution of the period. Chapter 2 is also concerned with the problem of genre. It discusses the uneasy and, one suspects, involuntary transition from epic to novel in Félix-Antoine Savard's *Menaud, maître-draveur*. Savard's text, I argue, is characterized by a generic indeterminacy which reflects a crisis of community and marks a shift to the "transcendental homelessness" with which Lukács identifies the novel form. Gabrielle Roy's *Bonheur d'occasion* gives rise, in chapter 3, to a discussion of the narrative problems involved when an outside observer tries to cross social boundaries in order to describe the everyday life of a working-class community. Comparing Roy's strategies with those George Orwell developed in the late thirties, I look at the thematic coherence of the critique of consumer capitalism contained in Roy's novel and the different ways in which she intervenes to mediate the relationship between her characters and the reader. Chapter 4 explores certain contradictions and epistemological uncertainties stemming from the use of a first-person, present-tense narrative in André Langevin's *Poussière sur la ville* and proposes a number of possible reading strategies which might be used to resolve (or, alternatively, not to resolve) the ambiguities generated by the form. From the question of narrativity and knowledge I pass, in chapter 5, to the problem of narratability and history, as it is raised in Hubert Aquin's *Prochain épisode*. Focusing on Aquin's critique of history as story (or anti-dialectical mythos) and on his analysis of cultural fatigue, the chapter discusses the stylistic implications of French Canada's historical difficulty of being and traces the complex relationship in the novel between narrative failure and the revolutionary politics of decolonization. Finally, in chapter 6, I analyse the way in which narrative voice functions in Anne Hébert's *Kamouraska* and touch on the current debate concerning the boundaries between modernism and postmodernism. Arguing against most accepted struc-

tural analyses of the novel, I contend that *Kamouraska* is perfectly
coherent and intelligible and only mildly subversive, insofar as its
stylistic excesses and narrative dislocations are all psychologically
motivated by the narrator's frame of mind, by her elaborate subterfuge
of hesitations, resistances, and projections.

R.D. Laing once wrote that there are not enough helpful books.
So let me say from the outset that I hope that this book may prove,
in the most modest of ways, a helpful one. Now I realize this may
seem a strange statement to make, a motherhood concept if ever
there was one, but not if one happens to believe that the main reason
there are not enough helpful books is that not enough writers –
especially, perhaps, of scholarly books – set out with that ambition;
in fact, to many minds, there is something vaguely improper about
scholarship that tries to be helpful, as though the imperatives of
"serious science" were somehow incompatible with the very notion
of "helping" (as in the vaguely supercilious way we speak of the
"helping professions"). Given the climate of research in the humanities
in the 1980s (and, one presumes, in the 1990s), to speak at all of
writing "helpful" books becomes, in however small a way, a political
gesture. I hope it will be read as such.

I also hope that this will be an interesting and engaging book,
since I believe these to be qualities that recent literary studies, in
their search for theoretical rigour, have on occasion been a little too
ready to sacrifice. I hasten to add that this should not be taken as
a condemnation of theory *per se,* but merely of sloppy or facile
theorizing. The line I wish to draw here is not between theory and
its rejection, but between its use and abuse, between theory as stim-
ulant and theory as analgesic. The "rush to the referent" which used
to characterize too much of our criticism has been replaced in certain
circles by a "rush to theory"; we do not spend enough time in literary
texts to get their measure; we do not, as Gaston Bachelard liked to
say, *live* in them, but pass from one to another, gathering quotes
much as bees collect pollen. The cross-fertilization can be exhilarating,
but all too often such busyness leaves us little time for thinking about
literature, and savouring it, for smelling the flowers so to speak. In
too many instances theory has become the crutch we reach for when
we are too tired to think, a mental grid which provides a semblance
of order, a lexicon which automatically generates "original" readings,
a rhetoric which produces the illusion of thought. At its best, theory
quickens our thinking and revitalizes debate; at its worst, it closes
our minds and drains our words of meaning.

It is perhaps symptomatic of the trials and tribulations of Canadian
criticism – of its own protracted difficulty of being – that the 1980s

have seen a groundswell of reaction against what is, in the name of "theory," disdainfully dismissed as "thematic" criticism. This occurs at precisely the same time as, elsewhere in the world, literary theorists have been making serious attempts to come to grips with the thorny problem of – that's right – thematics.[5] It would of course be unfair to see the recent contempt for thematic approaches simply as a phenomenon of fashion – though fashion, I suspect, is not the least factor in determining our critical tastes – just as it would be idle to lament the fact that Toronto is not Paris. Every institution (and literary criticism is most certainly an institution) must grow at its own pace according to its own internal dynamics and the dictates of the larger social and cultural context in which it is inserted. Purges are necessary when the system is sluggish and, although it might be thought unseemly to be seen chasing a bandwagon which has already disappeared from view, it must be borne in mind that, occasionally, such pursuit can lead to true dialectic, especially if we can manage not to lose sight of the fact that labels like "thematic" and "theoretical" are often simply academic shorthand for more or less complex positions and are not inevitably destined to degenerate into terms of ideological abuse.

This is not, however, a book about themes or thematics (though many of its insights, arguments, and conclusions are inevitably thematic in nature) and anyone looking here for a "death-of-theory" position will be disappointed. It is, in several different ways, a book about another notion much decried of late by those same "theoreticians" who deplore what they see as an endless diet of thematic readings. It is a book about *identity,* and I make no apologies for this since I believe that the best and most interesting literature to come out of Quebec has always been structured by ontological uncertainty, by that "certain difficulty of being" of which Fontenelle complained on his deathbed and which is at the very heart of what Miller calls the "narratable": "the instances of disequilibrium, suspense, and general insufficiency from which a given narrative appears to arise" (Miller 1981, ix).[6]

But why write a book in English about the Quebec novel? In the first place because there is still, despite the increased interest shown in Quebec literature of late, very little sustained criticism available in English. In fact, recent writing of any length and depth in English has been largely confined to two areas: feminism (and, more generally, women's writing studied as such) and comparative English-French studies. For the rest, as Philip Stratford pointed out not so long ago, English Canadians often know more about the literature of France than of Quebec (Stratford 1986, 3). In my own case, this was certainly true for a long time and quite possibly still is, though my situation in this respect is not exactly typical; for while my first encounters with Quebec literature took place fairly predictably in the context of university French courses, they were totally unmediated by any knowledge of the literature of English Canada. Since it is very likely that my sublime ignorance of the English-Canadian tradition at that time has had a lasting effect on the way I see my subject, it is probably worth taking the time to explain briefly the circumstances and to reflect upon their possible effects, if only in the guise of a *caveat lector.*

When I first came to Canada in 1973 I already held a degree in modern and medieval languages, so it was perfectly natural for me to extend my interest to the literature of Quebec. In this I was motivated not – as is presumably the case of most English Canadians who decide to explore the literature and culture of Quebec – by the desire to discover more about the "other side" of my national heritage but rather by those same obscure stirrings which had prompted me in earlier years to turn to foreign languages and literatures in pursuit of what J.P. Stern once called the "alien experience." For me, as I suspect for many others, the study of languages had been first and foremost a means of escape, a delightful excursion into other worlds and other lives. (As we see in the novels of John Le Carré, there is something vaguely disreputable about the linguist: the spy, the actor, and the student of languages – these are the habitual double agents of our time.) By the time I discovered the world of Quebec, my codes and habits as a reader were already, by and large, in place, and the horizon of expectation they provided was not in the least Canadian. I came to Quebec literature as a foreigner, an outsider. For someone living and working in Canada this position is not without disadvantages,[7] but it does have its compensations. Most significantly, it preserves me from the trap that even the best-intentioned of Canadian comparatists (and all English-Canadian students of Quebec are inevitably comparatists at some level of their being) find difficult to avoid, even when they are not ostensibly comparing. I am referring, of course, to the temptations of what Chantal de Grandpré has somewhat acerbically called the Canadianization of Quebec literature (de Grandpré 1985). Whatever assimilations and recuperations my essays ultimately practise, they are not those of Ronald Sutherland's "mainstreaming."[8]

A final remark is perhaps called for concerning the language of quotation, a question which has exercised me greatly during the preparation of my manuscript. On the one hand, I believe it is imperative that all quotation from primary sources be in the original French, not only because in many instances the kind of close analysis I practise here requires it but also because I am very conscious of wanting to maintain the essential foreignness of the "alien experience" I spoke of just now. I hope that those readers whose French is a little rusty will not be too inconvenienced by this, especially as I have chosen not to burden my text with English translations. On the other hand, I see no reason for slowing down the reading experience unduly and have therefore elected to use English for all quotation from secondary sources. Where references are given to the original French publication rather than to an English version, the translation is my own. This solution will not please everyone, but, then, no solution would.

A Certain Difficulty of Being

Saint-Denys Garneau nous a rendus conscients de notre difficulté d'être et de vivre en ce coin de pays qui est le nôtre et où l'homme n'est maître ni de soi, ni de sa terre, ni de sa langue, ni de sa religion, ni de ses dons les plus authentiques.

Anne Hébert

Le problème n'est pas d'écrire des histoires qui se passent au Canada, mais d'assumer pleinement et douloureusement toute la difficulté de son identité. Le Canada français, comme Fontenelle sur son lit de mort, ressent "une certaine difficulté d'être".

Hubert Aquin

CHAPTER ONE

"This is Not a Novel." The Rhetoric of Denial in Nineteenth-Century Quebec Novel Prefaces

Lorsqu'on fait un conte, c'est à quelqu'un qui l'écoute; et pour peu que le conte dure, il est rare que le conteur ne soit interrompu quelquefois par son auditeur. Voilà pourquoi j'ai introduit dans le récit qu'on va lire, et qui n'est pas un conte ou qui est un mauvais conte, si vous vous en doutez, un personnage qui fasse à peu près le rôle du lecteur, et je commence.   Diderot, "Ceci n'est pas un conte"

C'est icy un livre de bonne foy, lecteur.   Montaigne, *Essais*

Ceci (donc) n'aura pas été un livre.   Derrida, *La Dissémination*

The 26 June 1879 issue of *L'Opinion publique* contains the following good-humoured lament concerning the difficulties facing the would-be novelist in French Canada:

One needs ... an irresistible vocation to dare to write novels in Canada ... To win the untutored heart of a young girl; to focus the feelings of a wayward widow ... ; to conquer a mother-in-law; to obtain the hand of a princess ... what is all that compared to the writing of a Canadian novel! How many precautions, how much self-vigilance, what strictness in the treatment of character, what inner surveillance! I see only one way of getting round the problem: one would have to write a realistic novel, a true portrait of reality, everyday reality. Seeing itself in this newly placed mirror, our society would show indulgence for the errors of other societies; but woe betide the first author to hold up that mirror.

   Here is my much awaited conclusion: There is nothing easier in Canada than the not writing of novels. (Quoted in Dostaler 1977, 144–5.)

As the literary historians of the period have made us abundantly aware, the writer of this complaint is not overstating his case for satiric effect.[1] In fact, throughout the nineteenth century the novel is a beleaguered genre, constantly forced to defend itself against accusations of immorality, subversion, frivolity, escapism, lack of realism, realism, and, worst of all, naturalism – "that monstrous school," says Edmond Rousseau in his preface to *Les Exploits d'Iberville,* "of which Émile Zola is the pontiff and Jean Richepain the high priest" (Rousseau 1888). Small wonder, then, that faced with such hostility on the part of the shapers of public opinion, the novel is frequently ashamed to answer to its own name, preferring to pass itself off as something else. As Gilles Marcotte observed: "Thus was the novel born, in French Canada, in its own negation; it was not a welcome child" (Marcotte 1971, 12). In the following pages I will look at the kinds of discourse developed by the novelists themselves in the prefaces to their works and examine the rhetorical strategies on which they rely to defend themselves and their creations against actual or anticipated charges of un-Canadian activities.

I̶N A RECENT STUDY of what he calls the paratextual (or liminary) apparatus of works of literature, Gérard Genette argues that most of the themes and rhetorical strategies of the preface have been in place since the middle of the sixteenth century and that later variations derive not so much from any real evolution as from a series of selections made from within a repertoire that is much more stable than the writers of prefaces tend to think (Genette 1987, 152). Faced with a statement of this level of generality, it is reasonable to ask whether it is the fruit of long experience and careful research or whether, on the contrary, it stems from an *a priori* structuralist prejudice that would gladly do away with any complications of a diachronic nature. After all, Genette is a formalist and what he is offering us is essentially a typological essay. It is worth recalling that Henri Mitterand, speaking not only for himself but also for Claude Duchet, i.e., for two critics who are not known for their fear of history, once answered the question "Of what does the preface speak?" by stating that "it speaks *of literature,* and makes a universal statement about it. The minimal sentence which generates every preface is: *Literature is 'x'* or *is not 'x',* which comes to the same thing" (Mitterand 1980, 31). At the very least, Mitterand's claims should serve as a word of warning for one attempting to specify the distinctive features of the discourse developed by the nineteenth-century novel preface in Quebec. In this respect, the merit of Genette's study lies in the fact that it provides a descriptive norm against which to measure distinguishing deviations in the preface; armed with at least a rudimentary grasp of the rules of the genre, we can hope to avoid the trap of a facile historicism that might cause us to identify such and such a feature as being specific to such and such a context, when in reality what we are looking at is typical of the genre as a whole. For the moment, then, I am going to take Genette on faith and follow him in his analysis of what he calls "la préface auctoriale assomptive originale" (Genette 1987, 183), or the "original preface" for short; I will come back later to the questions of history and ideology that such an approach sets aside.

According to Genette, the cardinal function of the original preface is to ensure a correct reading for the text. This statement, however, incorporates two separate and distinct actions, the first of which is the necessary but insufficient condition of the second: the preface must first ensure a reading; it must then ensure that the reading is correct. These two goals determine two groups of functions, called by Genette "why" themes and "how" themes (themes which tell us *why* we should read this text and themes which tell us *how* to read it). If I start with the "how" themes, considering the preface as a set of directions on the proper use of the text, it is because they seem to be ideologically less loaded than the "why" themes.

The first of the "how" themes identified by Genette concerns the origins of the work, the circumstances and stages of its composition. Thus, in the opening chapter of *Les Anciens Canadiens* (1863), Aubert de Gaspé, Senior, tells a story to explain how, at the age of seventy-six, he crossed the Rubicon of writing. Almost thirty years earlier, his son had had the opposite problem: in the preface to *L'Influence d'un livre* (1837), generally considered to be the first French-Canadian novel,[2] de Gaspé, Junior, had told of a previous manuscript he had destroyed, thereby bestowing upon himself a certain respectability by creating a literary past for a young and apparently untried novelist – he was only twenty-three at the time – complete with apprenticeship and conversion: "Je croyais bien faire; mais je me suis aperçu que je ne faisais que reproduire de vieilles idées, et des sensations qui nous sont toutes connues. J'ai détruit mon manuscrit et j'ai cru voir un champ plus utile s'ouvrir devant moi. J'offre à mon pays le premier Roman de Moeurs canadien, et en le présentant à mes compatriotes je réclame leur indulgence à ce titre" (Aubert de Gaspé 1837, iii).

As can be seen in this example, any information offered about a work's genesis is closely linked to the author's image of his public; as he introduces himself to his reader, the author tries not only to guide the latter, but also to situate and define him (or her), often negatively, as in Antoine Gérin-Lajoie's foreword to his *Jean Rivard, le défricheur* (1874). "Jeunes et belles citadines qui ne rêvez que modes, bals et conquêtes amoureuses; jeunes élégants qui parcourez, joyeux et sans soucis, le cercle des plaisirs mondains, il va sans

dire que cette histoire n'est pas pour vous" (Gérin-Lajoie 1874, 1).[3]
This kind of address to a "frivolous reader"[4] can be associated with
a more general rhetoric that depends for its effect on a mechanism
of negative mediation and an appeal to a certain literary and moral
snobbery. If Joseph Doutre, in his preface to *Les Fiancés de 1812*
(1844), speaks only to the "few persons" who will understand him,
it is not so much in order to illustrate a situation which he deplores
as to transform it: "Telle est la généralité de ce préjugé en faveur
de l'étranger que, sur quarante milles hommes lettrés, on n'en trouvera
pas dix qui ne soient possédés de fureur pour les productions
européennes; et à peine en rencontrera-t-on mille qui liront avec
plaisir le travail d'un de leurs concitoyens, de quelque genre qu'il
soit" (Doutre 1844, v–vi). But the last word on this theme of the
happy few falls to Aubert de Gaspé, Senior, and it is a word that
Stendhal himself might have penned: "Ce livre ne sera ni trop bête,
ni trop spirituel. Trop bête! certes, un auteur doit se respecter tant
soit peu. Trop spirituel! il ne serait apprécié que des personnes qui
ont beaucoup d'esprit, et, sous un gouvernement constitutionnel, le
candidat préfère la quantité à la qualité" (Aubert de Gaspé 1899, 6).[5]

Perhaps the most important function of the original preface, according to Genette, is to set forth a declaration of authorial intent. Such
a function would embrace all the many claims made by nineteenth-
century novelists in their prefaces concerning the moral edification
of the reader. In his foreword to *Pour la patrie* (1895), for example,
Tardivel waxes lyrical about the mission of the writer as moral
gardener, who tends the spiritual values of his people and protects
the local flora from the proliferation of foreign weeds:

Dieu a planté dans le coeur de tout Canadien français patriote, "une fleur
d'espérance." C'est l'aspiration vers l'établissement, sur les bords du Saint-
Laurent, d'une Nouvelle-France dont la mission sera de continuer sur cette
terre d'Amérique l'oeuvre de civilisation chrétienne que la vieille France a
poursuivie avec tant de gloire pendant de si longs siècles. Cette aspiration
nationale, cette fleur d'espérance de tout un peuple, il lui faut une
atmosphère favorable pour se développer, pour prendre vigueur et produire
un fruit. J'écris ce livre pour contribuer, selon mes faibles moyens, à
l'assainissement de l'atmosphère qui entoure cette fleur précieuse; pour
détruire, si c'est possible, quelques-unes des mauvaises herbes qui menacent
de l'étouffer. (Tardivel 1975, 50–1)

The pontifications of the defenders of the moral ecosystem will
claim our attention later in this chapter; for the moment, I shall
look at another kind of declaration of intent which is common in

the prefaces to historical novels of the period and which calls for a new awareness of their past on the part of French Canadians. Thus, for example, Joseph Marmette in 1870 proposes to dramatize for popular consumption the "noble and glorious actions that every Canadian should know" (Marmette 1924, 18) and is seconded in this ambition by novelists like Honoré Beaugrand, Edmond Rousseau, and Napoléon Bourassa,[6] who are all anxious to "re-establish the truth" by making their compatriots aware of their own history. Joseph Doutre raises the same problem, but without claiming to have solved it: "L'historien sera quelquefois choqué du peu de respect que nous avons pour la vérité. Mais nous lui en voudrons de notre part pour ne nous avoir pas mieux instruits. Que connaît-on de l'histoire du Canada depuis l'avènement de la domination anglaise sur notre pays? Nous n'en avons aucun écrit, ou s'il en existe, ce sont tout au plus, quelques feuilles périodiques que le temps a détruites" (Doutre 1844, xix). Doutre's goal in writing *Les Fiancés de 1812* is thus to rouse French-Canadian literature from its slumbers in order to compensate for the lack of written history. This ambition will be widely echoed in other prefaces, like the one written by the publisher Cherrier for his 1853 edition of Chauveau's *Charles Guérin*. François-Benjamin Singer takes this argument a step further when, in the preface to his *Souvenirs d'un exilé canadien* (1871), he complains of his country's lack of history and adds that it is precisely for this reason that the Canadian novelist must have recourse to his imagination and to fiction.

The need felt by most novelists of the period to situate their novels in relation to some external reality, be it historical or contemporary, often leads to declarations concerning the last of the "how" themes I shall discuss here – the theme of genre. As Genette points out, the practitioners of well-established genres rarely feel it incumbent upon them to supply generic definitions, which become important only in times of transition or uncertainty. What is particularly interesting in the case of the nineteenth-century Quebec novel is not just that the authors seem to find generic definitions necessary, but that these definitions frequently take the form of generic denial (or denegation).[7] The 1874 preface to *Jean Rivard* is typical in that it presents all three of the "how" themes I have outlined – choice of public, declaration of intent, and definition of genre:

Le but de l'auteur était de faire connaître la vie et les travaux des défricheurs, et d'encourager notre jeunesse canadienne à se porter vers la carrière agricole, au lieu d'encombrer les professions d'avocat, de notaire, de médecin et les comptoirs des marchands, comme elle fait de plus en plus, au grand détriment de l'intérêt public et national. Afin d'en rendre la lecture moins aride, l'auteur crut devoir mêler à son récit certains détails de la vie intime et divers incidents qui ont eu l'effet de faire considérer ce récit comme une fiction. L'intention de l'auteur toutefois n'a jamais été de faire un roman, et il peut assurer que dans les faits et incidents qu'il raconte, il s'est appliqué avec un soin scrupuleux, au risque même d'ennuyer les lecteurs frivoles, à ne rien dire qui ne fût strictement conforme à la réalité. (Gérin-Lajoie 1874, vii-viii)

I shall come back to this question of denial in a moment, but first let us turn from the "how" themes to the "why."

According to Genette, the aim of the "why" theme is to persuade the reader of the text's importance or validity without alienating him (or her) by making extravagant claims about the author's abilities or credentials. This leads to a strategic and self-deprecating distinction between form and content: the book must be read for its subject, for the importance of what it deals with, even though its treatment might (inevitably) be found wanting (Genette 1987, 184). The subject is thus usually justified either in terms of its importance (and hence its utility) or in terms of its originality or novelty. The prefaces of the nineteenth-century Quebec novel rarely address the question of originality; on the other hand, they are full of protestations of virtue and high moral purpose. Javier Garcia-Mendez, in an excellent article, has grouped such examples into what he calls a topos of transformation: "Whether it be modifying the tendencies of the job market, purifying morals, defending the Catholic faith, re-establishing truth and defending the honour of compatriots in exile, reliving the heroism of the ancestral epic, transforming immediate historical circumstances, or promoting the emergence and development of a national literature – for the novelists of nineteenth-century Quebec, the goal of literary activity is always the modification of the world outside literature. The novel is constantly conceived in terms of its effect on the milieu; when they speak of the novel, these novelists are talking not about a book but about the influence of a book" (Garcia-Mendez 1983, 334).

However, if it is easy to agree with Garcia-Mendez concerning the emphasis placed in these prefaces on the pragmatic, extra-literary functions of the novel, the causal link he attempts to establish between this topos and two others – the lack of literary pretention and the plea for indulgence – would seem more problematic. Although these last two are undoubtedly constants of the literary preface, it is much less certain that the promotion of the pragmatic aspect of the text supposes, as Garcia-Mendez claims, "the subordination of the formal aspects of the message to the constraints of the communication situation" (Garcia-Mendez 1983, 338). In fact, as Genette's study shows, the emphasis placed on the importance of the subject and the corresponding de-emphasis of the way in which that subject is treated are part and parcel of a general rhetorical stance which is typical of any author's preface. To see these strategies as an indication of an ideological concern peculiar to the nineteenth-century Quebec novel would be to mistake their rhetorical nature and to fall into the trap of a naïve historicism. Moreover, the emphasis placed by Garcia-Mendez on these two topoi has the effect of displacing (or even suppressing) the ideological thrust of the topos of generic denial *(la dénégation du roman),* which is assimilated rather too rapidly to the other two.

According to Genette, the only claims that are discreet enough for an author to make in a preface about the treatment of the subject (as opposed to the merits of the subject *per se*) are those concerning the work's truthfulness, presumably because he believes truth to be a matter of conscience rather than talent. Garcia-Mendez has this kind of promise of veracity in mind when he invokes what he calls the true-to-life topos *(topos de la fidélité à la réalité),* a topos which is in evidence in Quebec as early as 1837: "J'ai décrit," says the author of *L'Influence d'un livre,* "les événemens tels qu'ils sont arrivés, m'en tenant presque toujours à la réalité, persuadé qu'elle doit toujours remporter l'avantage sur la fiction la mieux ourdie" (Aubert de Gaspé 1837, iv). The historical novels published later in the century exploit a variation on this motif, promising in their prefaces a fidelity to historical fact or truth. Thus Marmette in his preface to *François de Bienville:* "D'ailleurs, loin de fausser l'histoire, comme il arrive malheureusement dans le très grand nombre des romans historiques, je me suis au contraire efforcé de la suivre rigoureusement dans toutes les péripéties du drame. De sorte que le lecteur saisira facilement la ligne de démarcation qui, dans ce récit, sépare le roman de l'histoire" (Marmette 1924, 18). The dryness of some of the details of the novel, which might to some readers seem strange in a work of imagination, are explained by the fact that the author has deliberately used only enough plot as was necessary to enliven his story. At least, that is the theory.

The interesting thing about statements such as Marmette's is that they consistently set truth not, as one might expect, against lies or deceit but against fiction and, more particularly, against the novel. Which brings us to what Genette, after Lichtenberg, calls the preface as lightning conductor, as *excusatio propter infirmitatem* or, in Garcia-Mendez's terminology, as plea for indulgence. To illustrate his point, Genette quotes a curious dialogue taken from the preface to Nodier's *Les Proscrits* (1802), in which the author combines a clever defence with an even cleverer refusal to defend himself: "Your book will not win the support of persons of taste. – I'm afraid not. – You have sought to be new. – That is true. – And all you have been is bizarre. – That's possible. – Your style is uneven. – So are the passions. – And strewn with repetitions. – The language of the heart is not rich … – Your characters are ill-chosen. – They weren't chosen. – Your incidents badly invented. – Nothing was invented. – And you have written a bad novel. – It's not a novel." (Quoted in Genette 1987, 193.) This is the very heart of the rhetoric developed by the novel preface, the confluence of the why themes, emphasizing the importance of the subject and the truthfulness of its treatment, and the how themes, with their declarations of intent, their generic descriptions, and their attempts to define an audience. Central to all these concerns is the topos of denial with which Nodier aptly concludes his argument.

Writing in a similar vein, the Goncourt brothers preface their novel *Germinie Lacerteux* (1865) with a warning that promises the truth even as it begs the reader's indulgence and offers a generic description at the same time as it defines its public: "We must beg the public's pardon for giving it this book, and warn it of what it will find here. The public likes false novels: this novel is a true one." (As though the truth were some kind of noxious substance peddled in novels bearing the nineteenth-century equivalent of a surgeon-general's warning. "Vorsicht! Kunst!" – Beware! Art! – was the shrill message of a poster of unknown origin that I used to pass every day on my way to work.) The Quebec prefaces which interest me often bear a similar warning, but translate the Goncourts's formula – *Le public aime les romans faux: ceci est un roman vrai* – into Canadian French as *Le public aime les romans: ceci n'est pas un roman*. Or, in the form of a syllogism: Novels are false; this book is true; therefore this is not a novel. Once again the reader's indulgence is implicitly sought: the public loves novels, which are by definition false; this book is not a novel, since it is true; might this book even so find favour with the public or else create a public for itself?

This kind of reasoning – which is present in a diffuse, implicit, fragmentary, or displaced form in most of the novel prefaces considered here (for example in the echo of Montaigne we hear in the preface to *François de Bienville:* "Cecy, lecteurs, est un livre de bonne foy") – is found in its purest form in the author's foreword to *Jean Rivard:* "Ce n'est pas un roman que j'écris, et si quelqu'un est à la recherche d'aventures merveilleuses, duels, meurtres, suicides, ou d'intrigues d'amour tant soit peu compliquées, je lui conseille amicalement de s'adresser ailleurs. On ne trouvera dans ce récit que l'histoire simple et vraie d'un jeune homme sans fortune, né dans une condition modeste, qui sut s'élever par son mérite, à l'indépendance de fortune et aux premiers honneurs de son pays" (Gérin-Lajoie 1874, 1–2). However, this foreword is more complicated than at first meets the eye. In fact, this short text is composed of two parts, the second of which folds symmetrically back on the first. The first part sets forth the argument I have just analysed: this is not a novel and its hero is not of the romantic kind to be found in novels; therefore the book will find no favour with a certain kind of public. The second part, however, would seem to be trying to redeem this same hero in the eyes of this same public by arguing not only that he has all the necessary qualities of the hero of a novel but also that he could indeed have been that kind of hero had he not chosen a simpler and healthier way of life:

Hâtons-nous toutefois de dire, mesdames, de peur de vous laisser dans l'erreur, que Jean Rivard était, en dépit de son nom de baptême, d'une nature éminemment poétique, et d'une tournure à plaire aux plus dédaigneuses de votre sexe.

À l'époque où se passent les faits qu'on va lire, il approchait de la vingtaine. C'était un beau jeune homme brun, de taille moyenne. Sa figure mâle et ferme, son épaisse chevelure, ses larges et fortes épaules, mais surtout des yeux noirs, étincelants, dans lesquels se lisait une indomptable force de volonté, tout cela joint à une âme ardente, à un coeur chaud et à beaucoup d'intelligence, faisait de Jean Rivard un caractère remarquable et véritablement attachant. Trois mois passés au sein d'une grande cité, entre les mains d'un tailleur à la mode, d'un coiffeur, d'un bottier, d'un maître de danse, et un peu de fréquentation de ce qu'on est convenu d'appeler le grand monde, en eussent fait un élégant, un fashionable, un dandy, un cavalier dont les plus belles jeunes filles eussent raffolé.

Mais ces triomphes si recherchés dans certaines classes de la société n'avaient aucun attrait pour notre héros, et Jean Rivard préféra, comme on le verra bientôt, à la vie du lion de ville celle du lion de la forêt. (Gérin-Lajoie 1874, 2)

The invitation is clear: the gentle reader is to be allowed to have her cake and eat it too, at least in her fantasies where she can dream of what might have been.[8]

We are here in the realm of what Gerald Prince, in a recent article, has called the "disnarrated,"[9] by which he means "all the events that *do not* happen but, nonetheless, are referred to (in a negative or hypothetical mode) by the narrative text" (Prince 1988, 2). As Prince points out, "the disnarrated provides one of the important means for emphasizing tellability: this narrative is worth narrating because *it* could have been otherwise, because *it* usually is otherwise, because *it* was *not* otherwise" (5). In the context of the nineteenth-century Quebec novel, the rhetorical function of the disnarrated is particularly important because the contract offered by novelist to reader is often based on a specifically Canadian notion of verisimilitude which was apparently in conflict with what the French novel had accustomed the reader to consider as interesting or tellable. Ostensibly rejecting the melodramatic excesses of his French counterpart, the Canadian novelist attempts to impose a different set of norms or conventions for fiction-making, more in keeping with the pace of life he sees around him. Thus, Patrice Lacombe apologizes in the afterword to *La Terre paternelle* for the story he might have told but has not:

Quelques-uns de nos lecteurs auraient peut-être désiré que nous eussions donné un dénouement tragique à notre histoire; ils auraient aimé à voir nos acteurs disparaître violemment de la scène, les uns après les autres, et notre récit se terminer dans le genre terrible, comme un grand nombre de romans du jour. Mais nous les prions de remarquer que nous écrivons dans un pays où les moeurs en général sont pures et simples, et que l'esquisse que nous avons essayé d'en faire, eût été invraisemblable et même souverainement ridicule, si elle se fût terminée par des meurtres, des empoisonnements et des suicides. Laissons aux vieux pays, que la civilisation a gâtés, leurs romans ensanglantés, peignons l'enfant du sol, tel qu'il est, religieux, honnête, paisible de moeurs et de caractère, jouissant de l'aisance et de la fortune sans orgueil et sans ostentation, supportant avec résignation et patience les plus grandes adversités; et quand il voit arriver sa dernière heure, n'ayant d'autre désir que de pouvoir mourir tranquillement sur le lit où s'est endormi son père, et d'avoir sa place près de lui au cimetière avec une modeste croix de bois, pour indiquer au passant le lieu de son repos. (Lacombe 1972, 117–18)

It would be difficult to find a better illustration of Prince's claim that the disnarrated "institutes an antimodel in terms of which the text defines itself and indicates the aesthetics it develops and espouses, the audience it represents and aspires to, the matters, topics, and configurations this audience takes to be tellable" (Prince 1988, 6).[10] From Lacombe's description, it would appear that the antimodel in question – which sometimes, in keeping with the rhetoric of the day, takes on the proportions of the Antichrist – is the imported serialized novel *(roman-feuilleton)* that from the middle of the century on is devoured faster than it can be deplored. David Hayne notes, for example, that "when, around 1850, the accelerated rhythm of importation of French books provides an ample provision of nearly contemporary French novels, the enemies of the genre will think they see, in the works of the French serial writers, the confirmation of their worst suspicions, and will inveigh against 'the penny dreadful,' which they will often confuse with the novel *per se"* (Hayne 1971, 39). He goes on to quote an 1857 text by Louis-Wilfrid Marchand, for whom "these ruinous wild imaginings, for I cannot call them books, bring literature into disrepute ... All of these productions, with few exceptions, breathe evil and exude depravation." In a similar vein, Yves Dostaler quotes a somewhat later piece by J.-B. Caouette in the 29 October 1874 issue of *L'Opinion publique:*

The serial reeks of the novel a mile away ... It insinuates itself everywhere. The maid, on waking, snatches it from the hands of the babe who has found it under the dinner table ...; the clerk sees it hanging from the bell on the porte-cochère; the blacksmith on his anvil, the grocer on his scale ... the student squanders time on it which should be spent preparing his law or medicine ... even the poor man sets aside for it his habits of cheerful labour.

   Look at that window up there. Behind that little plantpot, under that cage, in which swings the proverbial parrot, the young girl with the azure eyes, with the candid brow, has dropped her needle ... Why? ... Ask that busy little fellow who, for a few pennies, has just tossed a little sheet, not yet dry, through the window to her. The girl is reading her serial. (Quoted in Dostaler 1977, 16–17)

Not to be outdone, Edmond Rousseau makes much the same complaint in the preface to his historical novel *Les Exploits d'Iberville:* "C'est un vrai déluge qui a envahi nos campagnes les plus reculées, je vous en parle en connaissance de cause. Et que lit-on? Le roman français du jour, c'est-à-dire, même parmi ceux qui sont réputés les moins mauvais, ce qu'il y a de plus dangereux pour le coeur et l'esprit de la jeunesse, un ramassis de songes creux, d'aventures impossibles et de doctrines subversives" (Rousseau 1888, vii). That the dilemma of the Quebec novelist remains unresolved at the end of the century is clear from the foreword to *Pour la patrie:* "Le roman, surtout le roman moderne, et plus particulièrement encore le roman français me paraît être une arme forgée par Satan lui-même

pour la destruction du genre humain. Et malgré cette conviction
j'écris un roman" (Tardivel 1975, 49).[11]

Joseph Doutre's preface to *Les Fiancés de 1812* is ambiguous in a
different way. As in the case of the preface to *Jean Rivard,* the text
develops different arguments in its two parts. The author starts out
by attacking the prejudice in favour of things foreign which, according
to him, is widespread amongst the many "dilettantissimis" who have
seen Paris and can no longer look upon the efforts of their fellow
citizens without a grimace of disdain (Doutre 1844, vi). However,
this condemnation of a hypothetical non-public – "Les Fiancés ne
sont pas écrits pour ces messieurs. Le coeur leur en soulèverait de
dégoût. Aussi se garderont-ils bien d'y toucher" (x) – is followed
by a vigorous defence of the novel in general and of Eugène Sue's
Les Mystères de Paris in particular. This profoundly ambivalent attitude
toward the French novel is also seen in the preface to *L'Influence
d'un livre,* which slips from a naïvely affirmative opening gambit
("This is a modern novel in the French style") to something more
tentative and much less confident ("This is, I hope and think, a
Canadian novel"). Such ambivalence would seem to be a politically
liberal and relatively clear version of the uneasiness informing most
Quebec novel prefaces of the period.

T HE DENIAL OF THE NOVEL as literary genre, which I have tried to
characterize by the formula "This is not a novel," is, as Charles
Grivel has shown, a normal part of the process of legitimation by
which the genre achieves its *effet de réel*.[12] However, as Garcia-Mendez has pointed out, in the case of the nineteenth-century Quebec
novel this rhetoric of refusal contains at least an element of denial
(of denegation) in the strong, psychoanalytic sense of the term. What
is denied, what is repressed in this way, is precisely the impossibility
of getting outside the codes of the French novel in order to create
a literary genre which would serve as a vehicle for a specifically
Canadian view of the world according to specifically Canadian criteria
of verisimilitude. Hence the uneasiness which seems to haunt prefaces
like the one written by Cherrier for Chauveau's novel:

Ceux qui chercheront dans *Charles Guérin* un de ces drames terribles et
pantelants, comme Eugène Sue et Frédéric Soulié en ont écrit, seront bien
complètement désappointés. C'est simplement l'histoire d'une famille canadienne contemporaine que l'auteur s'est efforcé d'écrire, prenant pour point
de départ un principe tout opposé à celui que l'on s'était mis en tête de
faire prévaloir il y a quelques années: *le beau, c'est le laid*. C'est à peine

s'il y a une intrigue d'amour dans l'ouvrage: pour bien dire le fonds du roman semblera, à bien des gens, un prétexte pour quelques peintures de moeurs et quelques dissertations politiques ou philosophiques. De cela cependant il ne faudra peut-être pas autant blâmer l'auteur que nos Canadiens, qui tuent ou empoisonnent assez rarement leur femme, ou le mari de quelque autre femme, qui se suicident le moins qu'ils peuvent, et qui en général mènent, depuis deux ou trois générations, une vie assez paisible et dénuée d'aventures auprès de l'église de leur paroisse, au bord du grand fleuve ou de quelqu'un de ses nombreux et pittoresques tributaires. (Chauveau 1978, 31)

But if the novel of France is, in relation to the norms of Canadian society, at once immoral and lacking in verisimilitude, the fact remains that it is enormously popular and that its codes determine in large part the expectations of the reading public. "La littérature canadienne est donc étouffée nécessairement dans son berceau," concludes Cherrier, "soit qu'elle s'efforce de revêtir l'idiome que la France nous a légué, soit qu'elle essaie de parler la langue de Shakespeare et de Byron" (29).[13] A similar problem is raised by André Belleau in his discussions of the interplay of social and literary codes in Quebec literature. Like most observers of the literary institution, Belleau derives his basic methodological concepts from Dubois (1978), whose seminal work can be situated in a French tradition which includes Sartre (1948), Barthes (1953), and, most importantly, the writings of Pierre Bourdieu. For all these authors, the emergence of an autonomous literary institution in France can be traced to the first half of the nineteenth century, though the precise date varies, with 1830 or 1850 being the most frequently cited. Similarly, all four writers see the autonomization of a literary field as being concomitant with the growing hegemony of the despised bourgeoisie in cultural as well as economic matters, although here again there is disagreement as to the exact nature of the relationship between a bourgeois ideology based on the notion of productivity and the refusal of the literary institution to allow the market to determine production. For Bourdieu (1971), literary activity can be divided into two spheres, a field of limited production and a field of large-scale production, each with its own institutional structure. In most studies after Bourdieu's, there is a tendency to identify the autonomous literary institution exclusively with the field of limited production.

There have been a number of attempts in recent years to apply this model to the literature of Quebec, and the essays collected in Lemire (1986a) and in a special 1987 issue of *Études littéraires* devoted to the autonomization of literature show that the debate concerning the use of the Bourdieu-Dubois model in Quebec is both lively and unresolved.[14] Belleau's most important contribution to this field of study lies in his contention that in Quebec there exists a fundamental conflict between the organizational function of the literary institution (the material base, the machinery of production, diffusion and reception) and the regulatory function (the *norms* of literary activity, which determine the literary status of both authors and texts); for while in certain sectors of what Bourdieu calls the "literary sphere" the machinery is indigenous to Quebec, the norms remain French. In other words, the literary institution in Quebec is double and the codes it generates frequently conflict: "I am convinced that we cannot understand our novelistic literature in any depth – regardless of the approach chosen – without taking into account the tensions and distortions produced by the coming together in a single text of the socio-cultural codes of Quebec and the literary codes of France" (Belleau 1981, 17–18).

Belleau's analysis bears primarily on the modern Quebec novel (post-1945), but it seems to me there is a very clear case of conflicting codes in the novel prefaces of the nineteenth century, which belong to what Belleau would probably call Quebec's literary prehistory. As I have tried to show, if the literary codes of the period are predominantly French, derived from canonical texts[15] as well as from the infamous *feuilleton,* the socio-cultural codes, especially after 1860, are resolutely Canadian and attempt to institute a national literature according to moral and political precepts (imposed by the Church in order to counter liberal tendencies in society) rather than to aesthetic precepts.[16] The conflict of codes is thus increasingly polemicized in texts like Casgrain's 1884 preface to *Angéline de Montbrun:* "Le plus grave inconvénient de sa manière actuelle, c'est qu'elle donne à son livre une physionomie trop européenne. Sa pensée habite plus les bords de la Seine que ceux du Saint-Laurent. On regrette de ne pas rencontrer assez de pages vraiment canadiennes, telles que celle du pélerinage d'Angéline au tombeau de Garneau. Notre littérature ne peut être sérieusement originale qu'en s'identifiant avec notre pays et ses habitants, qu'en peignant nos moeurs, notre histoire, notre physionomie: c'est sa condition d'existence." (Reprinted in G. Rousseau 1970, 69–70.) Thus, despite Gilles Marcotte's claim that in Quebec the institution precedes the works (1981), it is perfectly legitimate to ask, as do David Hayne (1986) and Maurice Lemire (1986b, 1987), whether the notion of an *autonomous* literary institution is applicable to the case of nineteenth-century Quebec, where the dominant socio-cultural codes are in such clear conflict with imported literary codes which they constantly attempt to censor and repress.

(Hayne's conclusion is that while we can indeed talk of a literary institution in the nineteenth century, we are at present almost totally ignorant of its origins; Lemire argues that since there is a visible struggle between rival factions to occupy the literary sphere as early as 1840, we have to situate the first aspirations toward autonomy then.)

EARLY IN THIS CHAPTER I quoted Henri Mitterand, for whom novel prefaces have a common kernel-sentence – "Literature must be 'x'" – which generates a syllogism equally characteristic of the genre: Literature must *be* or *do* 'x'; this novel does 'x'; therefore, you, the reader, must regard it as a book whose value is universal. In other words: This is what literature must be today and this is how what I have done conforms to that norm (Mitterand 1980, 24–5). While it is true that the same kernel-sentence and the same syllogism can be found in the novel prefaces of nineteenth-century Quebec, it is equally true that this situation is rendered more problematic by the presence of another discourse which has its source in the rhetoric surrounding the genre's ambiguous moral and social status. This discourse has its own kernel-sentence – *This is not a novel* – which gives rise to the following syllogism: The public loves novels, which are by definition false; this book is true; therefore this is not a novel and will probably fail to please the public. The conflict of codes (and of institutions) in this rhetoric of denial is clear. Unable to say with conviction, this is a novel (implying, *in the French style*), these novelists-in-spite-of-themselves are reduced to stammering, this is, I think, a Canadian non-novel, but with just enough novel about it not to be totally displeasing to the reading public.

A last remark is called for – a sort of postface to these reflections on the preface – which will also serve as a word of warning. Mitterand, for his part, reminds us that any sociocriticism of the novel based on the theoretical discourse of novelists cannot help but be incomplete and inexact, for while such discourse reveals the ideology of the preface writer, it blinds us to the ideology of the novelist: "Car il s'agit du même personnage, mais non de la même situation de communication, c'est-à-dire ni de la même énonciation, ni du même énoncé" (Mitterand 1980, 30–1). In other words, it is not possible to derive the ideology of *La Comédie humaine* from a reading of Balzac's preface; Balzac's practice as a novelist cannot be reduced to Balzac's theory as a preface writer. In *La Dissémination,* Derrida defines the preface as a "discursive anticipation," a "discourse of morality," thereby denouncing the reductive nature of any preface and demonstrating its radical non-pertinence to the text it introduces (Derrida 1972, 9–67). As Mitterand remarks, the literary preface, in trying to fix the meaning of a work, in trying to recapitulate before the fact, is always a lie or an illusion. This is not a novel, say the writers of prefaces. And of course they are right, for *this,* after all, is always and only a preface. But while prefaces might not tell the whole truth and nothing but the truth about the works they introduce, they do tell us a great deal about the literary institution specifying the conditions of production and reception of those works.

CHAPTER TWO

Between Epic and Novel: The Crisis of Community in Félix-Antoine Savard's Menaud, maître-draveur

The novel is the epic of a world that has been abandoned by God.   G. Lukács

To be legitimate, a style in art must connect itself with a style outside of art, whether in palaces or dance halls or in the dreams of saints and courtesans.

H. Rosenberg

In a patriarchal social structure the ruling class does, in a certain sense, belong to the world of "fathers" and is thus separated from other classes by a distance that is almost epic.   M.M. Bakhtin

In an essay entitled "Parable of American Painting," published in his *The Tradition of the New,* Harold Rosenberg evokes the scene of Braddock's Defeat as an emblem of the failure of a group to adapt its style to a new landscape: "I recall in my grammar-school history book a linecut illustration which shows the Redcoats marching abreast through the woods, while from behind trees and rocks naked Indians and coonskinned trappers pick them off with musket balls. Maybe it wasn't Braddock's defeat but some ambush of the Revolutionary War. In any case, the Redcoats march in file through the New World wilderness, with its disorder of rocks, underbrush and sharpshooters, as if they were on a parade ground or on the meadows of a classical European battlefield and one by one they fall and die" (Rosenberg 1959, 13–14).

According to Rosenberg, what defeated the Redcoats was their very skill, their military art; the assumptions of their technique and training as professional European soldiers prevented them from *seeing* the American trees. Blinded by their own style, they were incapable of adapting to the new configuration, or lack of configuration, of an unfamiliar terrain: "The Redcoats fall, expecting at any moment to enter upon the true battlefield, the soft rolling greenswards prescribed by the canons of their craft and presupposed by every principle that makes warfare intelligible to the soldier of the eighteenth century" (14).

For Rosenberg, Braddock's Defeat, or the "hallucination of the displaced terrain" (14), comes to stand for a mental condition which has haunted American painting and which Rosenberg calls Redcoatism: "the art-entranced Redcoat, in a succession of different national uniforms, dominates the history of American art. Like Braddock, painting in this country has behaved as if it were elsewhere – to the point where artists have often emigrated physically in order to join their minds in some foreign country" (15). In the pages which follow, I shall argue that Félix-Antoine Savard's *Menaud, maître-draveur* can be read as an interesting inversion of Redcoatism, which pits the tradition-bound *coureur de bois,* Menaud, against an invading enemy who contrives to remain invisible by the simple expedient of not showing up. Menaud's problem is not that he cannot see the trees, but that he can see nothing but the trees. For while the terrain remains unchanged, the power controlling it and the rules determining its use and exploitation do change. Savard's style, like Menaud's, cannot accommodate such displacements. The book he writes and the story he tells both bear witness to the anguish of this failure.

O N READING the secondary literature on Savard's novel, one is struck by the almost universal uneasiness among the critics before a text which seems somehow excessive, larger than life. In most cases, this uneasiness is attributable to their fundamental uncertainty concerning the literary genre to which the work belongs. From Maurice Hébert in 1937, for whom *Menaud* is more of a "poetic or poeticized story" (335) than a novel, to Madeleine Ducrocq-Poirier in 1978, for whom the poetic treatment of the story is at odds with the "novelistic substance" (332), the conclusion remains essentially the same: the work suffers from an interference between its poetic and its novelistic aspects, which are not well married in the text.[1] One of the most frequent complaints is that its highly stylized treatment seems strangely out of place in a work with a simple storyline consisting of only two threads: Menaud's impotent revolt against the encroachments of "foreigners" on his "ancestral" lands, a revolt which leads ultimately to isolation and madness, and his daughter Marie's hesitation between two suitors, the collaborator, le Délié, to whom she is physically attracted, and Menaud's heir apparent, the loyal *coureur de bois,* Alexis Tremblay (le Lucon).

In this respect, Réjean Robidoux and André Renaud are typical in their characterization of *Menaud* as a generic hybrid: "The systematic use of metaphor, the regular recourse to the epic manner, as well as the many lyrical movements, combine to make of *Menaud, maître-*

draveur an heroic fresco in which the realistic adventure of the characters is transformed into allegory" (Robidoux and Renaud 1966, 41). For them, as for others, the problem of genre is complicated but also illuminated by the different editions of the work. Thus, the first edition of 1937 is characterized by "a profusion of images, of metaphors rushing nervously, interweaving, criss-crossing, which deprive the prose of its novelistic feel" (43), whereas the revised and much sparer edition of 1944 achieves a better blend of poetry and novel. François Ricard speaks of the triumph of a certain classicism in the 1944 version over the drunken romanticism of the original, a triumph marked by a return to realism and a transition from lyric to narrative (Ricard 1972, 39–40).[2]

An interesting feature of many of these critical statements is the importance they attach to metaphor in the interplay of the two dimensions or tendencies manifested by the work. For Ricard, for example, it is through metaphor that the novel turns away from reality to take on the proportions and certain characteristics of the epic. "By opening the text up with metaphor, the writer builds around the simple adventure of a log-driver a whole network of relations which raise it to the level of a Herculean labour. It is primarily in this sense that *Menaud, maître-draveur* can be said to be epically inspired" (Ricard 1972, 29–30). But if metaphor is the sign of an epic transformation of the real, it must be borne in mind that this transformation remains totally subjective, dictated by the vision of the novel's hero which informs all aspects of Savard's prose style: "his vision is unabashedly inner-directed, metaphorical; it transposes rather than paints, celebrates instead of explaining" (Ricard 1972, 125). Metaphor becomes the stylistic manifestation of Menaud's own metaphysical and, hence, transforming vision of the world and, eventually, of his madness. An analysis of some characteristic images will clarify what is at stake in this process, before we go on to explore the implications for the larger structures and themes of the novel.

CONSIDER the following sentences:

A Et son esprit partit en course dans tous les sentiers de la forêt, multiple comme une meute sur des pistes de haut gibier. (*Menaud,* 156)
B Il lui passait des idées folles qui lui tricolaient dans tous les chemins du cerveau comme des jeunesses qui reviennent des noces, en ripompette. (166)

Perhaps what we notice first when the two sentences are placed side

by side is the striking symmetry between them, a symmetry that is
evident at more than one level. In terms of content, the state of
mind evoked is essentially the same in each case: in A we see
Menaud's excited anticipation as he rejoices in his decision to embark
on an adventure of liberation in the name of his people's heritage;
in B his daughter Marie is eagerly awaiting the visit of her young
beau, Alexis. From a formal point of view, we see the same binary
rhetorical structure of metaphor plus simile, with, from A to B, a
slight syntactical displacement of the element linking the two figures:
"multiple"/"en ripompette." Finally, within the metaphor itself, a certain semantic parallelism ("dans tous les sentiers de la forêt"/"dans
tous les chemins du cerveau") echoes and reinforces the symmetry
of the syntax. But if the similarities between the two sentences are
significant, so are the differences. The two similes introduce an
implicit contrast between the theme of hunting ("comme une meute
sur des pistes de haut gibier") and the theme of marriage ("comme
des jeunesses qui reviennent des noces"). Similarly, the two metaphors
conjure up the dialectical opposition of outer ("sentiers de la forêt")
and inner ("chemins du cerveau"), thus rehearsing, within the play
of the images themselves, one of the major thematic structures of
the novel. Finally, from a more general perspective, the two sentences
embody the conflicting topoï of departure ("partir en course") and
return ("revenir des noces").

This kind of differential analysis on the level of images leads
inevitably to an integral reading at a higher level. The differences
or oppositions at the level of phenomena – hunting and marriage,
forest tracks and pathways in the brain, departure and return – are
all dictated by certain structural features of the world of the novel:
the dialectic of outer and inner, the irreducible opposition of male
and female, the contrast between *coureur de bois* and settler (nomad
and sedentary) and between the masculine space of departure – "il
s'était fait une fête de partir" (181) – and the feminine one of waiting,
which is itself ultimately ambiguous – "la maison promise"/"une
cambuse funèbre" (170, 181). It is in this connection that one might
speak of metaphors rooted in metonymy or, to use an expression
coined by Gérard Genette in an essay entitled "Métonymie chez
Proust," of diegetic metaphors: "diegetic in the sense that their
'vehicle' is borrowed from the diegesis, i.e. from the novel's spatio-
temporal world" (Genette 1972, 47–8).[3] Since Genette's study is exem-
plary and provides insights that can be applied to Savard's use of
imagery, a summary of some of his main points may prove useful.

The critic begins with a warning: metaphor, he says, is so important
in Proust that the natural tendency, for both critic and author alike,

is to overestimate its influence to the detriment of other semantic relations. Genette is particularly interested in metonymic transpositions, such as transferred epithets and other synaesthetic figures, which Stephen Ullmann dealt with in his *Style in the French Novel*. Savard's "la grande paix dorée du soir" (19) is one example of Ullmann's category of images based on "the contiguity of the two sensations, their occurrence in the same mental context" (Ullmann 1957, 197). However, closer study of *Menaud* shows that Savard uses purely metonymic transpositions only rarely. In fact, rather than trying to isolate his examples of metonymy and set them up as a category of images in competition with metaphor, it may be more fruitful to follow Genette and study the role of metonymy *within metaphor,* showing how the elements interact and work together.

To illustrate his point, Genette compares two passages from Proust, one taken from *Du côté de chez Swann* and situated in Méséglise, the other taken from *Sodome et Gomorrhe* and situated in Balbec. The passages consist of descriptions of church steeples which are remarkably similar in their chief physical characteristics (Genette 1972, 43). It is precisely this apparently objective similarity that is puzzling, for the narrator uses two quite different images to describe the steeples, comparing one to an ear of corn, in the case of Méséglise, and the other to a fish, in the case of Balbec. On reflection, the reason for the difference becomes clear; in each passage it is the surroundings, the spatio-temporal context, which generates the image: "the earthiness of Méséglise, the maritime essence of Balbec" (44). The device, which could be described in terms of the regulating effect of relations of contiguity on the selection of metaphor, is typical of Proust.

In all the examples quoted by Genette, the relation of similarity between the two terms of the metaphors or similes discussed seems to be subject to a principle of proximity or contiguity, which can be spatial, temporal, or psychological in nature. This leads Genette to formulate the hypothesis that metaphor, in such cases, finds its support and its motivation in metonymy: "as though the *accuracy* of an analogy, i.e. the degree of similarity between the two terms, were less important to Proust than its *authenticity,* by which I mean its appropriateness to its spatio-temporal environment" (45). (Genette goes on to compare this principle of geographic "truth" with the culinary practice of matching certain regional dishes with a rigorously autochtonous sauce or garnish and serving it with a local wine, thereby creating a kind of metonymically "authentic" blend.)

In the sentences A and B quoted from *Menaud,* Genette's principle of authenticity is clearly at work. In each case, the aptness of the metaphor seems less important than its appropriateness in the diegetic context, which is largely a matter of character. Thus Menaud's ideas are likened to a pack of hunting dogs running through the forest in pursuit of the prey, whereas Marie's take the form of young folk coming back from a wedding. Both images depend for their effect on a process of motivation or naturalization: the similes appear "natural" in the context of the two characters and the differences pointed out in my brief analysis – the various oppositions and contrasts on the levels of form and theme – all flow from the fundamental opposition of man and woman, father and daughter.

We then have to ask if these examples are typical. Does Savard always motivate or authenticate his metaphors by grounding them in character? Examples c and d bear a certain resemblance to A and B in that they involve the same characters, Menaud and Marie, and a similar state of mental excitement:

c Mais dès que Josime eut passé la porte, ce fut dans la tête à Menaud comme un torrent d'avril. (157)
d Tout le long du jour, s'il en neigea des idées dans la tête de Marie! (165)

In both c and d, similar content finds a "vehicle" – "torrent d'avril/neige" – drawn from the natural world of the seasons. But how do we explain the choice, from within that symbolism, of two very different elements to express, by analogy, what is essentially one and the same thing? What determined the selection of the element "torrent d'avril" to describe Menaud's mental state, and the image of a snowstorm to suggest Marie's ideas? Can this be taken as a psychological indicator of character, as in A and B, or are there other factors at play?

To answer these questions, we need to reconstruct the immediate context of each sentence. It then becomes apparent that the choice of the "torrent d'avril" is motivated less by the opposition between father and daughter than by the thematic contrast this time between the *coureur de bois* Menaud and the farmer Josime:

Josime vint faire son bout de veillée.
Il reprit son sujet de la veille: la récolte, les labours d'automne.
Menaud, pour la politesse, répondait oui, non, à ce qui lui barrait ainsi l'idée, à ces versets aussi lents que des chars chargés de gerbes.
Mais dès que Josime eut passé la porte, ce fut dans la tête à Menaud comme un torrent d'avril. (156-7)

The "torrent d'avril" thus evokes, by metonymy, the season of the log drive, it is in opposition not to the winter snows but to the harvest, the "labours d'automne," and the "chars chargés de gerbes" which stand, again metonymically, for the character of Josime, the sedentary farmer. The choice of image thus reflects the work's primordial thematic opposition, so characteristic of the early novel in French Canada, which sets the nomadic against the sedentary, contrasting the freedom of the "fier coureur de bois" who never allows himself to be chained to hearth and home (23) with the "petite vie, étroite, resserrée" of the settler (171). This brings us back to the opposition, noted in examples A and B, between the space of departure and the space of waiting, since Josime is assimilated, according to the novel's logic, to the world of women. As for Marie's ideas being compared to a snowstorm, this is a simple case of contamination by proximity; the metaphor is suggested and prepared ("authenticated") by the snow which is falling all round the house. Thus the countryside is transformed into the very image of Savard's view of woman: "silencieuse et comme résignée" (165).

In example C, Menaud's thoughts are likened, according to a typically metonymic train of thought, to water. Elsewhere and more often in the novel, Savard prefers to use fire as an image of his hero's mental state:

E Au feu de cette lampe qui allumait des escarbilles en ses regards, il avait l'air d'un forgeron martelant des pensées de fer. (25)

F Aussi, son âme, ce matin, est-elle comme la cuve de forge quand le forgeron y plonge son fer rouge. (154)

Images such as these evoke not only the whole range of elementary meanings associated with fire (sacred, visionary, etc.) but also the various connotations of the word iron (iron hand, iron will, and so on). Moreover, the artisanal work and ideology evoked by the idea of the blacksmith contrasts with the impersonal and anonymous "ingénieur de la compagnie" (24) who, accompanied by an interpreter, comes to buy the services of the "lord and master" of the river.[4] The metaphor of the forge, and of the "thoughts of iron," is probably what generates or suggests, again metonymically, the new image of "words in arms" that occurs a few lines further on in the text:

G Mais voilà que, de cette diable de lecture, étaient sortis des mots en armes, et qu'avec eux toutes les voix du pays, de la montagne, des champs et des bois s'étaient engouffrées chez lui, ébranlant son âme et sa maison comme une bourrasque d'automne. (25)

The image of the "voices of the land," inherited from Louis Hémon's

Maria Chapdelaine will form a constant refrain throughout the novel. It is interesting that, already in this early passage, these voices are associated with the wind, in this instance an autumn squall which threatens the protective space of the house and sows seeds of unrest in the hero's mind. It is these voices, these "words in arms" (Hémon's), that are responsible for Menaud's agitated state and that incessantly enjoin him to leave, to renounce home comforts and the sedentary life of women and farmers:

H Sa femme avait tout fait pour enraciner au sol ce fier coureur de bois. Et lui, par amour pour elle, il avait défriché cette âpre terre de Mainsal, toujours prêt, cependant, à s'évader du regard vers le bleu des monts dès que le vent du Nord venait lui verser au coeur les paroles magiques et les philtres embaumés. (23)

The association of the north wind with the voices of the land is implicit in another characteristic image, which comes much later in the book:

I Tout y avait passé dans le pays, et depuis le commencement; et cette parole rude et forte avait fouaillé deux heures de temps dans la fumée des pipes, comme le noroît quand il fouette les nuages et découvre la vraie face de la terre. (162)

Far from being simple, the simile is constructed according to a formula dear to Savard, that of the four-term homology: "parole : noroît :: fumée des pipes : nuages." We find the same structure in the following image, where the analogy between word and fire is even more explicit:

J Voilà maintenant que cette parole flambait dans l'humble maison comme un feu d'abatis dans la clairière du printemps. (22)

Thus, we find the homology: "parole : feu d'abatis :: humble maison : clairière du printemps." A slightly more complex variant occurs on the same page:

K Puis, il ouvrit la porte toute grande; et, dans le soir immobile, il contempla la campagne endormie, laissant ses regards voler jusqu'aux horizons lointains, et revenir ainsi que des engoulevents au nid de ses pensées. (22)

The symmetry which should exist between the four terms of the homology ("regards : engoulevents :: horizons lointains : nid de ses pensées") is thrown out of kilter by the presence of two verbs ("voler, revenir"), instead of the usual one. Here again we have the dialectic of outer and inner, of open and closed ("horizons/nid"), as well as that of departure and return, all of which played an important part in examples A, B, and H. However, the articulation of these two dialectics is unbalanced by the fact that the terms of the simile ("regards" and "engoulevents") are the grammatical subjects of verbs which point in opposite directions: it is the looks which fly away and the nightjars which come back. The instability of the image can perhaps be explained in part by the ambiguity of the symbol of the bird in the novel, the nightjars of this passage finding themselves caught somewhere between the "oiselet que le vent bourru déniche" (199) and the "outarde qui regagne le Nord avec du vent neuf plein ses ailes" (181). Along the same lines, the dialectic of outer and inner is complicated by the fact that the sleeping countryside ("la campagne endormie") – which is metonymically related to the image of the great, golden peace of the evening spreading like a blanket a woman puts over a bed (19) – contrasts not with the closed universe of the house but with the man's world of distant horizons, of mountains, and of woods. In his article "Menaud ou l'impossible fête," André Brochu makes a similar point: "The whole novel will show, moreover, that the house and the natural world around it – the nature of fields and not of mountains – are intimately linked and together constitute the sphere of activity which has fallen to Woman ... the fields are an extension of the house, which itself is the extension of the room" (Brochu 1974, 257–8).

However, even woman, in the shelter of her room, is not entirely safe from that other nature, the wild nature which speaks through the wind, the mountain's very soul: "Ensuite, elle regagna sa chambre, saisie par cette bourrasque froide qui l'avait frappée au visage comme la première annonce des peines qui l'attendaient" (164). The image reappears a few pages later, this time bearing its full metaphorical weight. The voice of the land with its stern morality is still present in the wind but, more clearly than ever, it is a voice from the past; it mingles in Marie's mind with the memory of her mother, producing a vision at once more personal and more domesticated than Menaud's:

À tout instant la belle heurtait du regard contre les souvenirs de sa mère pieusement disposés çà et là.

Alors elle s'assit, toute figée, tandis que la bourrasque secouait la vieille maison, et que la poudrerie grêlait les vitres ...

Ça me reproche! pensa-t-elle ... ça me reproche! (167)

The moral reproach voiced by the wind will be heard once more in the same chapter, but this time by Alexis, as it strives to drown out the promise (or temptation) of Marie's words which still echo in his head as he leaves the house:

Mais les paroles de Marie sonnaient encore, sonnaient autour de lui comme les grelots d'une carriole de noces:

"Ce serait plaisant de vivre icitte … tranquille!"

Avant de prendre la dépente de la côte, il s'arrêta pour regarder la lumière de la maison promise; mais une bourrasque venue de la montagne lui jeta au visage un air froid, comme un reproche. (170)

We see here the same dialectic that informed examples A and B, transposed now in terms of Alexis's own dilemma: whether to stay or to leave, to marry and settle down or to answer the call of the land and of his race, to listen to the magical words, the "words in arms" which summon him, or to defend his heritage against the foreigners.

Genette's authentification of metaphor by metonymy, the grounding of analogy in the system of spatio-temporal and psychological relations which constitutes the world of the novel, is clearly, then, an important feature of Savard's prose style. What, for example, could be more "natural" than this vision of a people "fort comme le printemps lorsque le soleil descend sur le pays et donne des coups de pique sur les embâcles de l'hiver" (32)? Or the image used to describe Marie's state of mind after the arrival of her first suitor: "Mais le dialogue silencieux qu'échangeaient son coeur et la pensée de son père, ainsi qu'une laine fragile, était rompu" (27)? The idea of the silent communion between father and daughter being snapped like a length of yarn is related surely to the very name of Marie's admirer – le Délié – and its suggestion of a bond broken or undone. And the fact that the wool is so easily broken would seem, similarly, to be a reflection of Menaud's view of women as the weaker sex, ready to betray in their flesh the higher values of a noble race:[5]

Non, Menaud n'aimait point ce gars-là! De tout son instinct d'homme libre et jaloux du sol. Pour lui, le Délié était un de ces traîtres, un de ces vendus qui livrent, pour de l'argent, la montagne et les chemins à l'étranger.

Cette espèce-là, sans doute, quand on en aurait assez … tout le pays, toute la race la renieraient.

De penser que sa fille, le sang de son sang, pourrait un jour … épouser …

Cela, non! Jamais! (29)

The authenticity of the image is, then, overdetermined, not only by the network of themes it embodies, but also by the simple fact that in this scene Marie is sitting at her loom, weaving.

As well as functioning as a metonymy for woman in the novel, the loom is itself endowed with metaphorical meaning:

Et l'on n'entendait plus que le frappement du ros qui tassait la tissure entre les fils de la chaîne.

Un rythme la berçait de droite à gauche. De ses deux bras harmonieusement levés l'un après l'autre, elle semblait battre la mesure à quelque mystérieuse musique, cependant qu'à la trame de cette lourde étoffe grise, elle insérait toute la chaleur de son être pour son père, pour Joson, qu'elle protégerait ainsi contre le froid qui glace là-bas le coeur des hommes.

Et c'était sa manière à elle de dire à chaque coup de marchette: "Une race qui ne sait pas mourir!"

Ce qu'elle faisait là, sa mère et bien d'autres femmes l'avaient fait avant elle, entremêlant aux laines de subtils sentiments de force, de résistance, et des prières même. (26)

Thus, the image of the fragile yarn links up – by a process which is at once metonymic and metaphoric (wool/weaving/bonds with the past) – with an apparently quite different image, that of the sun transformed into log-driver: "Et ce fut alors comme s'il l'eût vue, cette race, non dans les livres, mais vivante, mais dans sa chair dressée là, devant lui; et cette race, elle devenait comme un grand peuple libre, debout, enfin, dans sa lumière, et fort comme le printemps lorsque le soleil descend sur le pays et donne des coups de pique sur les embâcles de l'hiver" (32). In the last analysis, it is this vision of the race – and the ideology of survival and fidelity to which it gives rise – that informs, through a network of thematic oppositions, all the images presented here. But if the work's *coherence* resides above all in the metaphoric relation, which bridges the world of the novel and a metaphysical world of myths and heroic visions, its internal *cohesion* depends more on the logic of metonymy, which forges the links – horizontal rather than vertical – between the various elements of the diegesis.

IN THE PRECEEDING discussion, I have tried to capture the interplay of metaphor and metonymy at the level of the images themselves, dwelling on the naturalizing role of metonymy *within* metaphor. The metaphor/metonymy distinction can, however, be generalized to coincide with the more fundamental distinction between the paradigmatic and syntagmatic axes of language – the axis of selection and the axis of combination. As Roman Jakobson argues in his classic study of aphasia, it is by the manipulation of these two aspects of language that the individual asserts his own personal style, his way of being in language: "The development of a discourse may take place along two different semantic lines: one topic may lead to another either through their similarity or through their contiguity. The metaphoric way would be the most appropriate term for the first case and the metonymic way for the second, since they find their most condensed expression in metaphor and metonymy respectively" (Jakobson 1956, 76).

According to Jakobson, cases of aphasia can be divided into two categories, depending on whether the disorder is primarily one of selection or of combination. The first type is referred to by Jakobson as similarity disorder, the second as contiguity disorder. For someone suffering from similarity disorder, the context (both linguistic and referential) becomes an indispensable factor. This kind of patient will have no difficulty completing sentence fragments or answering questions, since his speech is merely reactive, but he will find it very difficult to start a conversation or to deliver (or even understand) a monologue or other closed forms of speech. Naming an object and defining (or even repeating) a given word can become impossible tasks, though the patient will have no problem using the same words in context. The subject of the sentence is often omitted and key words may be dropped or replaced by abstract anaphoric substitutes, while "words with an inherent reference to the context, like pronouns and pronominal adverbs, and words serving merely to construct the context, such as connectives and auxiliaries, are particularly prone to survive" (64–5). These "connecting links of communication," which constitute the framework of speech, will be the last elements to remain intact in this type of aphasia.

Contiguity disorder, on the other hand, is "contexture-deficient" and manifests itself in an inability to construct propositions or, more generally, to combine simple linguistic entities into more complex ones:

The syntactical rules organizing words into a higher unit are lost; this loss, called agrammatism, causes the degeneration of the sentence into a mere "word heap," to use Jackson's image. Word order becomes chaotic; the ties of grammatical coordination and subordination, whether concord or government, are dissolved. As might be expected, words endowed with purely grammatical functions, like conjunctions, prepositions, pronouns and articles, disappear first, giving rise to the so-called "telegraphic style," whereas in the case of similarity disorder they are the most resistant. The less a word depends grammatically on the context, the stronger is its tenacity in the speech of aphasics with a contiguity disorder and the sooner is it dropped by patients with a similarity disorder. (71–2)

Is there anything in Savard's literary style which would lead us to characterize it in terms of a tendency toward either the metaphoric or the metonymic pole of language as described by Jakobson? François Ricard's stylistic analysis of *Menaud* in his excellent study of *L'Art de Félix-Antoine Savard* serves as a useful starting point. The section on grammatical linking (79–87) is particularly revealing. Ricard starts by pointing out the extraordinarily large number of lists or enumerations in the novel, the apparent object of which is to build up and amplify the descriptions while at the same time intensifying the emotions. However, this technique is not without its dangers and, as Ricard observes, an attentive reading of *Menaud* quickly reveals the secrets of the style, secrets which, once disclosed, can degenerate rapidly into formulae. The dazzling impression created on a first reading begins to give way to feelings of boredom or lassitude as the relentless repeating of the device becomes all too predictable. The reader may begin to sense that the constant multiplication of synonyms betrays a fundamental inability to choose and reveals the author's incapacity to come up with the one word that might have done the job (Ricard 1972, 81).

Such a style depends for its expressive power on an absence of coordination. The author prefers simple juxtaposition; sentences are linked (or not linked) in the same way, the prose progressing for the most part by the juxtaposition of independent clauses (Ricard 1972, 82–3). Subordinate clauses, with the exception of relatives and comparatives, disappear almost entirely, a reflection of Savard's preference for minimal logical linkage. The same is true of the larger stylistic patterns of the work. More often than not paragraphs are formed of a single, autonomous sentence, thus allowing no elaboration of ideas or complexity of thought. Ricard sees in this technique of short, self-contained, grammatically unlinked paragraphs, a kind of literary pointillism which, when carried to extremes, can be disorienting or simply annoying: "Eventually, as he passes from one paragraph to another, the reader starts to wonder where he is going" (86).

If Savard sins by excess, it is clear that his excess is on the side of metaphor rather than metonymy. The paradigmatic relations of similarity associated with the metaphoric pole of language are systematically promoted in *Menaud* over syntagmatic continuity and

coordination. This vertical rather than horizontal style, which results
in moments of poetic ecstasy and set pieces destined for preservation
in anthologies of French-Canadian literature, constantly runs the risk
of drying up the slow trickle of the story and putting a stop to any
narrative development. Interestingly enough, Yvon Malette uses the
distinction between vertical and horizontal in examining *Menaud*
and *Maria Chapdelaine* (Malette 1968, 23–4). While he describes
Hémon's style as being "at once descriptive, narrative and realistic,"
Savard's is "at once lyric, poetic and epic" (21). This brings us to
another aspect of the metaphor/metonymy distinction, since for Jakobson the dominance of one or the other of these two tendencies can
function as an indication of the literary genre to which the work
belongs: "The primacy of the metaphoric process in the literary
schools of romanticism and symbolism has been repeatedly acknowl-
edged, but it is still insufficiently realized that it is the predominance
of metonymy which underlies and actually predetermines the so-called
'realistic' trend, which belongs to an intermediary stage between the
decline of romanticism and the rise of symbolism and is opposed
to both. Following the path of contiguous relationships, the realistic
author metonymically digresses from the plot to the atmosphere and
from the characters to the setting in space and time" (Jakobson 1956,
77–8). We are thus back to our starting point in the uneasiness felt
by critics faced with the conflicting tendencies of Savard's text. It is
time now to look fairly and squarely at this problem by relating
the work's formal structures to its thematic ones.

ANY THEMATIC STUDY of *Menaud, maître-draveur* must start with
the question of intertextuality and, more specifically, with the
use made in the novel of the passages quoted from *Maria Chapdelaine*. François Martineau has argued persuasively that the way
these extracts function in Savard's novel implies a transformation not
only of their original meaning but also of the larger thematic structures
of Hémon's work. Paying particular attention to the sentence "Autour
de nous des étrangers sont venus," Martineau claims that, for Hémon,
"autour de nous" does not mean *here,* in Quebec.[6] For Savard, on
the other hand, the foreigners are well and truly *here,* not so much
"around us" as "amongst us," a reading which is supported by the
fact that the abbreviated form, "Des étrangers sont venus," is used
twelve times in *Menaud,* whereas the words "Autour de nous" appear
only once.

One consequence of this change in historical situation (or interpretation) is reflected in the thematic displacement that takes place

between the dilemma of Maria and that of Marie. It could be argued that had Maria yielded to the "American temptation" represented by marriage to Lorenzo Surprenant her decision would not have had particularly serious consequences; she would simply have left her country, becoming another statistic in the so-called emigration problem. For Savard, however, the problem is quite different. It is caused by the presence of the foreigner *here,* within the country, as a result of which the community itself is fragmented, split against itself. It would appear that, from *Maria Chapdelaine* to *Menaud, maître-draveur,* the thematic and moral values associated with the dialectic of here and there have changed. For Hémon, the simple fact of staying was an affirmation of continuity and solidarity with the past, while leaving was to leave for the United States and thus a betrayal of the cultural heritage. For Savard, on the other hand, the verb *to leave* always has a positive connotation, associated as it is with the nomadic life of the *coureur de bois.* To leave is to leave not for the United States but for the mountains, that mythical place which finds itself in thematic and ideological conflict with the houses and fields of the sedentary population. In *Menaud,* it is thus *leaving* that becomes an affirmation of fidelity to the ways and values of one's forebears and *staying* that, paradoxically, is seen as a betrayal of those same values. As Martineau points out, Savard is writing out of his great concern for a community threatened with disintegration, a community in which many of the certainties of 1914 have, by 1937, already been lost.[7]

It would, however, be misleading to speak of a generalized ideological split between the two groups (farmers and *coureurs de bois*) in Savard's novel, since the whole point of *Menaud* lies in the hero's failure to rally a community of the faithful against the encroachments of the foreigner. In the century between 1837 and 1937 many things changed, which is probably why André Brochu prefers to situate the opposition on a different level, distinguishing between a community in space, that of the present, and a community in time, a community of race and of ancestral heroes (Brochu 1974, 254). The distinction between the horizontal and vertical dimensions of the work can thus be given, in Brochu's study, a purely thematic formulation: having established an opposition between, on the one hand, an alliance of woman, foreigner, and horizontal nature and, on the other, a configuration of man, ancestors, and ideas, Brochu goes on to remind us that it is in the mountains that Menaud feels closest to his forefathers and that "height in space is linked to depth in time, both implying the same refusal of surface, i.e. of the foreigner and, more secretly, of woman" (264).

Is there, then, any correlation between the formal and thematic aspects of the opposition of vertical and horizontal? In an article written for the *Dictionnaire des oeuvres littéraires du Québec,* François Ricard describes what he calls the lyrical dimension of *Menaud* – made up of metaphors, visions, and the voices from *Maria Chapdelaine* – in terms of a "vast imaginary universe super-imposed on the immediate world of things and events which the characters inhabit" (Ricard 1980, 695). The reader is thus constantly solicited to pass from the "real" time and space of the characters to an ideal or superhuman parallel world which serves as an heroic backdrop to their story. The stylistic distinction between vertical and horizontal (lyrical and narrative, poetic and realistic, etc.) is thus amplified to embrace an opposition between, on the one hand, a universe of symbol, memory, and myth and, on the other, the everyday world of the characters. Clearly, this is only a short step away from the thematic distinction made by Brochu between the community in time (that of the race) and the community in space (that of the characters). To make the connection even clearer, one might reformulate Brochu's distinction and speak of an opposition between a metaphoric space-time, made of relations *in absentia* and oriented towards a mythical past, and a metonymic space-time, made of relations *in praesentia* and oriented towards the present of the diegesis. (In another essay published in *Figures III,* "La rhétorique restreinte," Genette points to the possibility of a theological inter-pretation of the metaphor/metonymy couple, in which it is tempt-ing to see the opposition between the spirit of religious transcendence and the spirit of a down-to-earth immanence. In Genette's image, metaphor would be the Mary of tropes and metonymy the Martha.)

It is to this tension between two different prose styles that Ricard attributes the difficulties experienced by critics trying to assign a generic label to *Menaud.* The ambiguity, he suggests, stems above all from the work's peculiar style, the constant mixing of narrative and lyric, the abundance of poetic devices in a text which nevertheless retains the general appearance of a novel with a story, characters, dialogue, etc. (Ricard 1980, 696). However, this "stylistic" explanation needs to be qualified, since, as we have seen, on the level of the images themselves metonymy plays an important part in grounding the metaphors and similes in the diegesis. In fact, the sources of the ambiguity (and of the critics' uneasiness) reside not in the style, in the narrow sense of the term, but at a deeper level.

André Brochu points us in the right direction when he writes that *Menaud* is not, as some have maintained, an *epic* work. In an epic the "villains" are present in concrete form and enter into real combat with the hero, whereas in *Menaud* the foreigners remain a diffuse and anonymous power (Brochu 1974, 253). There is, however, little doubt in my mind that Savard, had he been allowed to choose, would have loved to make *Menaud, maître-draveur* the French-Canadian epic, a celebration of the triumph of his people over a society which had become anonymous and impersonal, which had betrayed the spiritual values of the community once known as New France. But, when he came to write his epic, Savard encountered an obstacle in the form of historical reality – and that obstacle proved insurmountable. As Lukács argues in his *Theory of the Novel,* "the epic and the novel ... differ from one another not by their authors' fundamental intentions but by the given historico-philosophical realities with which the authors were confronted. The novel is the epic of an age in which the extensive totality of life is no longer directly given, in which the immanence of meaning in life has become a problem, yet which still thinks in terms of totality" (Lukács 1971, 56). How, then, is it possible for Savard to tell the tale of the epic hero Menaud, when Menaud the individual is crushed by the evidence of his historical situation?[8] Lukács is quite clear on this point: "The epic hero is, strictly speaking, never an individual. It is traditionally thought that one of the essential characteristics of the epic is the fact that its theme is not a personal destiny but the destiny of a community. And rightly so, for the completeness, the roundness of the value system which determines the epic cosmos creates a whole which is too organic for any part of it to become so enclosed within itself, so dependent upon itself, as to find itself as an interiority – i.e. to become a personality" (Lukács 1971, 66). As Ricard argues, the old master-driver Menaud tries to bend the historical present to his atemporal vision, to make the real world around him conform to a particular rhetoric of the ideal (Ricard 1972, 113). It is Menaud's impotence, his inability to carry out this project, which will lead him into madness and turn Savard's frustrated epic into a novel.

The confrontation with the enemy, the showdown that Menaud so desperately needs in order to justify his own existence, will never take place. The terms as well as the stakes of the struggle have changed. Menaud still lives in the world of heroic gestures, the world of the epic or, perhaps more aptly, of the Hollywood western in which a Gary Cooper is still capable of single-handedly rescuing the community. But the world has changed: oppression and exploitation have become impersonal and anonymous; they no longer wear a particular, recognizable face but hide behind the company, the economy, the law. As for the two villains of the piece, Menaud's adversary, le Délié, is simply an empty symbol, a scapegoat, and the foreigner is conspicuous by his absence – he never deigns to set foot in the world of the novel, will not leave the boardrooms of Bay Street or Wall Street. And that is what Menaud does not understand, for Menaud is himself an anachronism. His community, the one he believes in and would gladly die for, belongs to an essentially tribal past and has nothing to do with the realities of modern society. When he finally arrives in his mountain retreat, ready to fight, to defend his heritage against an eternally absent enemy, the warrior-hero is transformed overnight into a pathetic old man who will live the rest of his life in the past conditional, in the mode of impotence and failure, the mode ultimately of madness:

Il s'était représenté cent fois la scène: la sommation d'abord, ensuite, sa réponse droite et fière. Puis, la pourchasse de l'intrus jusqu'au bas de la montagne, quelque chose comme une débâcle de toutes les colères que le pays avait sur le coeur depuis les années de servitude.

Triomphant, il aurait ensuite regagné ses chasses, les sanctuaires profonds de son domaine, les aires étincelantes de ses lacs; il aurait bu le coup de la liberté à même l'air frais et vierge des monts.

Le soir, il se serait enfin reposé en tête à tête avec ses morts consolés. (*Menaud,* 181–2)

Madness, here, is an exile, a fall from grace. To appreciate the nature and the full import of Menaud's madness, it is necessary to understand the state from which he has fallen, a state which seems to approximate what Lukács, in a famous passage, describes as the age of the epic:

Happy are those ages when the starry sky is the map of all possible paths – ages whose paths are illuminated by the light of the stars. Everything in such ages is new and yet familiar, full of adventure and yet their own. The world is wide and yet it is like a home, for the fire that burns in the soul is of the same essential nature as the stars; the world and the self, the light and the fire, are sharply distinct, yet they never become permanent strangers to one another, for fire is the soul of all light and all fire clothes itself in light. Thus each action of the soul becomes meaningful and rounded in this duality: complete in meaning – in *sense* – and complete for the senses; rounded because the soul rests within itself even while it acts; rounded because its action separates itself from it and, having become itself, finds a centre of its own and draws a closed circumference round itself. "Philosophy is really homesickness," says Novalis: "it is the urge to be at home everywhere." (Lukács 1971, 29)

It is from this kind of homesickness that Menaud suffers and for which Alexis seeks a remedy in his ideal of freedom, his dream of a community of ever open doors where there is no philosophy but where all men are philosophers: "Etre libre, c'était, en quelque endroit qu'on allât où les pères étaient allés, sur tous les visages reconnaître quelque chose du visage des siens, dans les moeurs, quelques traits de ses moeurs; c'était voir toute porte s'ouvrir, c'était entendre dans sa langue: 'Entrez! vous êtes chez vous!'" (*Menaud,* 172–3). But, in the world of *Menaud,* such a dream is just that – a dream and nothing more. The "totality of life that is rounded from within" (Lukács 1971, 60) and which is the domain of the epic, is no longer a given. What is left to the novel to express is a state of "transcendental homelessness" (41).

Menaud's madness – of a kind unknown in the epic[9] – is a manifestation of this homelessness. It is a sign of the type of disjunction of soul and world that Lukács associates with abstract idealism and which consists of a narrowing of the soul: "The hero's soul is at rest, rounded and complete within itself like a work of art or a divinity; but this mode of being can only express itself in the outside world by means of inadequate adventures which contain no counter-force within them precisely because the hero is so mani-acally imprisoned in himself; and this isolation, which makes the soul resemble a work of art, also separates it from all outside reality and from all those other areas of the soul which have not been seized by the demon. Thus a maximum of inwardly attained meaning becomes a maximum of senselessness and the sublime turns to madness, to monomania" (Lukács 1971, 100). Menaud's soul is like a work of art, but a work of art which corresponds to no reality in the outside world. Exiled in an unhappy age, Menaud is con-demned to wander in search of meaning. The paths he treads are not those of the glowing world of the epic but the "chemins du cerveau," the paths of inner exile which belong to the novel and to madness:

Il referma brusquement la porte.
Cette fête-là n'était plus pour lui.
Il n'était qu'un intrus maintenant, un rôdeur sombre, furtif, le dépossédé, revenu, malgré les lois, s'emplir une dernière fois les yeux au bord de la fête interdite. (*Menaud,* 182–3)

Reduced to the status of an impotent spectator, Menaud can only look on and wait for the night of madness to shroud his pain. His participation in the world is over.

To sum up. On the level of the images, metonymy in *Menaud* serves to authenticate and naturalize the metaphors and to ground them in the diegesis. However, the diegesis is itself already strongly metaphoric, given the cycle of the seasons, the thematic and ideological role of spatial figures (land, forest, mountains, fields, house, cabin, etc.), and there is no doubt which mode is dominant: metonymy plays an important but secondary role. On the level of style in the wider sense of the term, Savard's predilection for metaphor and for a "vertical" *écriture* is reflected in his struggle against time "by inscribing things above its course." [10] In this respect, the author's thwarted ambitions are inscribed in his language; though he aspires to the abolition of time characteristic of Lukács's description of the epic, he is constantly brought up against historical reality: "In the epic the life-immanence of meaning is so strong that it abolishes time ... In the novel, meaning is separated from life, and hence the essential from the temporal; we might almost say that the entire inner action of the novel is nothing but a struggle against the power of time" (Lukács 1971, 122). Bakhtin, for his part, emphasizes not so much the timelessness of epic as the absolute nature of the past it represents and the absolute distance that separates the epic world from contemporary reality. [11] This distance informs the style and tone of epic discourse and constitutes a limit which cannot be transgressed without crossing over into the novel. [12] According to this view, one could argue that Savard was tempted by the "epic incorporation of the contemporary hero into a world of ancestors and founders," by the desire to transfer to contemporary events "the time-and-value contour of the past, thus attaching them to the world of fathers, of beginnings and peak times – canonizing these events, as it were, while they are still current" (Bakhtin 1981, 14–15).

Savard's preference for exalted language (over the demands of a realism anchored in a believable story) would be less problematic if his themes were better suited to such a style, if the work were indeed a celebration of epic deeds accomplished in the name of a unified ideology. What becomes evident in the course of the narrative is that modern society is no longer capable of nourishing such a vision or of sustaining such a style. It is this shattering of the metaphoric illusion which leads to Menaud's madness, a madness which is every bit as *literary* as Don Quixote's. [13] Yet even here, metaphor is never very far away: "Ce n'est pas une folie comme une autre!" says Josime. "Ça me dit, à moi, que c'est un avertissement" (*Menaud*, 205). In other words, it is a madness with a messsage. The writing never allows the world of the novel simply to come into being, to be produced as an *effet de réel;* instead it prefers, stylistically, to take refuge in the sibylline oracles of madness in order to figure the failure of the metaphoric coherence of the hero's vision. Metaphor is not the mark of the epic – the epic being, like the novel, a predominantly metonymic genre – but it becomes, in *Menaud,* the sign of the epic's impossibility, a monument to the failure of myth to fill the gap left by the loss of history. But though the aspiration to epic meaning may be thwarted, it is never wholly set aside.

In François Ricard's words, Menaud is an epic hero flung into the world of the novel: "In other words, a being dominated by a profoundly mythical cast of mind, who finds himself plunged into a negating universe, in which his dearest aspirations come to grief on the obstacle of a devastating reality" (Ricard 1972, 117). The path trodden by Menaud leads, without ever arriving, from one vision and one genre to something else: from the world of the epic to that of the novel. For Savard, it was not a chosen path, any more than it was for Braddock's Redcoats, but it is a path which points, perversely enough and in spite of itself, towards the modern Quebec novel. Of course, I do not wish to suggest that *Menaud* is a "modern" novel or that there is any real compatibility between its author's worldview and the spirit of the Quiet Revolution.[14] It is not so much a case of Savard's nationalism foreshadowing the novels of the sixties as of the failure of his text to provide adequate compensation for the loss of history, thereby implying the existence of a literary field independent of other social institutions. So *Menaud, maître-draveur* becomes literature in a way not previously seen in Quebec. As Marie-Andrée Beaudet argues, the year 1937 marks a shift to a typically modern form of relatively autonomous literary activity (Beaudet 1987, 63). In this sense, then, one might be tempted to argue that *Menaud* is, contrary to certain appearances, a modernist text and to recall the debate between Frank Kermode and Joseph Frank over the latter's notion of spatial form, which Kermode identified with the denial of history characteristic of the political and cultural fascism frequently associated with the modernist movement (Frank 1981, 215–27, and Mitchell 1986, 96–8).

As one critic has said, it is difficult for a work of literature "to live an inner action which has strayed from the path of its initial project" (Ducrocq-Poirier 1978, 333). However, the fact remains that

the peculiar interest, at once literary and historical, of *Menaud* lies
precisely in its difficulty of being, in the ontological struggle it
embodies that was to be taken up explicitly and paradigmatically
almost thirty years later by the young (and revolutionary) author of
Prochain épisode. Robert Major, who compared Savard's and Aquin's
novels in 1983, saw a profound paradox in the many parallels between
the works of these two authors, who come from opposite ends of
the political spectrum. The paradox disappears, of course, as soon
as we accept the hypothesis that Aquin, writing in the mid-sixties,
is in fact proposing a self-conscious critique of the French-Canadian
myths which underlie *Menaud*. Thus, for example, the theme of the
absent enemy, seen so clearly in Menaud's desperate need for a
face-to-face confrontation with a real adversary, is developed by
Aquin – "J'ai besoin de H. de Heutz. S'il n'arrive pas, que vais-je
devenir?" – with an intertextual awareness bordering on parody. I
shall examine the modalities of Aquin's critique in chapter 5.

CHAPTER THREE

On the Outside Looking In: The Political Economy of Everyday Life in Gabrielle Roy's Bonheur d'occasion

And there is the girl behind the counter too – I would as soon have her true history as the hundred and fiftieth life of Napoleon or seventieth study of Keats and his use of Miltonic inversion which old Professor Z and his like are now inditing.   Virginia Woolf, *A Room of One's Own*

Jam tomorrow, never jam today.   John Maynard Keynes

Nearly fifty years ago a posh, lanky young man packed his bags and made off into the undergrowth of England. Like a mountaineer conquering his own nightmare, he embarked on a two-month personal encounter with the unknown – the working class, who populated his childhood memories as a spectre of fear and loathing. He made a sentimental journey – it was a conjugation of the personal and the political – amidst the supposedly silent majority, the people excluded from politics who appeared as vagrants on the doorstep of democracy. (Campbell 1984, 1–2)

That man was, of course, George Orwell, described here by Beatrix Campbell in her *Wigan Pier Revisited*. His own book, *The Road to Wigan Pier*, had appeared in 1937, the same year in which Félix-Antoine Savard had published the original version of *Menaud, maître-draveur*. The distance between the two worlds, between the ancestral forests of Charlevoix and the urban decay and dire poverty of England's industrial North, would seem at first glance to be historically, ideologically, and aesthetically unbridgeable. And yet, only a few short years later, in the summer of 1941, a young journalist from Saint-Boniface was already at work on a very different kind of French-Canadian novel as she tramped the streets of her adopted city, discovering in the slums of Saint-Henri a landscape far closer to Orwell's Wigan and Barnsley and Sheffield than to anything that might have haunted the dreams, or even the wildest nightmares, of Savard's mad Moses.

In her address to the Royal Society of Canada on the occasion
of her induction into that august body in 1947, Gabrielle Roy recounts
how little things have changed in the intervening years, as she gives
directions for how to enter that world on the other side of the
tracks: "You go down Atwater Street and come almost at once to
the populous Notre-Dame. And there before you lies the same grey
village within our great city, the village that is found in all the great
cities of the world, where, in dust and smoke and overcrowding,
in a lack of air and green space, live the majority of human beings
... I arrived on the poor hillock where Saint-Henri tries to get above
the noise, the racket, the unclean air, and stretches toward the sky,
past the steel and the exasperated sound of bells, past tree branches
heavy with soot and dust. From the little summit, I could see that
Saint-Henri had not changed in any way. There were still no decent
houses to shelter its families, there was still no beauty, there were
no amenities in the workers' lives" (Roy 1982, 157–8).

One measure of the distance between Savard's self-destructing epic
and Gabrielle Roy's foray into urban realism lies in the transformation
of the nomad figure. In *Menaud, maître-draveur,* the nomad, in the
shape of the *coureur de bois,* is the positively valued term in a
series of binary oppositions which define the ideological space of
Savard's world. In *Bonheur d'occasion,* however, the nomad has
been stripped of any archetypal romance to become the modern
déraciné par excellence, the unemployed urban worker transformed,
at best, into taxi driver, at worst, into cannon-fodder to be shipped
off to Europe as part of the great twentieth-century epic. "Did not
the soldiers become the true travellers in this world, pilgrims of
universal brotherhood, they who left to fight the enemies and found
everywhere nothing but artisans and workmen like themselves – and
often the unemployed, just as they had been?" (Roy 1982, 163). In
the world of *Bonheur d'occasion,* the nomads – in Beatrix Campbell's
phrase, those "vagrants on the doorstep of democracy" – are called
Azarius and Ernest and Pitou. But, inconceivable in Savard's universe,
the nomad is also called Rose-Anna, a woman who walks the streets
of Saint-Henri every spring, pregnant yet again, in search of a house
to rent. Rose-Anna is "almost fifty now and has never lived more
than two years in the same house" (Roy 1982, 161). And, on a
different level, the nomad is Gabrielle Roy herself, like Orwell, a
writer in exile – temporarily at least – from her home and from
her class, as she makes a sentimental journey not into the forests
of Charlevoix, but into the undergrowth of Montreal.[1]

There are, of course, many differences between Orwell and Roy,
and I shall come to some of them shortly. One thing they have in

common, though, and which sets them apart from Savard, is the conscious need to ground their writing in historically defined personal experience. Which is not to say that Savard was not close to his subject; his problem in writing *Menaud* was that he chose a form which implied a unified ideology that was not materially grounded, with the result that both author and protagonist seem to be taken by surprise by a historical reality that ends up invading and cracking a literary structure not designed to contain it. In the case of both Roy and Orwell, however, there is an awareness of stepping outside of one's own immediate reality in search of both another world and a literary form capable of rendering one's experience of that world. The danger, of course, is that the writer will prove to be nothing more than an ethnographic reporter, a scientific "observer" recording the curiosities found in the "other" culture. Indeed, this side of Orwell was suspected by at least one friend of his during the period after his return to England from Burma in 1927. "I never took his tramping seriously," says Dennis Collings. "His tramping was like his hop picking: it was an anthropological experience he wanted to go through, in the end leading to something that could be written about" (Wadhams 1984, 36). But this is a comment about the man rather than about the writer, and the case of Orwell is sufficiently instructive for us to spend a little time recalling the strategies he developed for dealing with the specific problem of *writing* about a community from the outside.

Raymond Williams has argued convincingly that the conventional division of Orwell's writing of the thirties into the "documentary" and "factual" work, on the one hand, and the "fictional" and "imaginative" work, on the other, is superficial and misleading: "Literature used not to be divided in these external ways. The rigid distinction between 'documentary' and 'imaginative' writing is a product of the nineteenth century, and most widely distributed in our own time. Its basis is a naïve definition of the 'real world,' and then a naïve separation of it from the observation and imagination of men" (Williams 1984, 41). In fact, as Williams shows, all of Orwell's writing of the period draws on essentially the same material, and his "documentary" work is every bit as "literary" (i.e., shaped and organized) as his novels. The problem is not, then, one of "fact" versus "fiction" but rather of the capacities of different literary methods and forms to render the fundamental problem of social relationship: how does a "cultivated man" go about describing the life of the "man in the street"? Orwell's solution in the novels, in *Burmese Days, A Clergyman's Daughter,* and *Keep the Aspidistra Flying,* is to create "the figure of the intermediary (the 'shock-absorber of the bourgeoisie' as he once referred to people like himself). Instead of direct realisation of what was observed, he created the intermediary figure who goes around and to whom things happen" (Williams 1984, 47–8). From a social point of view, the problem with this structure is that, though it allows Orwell to describe the things that happened to him, it remains essentially passive and allows for no intervention in the social and political process. In his essays of the period, by contrast, Orwell is present – the Orwell who, let us not forget, was a successful literary creation of Eric Blair's. "Instead of diluting his consciousness through an intermediary, as the mode of fiction had seemed to require, he now writes directly and powerfully about his whole experience. The prose is at once strengthened, as the alternation between an anxious impersonation and a passively impersonal obser- vation gives way to a direct voice, in which there is more literary creation than in all the more conventionally 'imaginative' attempts" (Williams 1984, 49). The authority of "personal experience" established through the creation of the isolated independent observer who has "seen for himself" can be used to political effect in the ensuing debate on the possibilities and limitations of socialist intervention. In such a structure the political point, as Williams himself concludes, *is* the literary point. "Intermediate characters and experiences which do not form a part of this world – this structure of feeling – are simply omitted. What is left in is 'documentary' enough, but the process of selection and organisation is a literary act: the character of the observer is as real and yet created as the real and yet created world he so powerfully describes" (52).

In *Bonheur d'occasion,* Gabrielle Roy is faced with much the same problem as Orwell, but her response is quite different. In the first place, she chooses not to intervene directly in the world she describes, as Orwell had done in the "documentary" *Road to Wigan Pier.* (This statement will have to be qualified later, when I discuss the question of the narrator's presence in the novel.) But, unlike the Orwell of the novels, she does not compensate for her own absence by creating a single intermediary figure to act as the passive surrogate for her experience as an observer. Instead, she opts for a technique of what might loosely be termed omniscient third-person narration with shift- ing focalization; she creates a number of different characters who observe each other as well as the world they live in, so that we have a narrative structure which is intrinsically polyphonic and dia- logic.[2] Setting out to give a voice and a point of view to the people whose desperate plight she describes, Roy achieves something which Orwell was probably incapable of, judging from this comment by a close friend, Brenda Salkeld: "I said, 'Never write about people, you don't understand them. Even about yourself you haven't a clue.' He might as well have been in a glass case. He didn't understand people at all" (Wadhams 1984, 39).

Within this basic and very fluid form, two characters stand out in *Bonheur d'occasion*. The first is Rose-Anna, who is the sentimental focus of the novel and who, according to Gabrielle Roy, had forced her creator's hand in much the same way as history had forced Savard's: "This little working-class woman, gentle and imaginative – I can admit this to you today – almost forced her way into my story, then turned the plot upside down and, finally, managed to dominate the book through her very un-literary quality of tenderness. And I'm very grateful today to Rose-Anna for having forced my hand, because without the humility and strength of her tenderness I doubt that my story would have had the gift of touching the heart" (Roy 1982, 159–60). For all her powerful presence in the novel, Rose-Anna remains, on the larger stage, a passive character. She is all understanding but she does not comprehend what is happening to and around her; like Menaud, she is confused by the changes she sees in her world and which she is powerless to stop or influence in any meaningful way. This is why Roy required another character to articulate Rose-Anna's intuitively compassionate vision, to act as the novel's intellectual and ideological focus. That character is Emmanuel. Like Orwell, and like Gabrielle Roy herself, Emmanuel is something of an outsider; he dreams of "a new social order based on the dignity of work and a just division of wealth" (Roy 1982, 170). He is the head to Rose-Anna's heart, the mind to her body. He goes to war at the end of the novel in much the same way as Orwell had gone to Spain in 1937 after the writing of *Wigan Pier*, in order to "see what was happening" and to fight, not for the preservation of the old order, but for the establishment of a new one.

Emmanuel leaves Saint-Henri by train: "Le visage collé à la vitre, Emmanuel vit fuir les barrières du passage à niveau, le Sacré-Coeur de bronze, l'église, la cabine de l'aiguilleur montée sur pilotis. Il aperçut un arbre, dans un fond de cour, qui poussait ses branches tordues entre les fils électriques et un réseau de cordes à linge. Ses feuilles dures et ratatinées semblaient à demi mortes de fatigue avant même de s'être pleinement ouvertes" (*Bonheur,* 386). The image of life strangled and stunted by urban growth is clear and strong. As often, however, the novelist cannot resist pushing metonymy over into metaphor to make her point and taking back the point of view she had given on loan to her character. In the process she echoes the closing "avertissement" of *Menaud:* "Très bas dans le ciel, des nuées sombres annonçaient l'orage."

It is by train, too, that George Orwell leaves Wigan, through a landscape every bit as desolate:

The train bore me away, through the monstrous scenery of slag-heaps, chimneys, piled scrap-iron, foul canals, paths of cindery mud criss-crossed by the prints of clogs. This was March, but the weather had been horribly cold and everywhere there were mounds of blackened snow. As we moved slowly through the outskirts of the town we passed row after row of little grey slum houses running at right angles to the embankment. At the back of one of the houses a young woman was kneeling on the stones, poking a stick up the leaden waste-pipe which ran from the sink inside and which I suppose was blocked. I had time to see everything about her – her sacking apron, her clumsy clogs, her arms reddened by the cold. She looked up as the train passed, and I was almost near enough to catch her eye. She had a round pale face, the usual exhausted face of the slum girl who is twenty-five and looks forty, thanks to miscarriages and drudgery; and it wore, for the second in which I saw it, the most desolate, hopeless expression I have ever seen. It struck me then that we are mistaken when we say that "It isn't the same for them as it would be for us," and that people bred in the slums can imagine nothing but the slums. For what I saw in her face was not the ignorant suffering of an animal. She knew well enough what was happening to her – understood as well as I did how dreadful a destiny it was to be kneeling there in the bitter cold, on the slimy stones of a slum backyard, poking a stick up a foul drain-pipe. (Orwell 1962, 16–17)

A comparison of these two paragraphs shows how Orwell profits from his "documentary" method. Since he is already there, centrally present in the text, he has no need to shift into an overtly meta-phorical mode to make sure that he is getting his point across. Both voice and vision are explicitly his, and the passage from story to discourse, from detail to generalisation, is both natural and easy and is effected without any impairment of the powerful and haunting visual image. Besides, Orwell's train is taking him out of the "other" world and back to civilization, back from Wigan to *Wigan Pier*, to the writing of the book and the possibility – however vague, however deferred – of active intervention in the lives of those whom he has been describing, "back to an indifferent and sleepy and uncaring world, which has to be told about the isolation and the suffering" (Williams 1984, 53). Emmanuel, on the other hand, is being sent off by his creator not to tell his story but to fight in a war whose outcome is uncertain and whose point is, at best, ambiguous. Instead of opening onto the possibility of social and political action, *Bonheur* seeks metaphorical closure in the gathering storm clouds that herald the end, if not of narrative, at least of this narrative.

It is this feeling of having failed to intervene, of having abandoned her characters to a world where there is no possibility of change, that haunts Gabrielle Roy's address to the Royal Society in 1947. "The novelist, impelled to describe certain misfortunes he has seen, can be overwhelmed with a sense of futility if he sees the same misfortunes on the point of being repeated" (Roy 1982, 159). In a sense, her address can be seen as a postscript to the novel; it functions in much the same way as Orwell's documentary technique, exploiting the authority of personal experience and observation of a given community to demand change. Roy's tactic in this short piece is to take the road back to Wigan, back to Saint-Henri and to the characters she had left there, but this time as herself. The message she delivers in her own voice to the members of the Royal Society is that the problems of poverty and injustice have not been solved by the relative prosperity of the war years and that, far from being local historical accidents, they are in fact endemic to her society's economic system:

The textile workers have been on strike in Saint-Henri. They wanted to bring their salaries in line with the rising cost of living. But immediately the cost of living went up again, so that after all the suffering of the strike, the condition of workers' lives has not changed an iota.

"But the workers are making good money!" Rose-Anna hears from all sides. "They're going to ruin industry, upset the economy." Funny thing, Rose-Anna muses, it's always the workers who get the blame when prices rise. Why not put some blame on those invisible people we find it so hard to imagine, behind the high walls of the spinning mills and factories of Saint-Henri, far beyond these ramparts of smoke and steam and the rumble of machinery? But Rose-Anna always gets confused by such thoughts, and quickly comes back to the problems closest to her: milk at sixteen cents a quart and meat at a price she can barely afford; shoes fifty per cent dearer; even bread is going up. She has never felt so baffled by this doubtful equilibrium of profit that keeps our social system going. (Roy 1982, 161–2)

This is the theme, uttered loud and clear, that will run right through the 1947 text as Roy listens to one character after another: that society's woes are economic and that the remedies must be economic too. And though her spokesman of choice is, we are told, dead – dead of starvation in a Hong Kong prison camp – his vision can still be invoked and is invested now with the peculiar authority of martyrdom: "And in this society Emmanuel imagined there were no more reasons for strikes or the squandering of foodstuffs, because an intelligent government would ensure for workers conditions and salaries that were equitable. Moreover, industry was no longer to be uniquely concerned with selling products with no regard for the people's real needs; and, finally, the exploitation of our resources would be undertaken in the interest of the greatest number" (Roy 1982, 170). It seems to me that Gabrielle Roy goes further than George Orwell in her denunciation of consumer capitalism and its dehumanising effects, perhaps because Orwell's criticisms always seem to get sidetracked by the complexity of the class structures he describes and his own highly ambivalent attitude toward them. For, so long as it is possible to describe class and social structure mainly in terms of relatively external and superficial differences in social behaviour such as accent and personal taste, the underlying economic relationships which shape them will remain masked. Raymond Williams points to Orwell's curious equivocations on this score, stating he was blinded by his sentimental image of England as a "family with the wrong members in control": "It is strange to have to make this point about an Orwell whose emphasis on the determining fact of money is so intense and even at times (in the thirties) extreme. But there's money in the pocket, and more money in more pockets will mean precisely the classlessness he refers to. There's also, however, that quite different 'money' which is capital, which is the ownership and creation of the means of social life itself. Here any question about control is inevitably a question about this ownership, which can indeed remain unaltered in any major way during a period in which the visible signs of 'class,' the small change of the system, have been if not wiped out (for there is no sign of that happening, thirty years after Orwell wrote) at least modified, moderated, and evolved" (Williams 1984, 24). Coming from a society in which class relationships are, on the whole, more transparent and less totalitarian, Gabrielle Roy has little difficulty in seeing through the patriarchal ideology of the "family" (which she dissects with remarkable hardheadedness in *Bonheur d'occasion*[3]) to the economic realities of systemic exploitation which lie beneath. I shall argue in the remainder of this chapter that *Bonheur d'occasion* is indeed a novel about money and that its principal thematic and semantic structures flow from the economic relationships that shape its fictional world.[4]

As a GEOGRAPHICAL entity, the Saint-Henri of the forties can be defined as a transitional space not only between town and

country but also between the relatively new way of life associated
with industry, large urban centres, and the traditional values and
rhythms of rural Quebec.[5] As a *faubourg* of Montreal, Saint-Henri is
a village which has been swallowed up by the city in its relentless
growth but which retains some of the characteristics of village life,
such as a sense, however diluted, of community. Despite the fact
that life here continues on a scale which remains recognizably
human, the scars of accelerated industrialization are everywhere
apparent, and the countryside is transformed in the memories of
these city-dwellers into an earthly paradise from which they have
been driven.

Moreover, in the city poverty and hardship are experienced in a
different way, as not only a physical but also a moral degradation,[6]
perhaps because here all human relations are mediated by money.
(And not only human relations – deals are also made with God,
the Virgin Mary, and the saints [*Bonheur,* 124, 144, 205].) This is
particularly clear within the most sacred of French-Canadian institutions, the family; in *Bonheur d'occasion* not a single relationship is
spared from the impact of money or lack of it. A single example
will suffice. When Eugène Lacasse tells his mother that he has joined
the army and that she will receive twenty dollars a month in pay,
Rose-Anna struggles to set the sum of money out of her mind but
finds herself unable to keep it out for long: "Elle repoussa cette
idée avec énergie, serrant un peu les lèvres … Un peu plus tard,
elle s'aperçut que ces vingt dollars étaient déjà engloutis, qu'elle les
avait, dans son imagination, dépensés jusqu'au dernier sou. Elle
haleta doucement, honteuse et quand même soulagée" (99–100). In
this world, no human emotion or bond is proof against the all-per-
vasive influence of money.

The urban space is itself divided along lines of economic activity
and social class; Saint-Henri (the space of work, unemployment, and
domestic poverty) is defined in relation to both Westmount (capital
and economic power) and rue Sainte-Catherine (the temptations of
the consumer society). The bitter irony of an economy of abundance
and excess[7] which founds its wealth on the exclusion of a whole
segment of society is brought home most powerfully in the remarkable monologue of a minor character, Alphonse Poirier:

Avez-vous déjà marché, vous autres, su la rue Sainte-Catherine, pas une
cenne dans vot' poche, et regardé tout ce qu'y a dans les vitrines? Oui,
hein! Ben moi aussi, ça m'est arrivé. Et j'ai vu du beau, mes amis, comme
pas beaucoup de monde a vu du beau. Moi, j'ai eu le temps de voir du
beau: pis en masse. Tout ce que j'ai vu de beau dans ma vie, à traîner

la patte su la rue Sainte-Catherine, ça pourrait quasiment pas se dire! Je sais pas, moi, des Packard, des Buick, j'en ai vu des autos faites pour le speed pis pour le fun. Pis après ça, j'ai vu leurs catins de cire, avec des belles robes de bal sur le dos, pis d'autres, qui sont pas habillés une miette. Qu'est-ce que vous voyez-t-y pas su la rue Sainte-Catherine? Des meubles, des chambres à coucher, d'aut' catins en fanfreluches de soie. Pis des magasins de sport, des cannes de golf, des raquettes de tennis, des skis, des lignes de pêche. S'y a quelqu'un au monde qu'aurait le temps de s'amuser avec toutes ces affaires-là, c'est ben nous autres, hein?

Mais le seul fun qu'on a, c'est de les regarder. Pis la mangeaille à c'te heure! Je sais pas si vous avez déjà eu le ventre creux, vous autres, et que vous êtes passés par un restaurant d'iousque qu'y a des volailles qui rôtissent à petit feu su une broche? Mais ça, c'est pas toute, mes amis. La société nous met toute sous les yeux; tout ce qu'y a de beau sous les yeux. Mais allez pas croire qu'a fait rien que nous mette sous les yeux!

Ah! non, à nous conseille d'acheter aussi. (59–60)

The passage is particularly interesting because it raises, in a more forthright and critical way than Orwell manages to do, the question of society's production and regulation of desire through the economic system. Moreover, it does so in terms of two thematic and narratological categories which are of prime importance in the novel's construction: time and vision.

The importance of vision, of looking, in *Bonheur d'occasion,* is something of a commonplace in the critical literature on the novel.[8] Rather than go over ground already covered by earlier commentators, I shall go straight to what is of immediate interest to me here – the transformation of the individual by the gaze into sign or object. This process, which is perfectly consistent with Alphonse's description of the spectacle of vicarious consumption, is particularly apparent in the visual exchanges which take place between Jean Lévesque and Florentine Lacasse in the early parts of the novel. Take, for example, the account of what Florentine registers as she observes Jean steadily through half-closed lids:

Le vêtement d'étoffe anglaise ne rappelait pas les magasins du faubourg. Il lui apparut que ce seul vêtement indiquait un caractère, un genre d'existence comme privilégiés. Non que le jeune homme fût vêtu avec recherche; au contraire, il affectait une certaine nonchalance: sa cravate était à peine nouée, ses mains quelque peu tachées de cambouis, et sa chevelure, qu'il ne ménageait en aucun temps, allant toujours nu-tête à la pluie ou au soleil et par les plus grands froids, se montrait indocile et touffue. Mais justement, ce manque de soin dans les petits détails donnait plus d'importance aux choses coûteuses qu'il portait: la montre-bracelet dont le cadran miroitait à chacun de ses gestes, le foulard de riche soie enroulé négligemment autour de son cou, les gants de fine peau sortant un peu de la poche de son complet. Il sembla à Florentine que, si elle se penchait vers ce jeune homme, elle respirerait l'odeur même de la grande ville grisante, bien vêtue, bien nourrie, satisfaite et allant à ses divertissements qui se paient cher. Et soudain, elle évoqua la rue Sainte-Catherine, les vitrines des grands magasins, la foule élégante du samedi soir, les étalages des fleuristes, les restaurants avec leurs portes à tambours et leurs tables dressées presque sur le trottoir derrière les baies miroitantes, l'entrée lumineuse des théâtres, leurs allées qui s'enfoncent au-delà de la tour vitrée de la caissière, entre les reflets de hauts miroirs, de rampes lustrées, de plantes, comme en une ascension si naturelle vers l'écran où passent les plus belles images du monde: tout ce qu'elle désirait, admirait, enviait, flotta devant ses yeux. (21)

The description is remarkable in its assimilation of the person observed to the society which produces him as object, as object of desire. For Jean is just that: a product, a commodity, a department store mannequin, an image on the cinema screen of consumer capitalism. And Florentine, of course, cannot afford him, can only look. Or buy a moment of his time with her own body and her own future.

When Jean finally does take her out to a restaurant, waylaying her unexpectedly as she leaves her work, she is distressed that the image she sees reflected in his eyes is not the one she would have wished to create, is not sufficiently *produced:*

Elle rencontra son regard; elle s'y vit comme dans une glace, et ses mains s'activèrent pour rétablir l'équilibre de son petit chapeau. Sa pensée trottait. Elle avait imaginé, bien sûr, qu'elle sortirait ainsi un jour avec le jeune homme, mais mise en ses plus jolis atours. Elle pensa avec détresse, avec une réelle détresse, à sa jolie robe neuve, très ajustée à la taille, qui lui faisait des seins ronds, tout petits, et des hanches juste assez saillantes. Avec un serrement de coeur, elle passa en revue tous les petits bijoux de son coffre dans lequel elle aurait pu choisir une épingle pour ses cheveux, des bracelets, quatre ou cinq qui auraient sonné à son bras, et peut-être aussi une broche pour son corsage. N'était-ce vraiment pas navrant, pensait-elle, d'aller en ville dans sa pauvre petite robe de travail et sans aucun bijou? (79)

Seeing herself as an object to be manufactured and displayed, to be sold and consumed, she panics at the thought she might have forgotten her lipstick, and her heart sinks when she realizes that she has a run in her stocking. For here production is at once industrial and theatrical – the production of images, of commodities divorced from everyday life, of the world as department store window or cinema screen. What Florentine, in her eagerness to be a part of the play, does not realize is that the beautiful illusion depends on the careful elimination of all trace of the means of production. Thus, when she starts to rummage through her purse and spread out on the restaurant table "tout son attirail de beauté" – lipstick, comb, and powder compact – Jean's look of embarrassed horror speaks eloquently of the immense distance separating the people of Saint-Henri from the society which is built upon their labour but which excludes them so cynically.

As Jean himself points out, Florentine is caught between two worlds: "Florentine ... Florentine Lacasse ... moitié peuple, moitié chanson, moitié printemps, moitié misère ..." (31). One way of examining this division is precisely through the transformation of merchandise into spectacle associated with the shift to consumer capitalism. In France this shift occurred with the development of the department store in the second half of the nineteenth century, but, in a clergy-dominated Quebec, which was still clinging to its rural power base well into our own century, the shift took place consid-erably later. As Rachel Bowlby argues in her study of Zola, Gissing, and Dreiser, "The second half of the nineteenth century witnessed a radical shift in the concerns of industry: from production to selling and from the satisfaction of stable needs to the invention of new desires" (Bowlby 1985, 2). Florentine Lacasse is typical of her social class in this transitional period in that she finds herself caught between two systems, between an economy of need and an economy of desire, between her everyday life of work and family in Saint-Henri and the dream factories of rue Sainte-Catherine.

An excellent illustration of the way the opposition between need and desire functions in the novel is to be found in chapter 9, in which Rose-Anna wanders into the *Quinze Cents* where her daughter works at the lunch counter. Surprised to see her mother outside her usual domestic setting, Florentine decides to treat her to a hot meal: "Y a justement du poulet à quarante cennes aujourd'hui. M'en vas te payer la traite" (120). But things are not so simple for Rose-Anna, and the invitation throws her into turmoil. Horrified by the price, she is nevertheless tempted by the sheer extravagance which, for her, has the force of a transgression: "Toute sa vie, elle, qui connaissait si bien le prix des aliments, elle, qui avait appris à composer des repas solides et peu coûteux, avait gardé une répugnance de paysanne à payer dans les restaurants un repas qu'elle aurait pu préparer – elle ne se défendait pas d'en faire le calcul – à un prix tellement plus modique. Mais toute sa vie aussi, elle avait refoulé la forte tentation de s'accorder une fois en passant ce plaisir qu'elle jugeait si extravagant" (121).

In Rose-Anna's case, we are led to believe, the conflict between the two systems – of need and desire – can be explained in terms of the transition from an agrarian economy, with its relative self-sufficiency of the family (her "farmer's repugnance" for spending money in a restaurant on food she could prepare at home), to an urban economy which seduces consumers according to a social logic that first creates desires, then transforms them into needs. Rose-Anna finally succumbs to temptation and lets Florentine bring her the chicken, though with little enough good grace:

Mais elle ajouta, plusieurs fois, avec cette sourde ténacité qui lui gâtait la moindre extravagance:
– C'est trop cher, par exemple, sais-tu, quarante cennes. Me semble que ça vaut pas ça. Pense donc, Florentine; c'est cher!
Quand elle eut mangé le poulet, Florentine lui coupa un morceau de tarte.
– Ah! je peux plus, dit Rose-Anna. C'est déjà ben trop.
– C'est tout compris dans le repas, insista Florentine. Ça coûte pas plus cher.
– Ben, je vas y goûter d'abord, dit Rose-Anna. Mais c'est plus la faim.
(123)

Having stepped out of the world of needs ("c'est plus la faim"), Rose-Anna is incapable of enjoying a few minutes in the world of desire without being nagged by her conscience. So when Florentine, in a sentimental moment of generosity, makes Rose-Anna a present of the two dollars she had been saving to buy a pair of silk stockings, Rose-Anna turns bright red but takes the gift anyway, turning it with her words into something quite different, something akin to a welfare payment: "Pour te dire vrai, avoua Rose-Anna, j'en avais quasiment drette besoin" (124). Failing to grasp the spirit of the gift, she brings it into the only world she understands, into the system of needs, and Florentine's moment of satisfaction is ruined: "Alors, brusquement, toute la joie que Florentine avait éprouvée se changea en fiel. Ce ravissement qu'elle avait ressenti à être généreuse, sans motif d'intérêt, ce ravissement infini laissait place en elle à une espèce de stupeur douloureuse. C'était une pure perte, cet acte, il ne servait à rien. C'était une goutte d'eau dans l'aridité de leur existence" (125). Rose-Anna trudges off "attentive à tant de choses qu'elle s'était défendu de regarder, et les désirs croissaient en elle, vastes et multiples, elle s'éloignait avec l'argent bien caché et qui avait fait naître tant de désirs, plus pauvre certainement qu'à son entrée dans le magasin" (125). She is poorer because the two dollars have opened up a whole new world of possibilities of which she had not even been aware. What should she buy? she wonders, as she makes her way out through the store, stopping at the toy counter to examine a shiny tin flute which would be perfect for her little boy, Daniel, who is sick. "Achèterai-je la flûte brillante, la flûte mince et jolie, ou les bas, le pain, les vêtements? Qu'est-ce qui est le plus important? Une flûte comme un éclat de soleil entre les mains d'un petit enfant malade, une flûte joyeuse, qui exhalera des sons de bonheur, ou bien, sur la table, la nourriture de tous les jours?" The question, of course, is unanswerable since there is no common measure for the two orders. Rose-Anna, however, is not to know that and has no defence against the torment of her moral dilemma.

The theme of the gift of money is repeated in chapter 19, but this time the circumstances are, in a sense, reversed. Here it is Rose-Anna who "lends" ten dollars to her son Eugène, knowing full well that she will never see the money again. This time, however, the sacrifice does not involve a luxury – a pair of silk stockings or some other object of desire – but one of life's necessities, for the ten dollars represent her rent money. Then, before going out on the town, Eugène scatters small change to the children, creating a carnivalesque mood not out of place in one who will soon be going to war. But Rose-Anna finds it unbearable: "Et il y avait vraiment dans la maison une gaieté brûlante tout à coup, une excitation intense. Les enfants comptaient leurs pièces en se bousculant, déjà prêts à se talocher sournoisement. Puis, Rose-Anna, accablée de surprise et de gêne, les vit partir à la course vers le magasin du coin. Eugène, à son tour, se glissa au dehors. Seule avec la petite fille qui chantonnait, réfugiée sous une chaise, elle s'appuya à la table et se laissa aller à un moment de tristesse poignante. Elle avait eu du mal, un mal infini, à voir cet argent voler en l'air" (241). Unlike his mother who remains incapable of buying the child's flute, Eugène is not afraid to spend money; despite his good intentions concerning his mother, a few pages later he is striding off in pursuit of a faceless, impersonal pleasure: "L'image de Rose-Anna recula très loin dans son esprit. Il jeta sa cigarette et, sifflotant, vint à travers le square à la rencontre de cette robe claire, collante et flamboyante" (247). The metonymic substitution of dress for girl reflects her status as merchandise, as a commodity in the circuit of economic exchange. For Rose-Anna, on the other hand, the ten dollars buy nothing; the money has been given away, lost, consumed, its use value destroyed for ever.

That, of course, is one way of explaining the shift from "the satisfaction of stable needs to the invention of new desires" – by evoking Marx's analysis of commodity fetishism and the ascendancy of exchange value over use value. What is interesting in *Bonheur d'occasion,* however, is the way in which different characters live this situation in different ways. In this respect the clear parallel between the themes of time and money underlines the coherence of the novel's semantic structure. Thus, for example, Jean Lévesque is presented in terms of the dynamic time of the social climber, for whom the present moment is entirely subordinated to future plans. In his world the past exists only as an image of his own weakness, of the vulnerability of the "foundling,"[9] and he will spend his whole life trying to forget it. For this capitalist in the making, work is a way of mastering time, of translating it into money. As a twentieth-century version of *homo oeconomicus,* it is not surprising that he is compared, implicitly, to Robinson Crusoe whose Calvinist work ethic he embodies: "Il atteignait une époque relativement calme où, comme un naufragé dans une île déserte, il regardait toute ressource autour de lui avec le besoin de la plier à ses fins. Il se vouait à des années de lutte et de misère au bout desquelles il n'aurait qu'à étendre la main pour saisir le fruit de son travail et de son renoncement" (207).

The opposite of the capitalist, in this scheme of things and in the context of the novel, is the etymologically "prolific," proletarian, who produces a large number of children (her only capital – an ironic commentary on the nationalist ideology of the "revenge of the cradle") and who lives from day to day, spending what she earns. Thus Rose-Anna's only escape from the "long, dull, grey journey" of her life, from the unbearable day-to-dayness of the present, are her nostalgic retreats to the lost paradise of a childhood spent in the country. Florentine is a creature of the city, born and bred: she lives on the surface of things and people in a present which contains both work and play but which has one eye on the future, on the only escape route possible for a girl of her condition, through a Jean Lévesque or an Emmanuel Létourneau. Seen in this light, the ambiguity of the "seduction scene" in chapter 16 becomes apparent. For Jean, the seduction is a kind of exorcism, a way of ridding himself of a burdensome past and of the "smell of poverty," a way of wiping out a certain image of himself as a "sickly orphan" so that he can get on with the business of climbing up the social ladder. For Florentine it is part of a social masquerade: putting on her make-up and her jewellery, playing the parts of housewife and *ingénue,* she tries to construct, through the mediating gaze of Jean, an identity, an image of herself as object of desire, as a commodity on the marriage market.

The work of the capitalist and that of the proletarian derive, then, from different orders. The proletarian works in order to spend and in order to satisfy the needs of her family; the capitalist works in order to accumulate wealth and to assure the growth of the means of production. The work of the capitalist will bear fruit in the future; the labour of the proletarian centres around childbirth and can never escape the cycle of life and death.[10] As the song says, the rich get richer and the poor get ... children. But what are the immediate products of these two kinds of work? Or, more exactly, what is bought with the money they generate? For the most part, as we have seen, Rose-Anna spends her money (and Florentine's) on things that can be defined fairly narrowly in terms of their use value – food, clothing, and shelter. Within this system of stable needs and uses, however, there appear here and there, acts and objects that transgress its logic and its rules. The sacrifice entailed in the act of giving can be seen as one such transgression. In this respect, certain objects associated with Daniel – a tin flute, a new coat – acquire a special status in the novel. A few days before his death in the hospital, his sister Yvonne brings him an orange: "À l'hôpital, on lui avait donné souvent dans un verre un jus qui avait le goût de l'orange. Mais une orange, ce n'était pas un jus, ce n'était pas dans un verre; c'était un fruit qui rappelait Noël. C'était un fruit que l'on trouvait dans son bas au matin de Noël et que l'on mangeait, quartier par quartier, en le faisant durer tant qu'on le pouvait. Une orange, c'était comme un manteau, c'était comme une flûte brillante; on en avait grande envie, on la demandait souvent, et puis enfin, quand on l'avait dans la main, on n'y tenait plus" (357).

Such objects seem to elude the logic of economic exchange; deriving their value from the interpersonal relations in which they are given and received and which they themselves create or maintain, they cannot be possessed or hoarded since they have no meaningful existence outside those relations. In Jean Baudrillard's terminology, such objects are defined in terms of their *symbolic* value:

In symbolic exchange, of which the gift is our most proximate illustration, the object is not an object: it is inseparable from the concrete relation in which it is exchanged, the transferential pact that it seals between two persons: it is thus not independent as such. It has, properly speaking, neither use value nor (economic) exchange value. The object given has symbolic exchange value. This is the paradox of the gift: it is on the one hand (relatively) arbitrary: it matters little what object is involved. Provided it is given, it can fully signify the relation. On the other hand, once it has been given – and *because* of this – it is *this* object and not another. The gift is unique, specified by the people exchanging and the unique moment of the exchange. It is arbitrary, and yet absolutely singular. (Baudrillard 1981, 64)

In consumer society, however, the object tends increasingly to become autonomous, to be reified as a *sign* in the code regulating the social logic of exchange:

Instead of abolishing itself in the relation that it establishes, and thus assuming symbolic value (as in the example of the gift), the object becomes autonomous, intransitive, opaque, and so begins to signify the abolition of the relationship ... Whereas the symbol refers to lack (to absence) as a virtual relation of desire, the sign object only refers to the absence of relation itself, and to isolated individual subjects.

The sign object is neither given nor exchanged: it is appropriated, withheld and manipulated by individual subjects as a sign, that is, as coded difference. (Baudrillard 1981, 65)[11]

These are the objects of Jean Lévesque's world, the signs he wears on his person and which transform him, in the eyes of Florentine, into a commodity on the futures market: "Jamais elle n'avait rencontré dans sa vie un être qui portât sur lui de tels signes de succès. Il pouvait bien, ce garçon, n'être qu'un mécanicien en ce moment, mais déjà elle ne doutait pas plus de sa réussite dans l'avenir, dans un avenir très rapproché même, que de la justesse de l'instinct qui lui conseillait de s'en faire un allié" (22). As Emmanuel will discover on his walk through Westmount towards the end of the book, in the alienated world of signs it is people who are dispensable:

La pierre, les grilles de fer forgé, hautaines et froides, les portes de vieux chêne, les lourds heurtoirs de cuivre, le fer, l'acier, le bois, la pierre, le cuivre, l'argent semblaient s'animer peu à peu et semblaient dire d'une voix creuse, avec un ricanement léger qui se communiquait aux arbustes, aux haies émondées, et franchissait la nuit:

"Qu'est-ce que tu oses penser, toi, pauvre être humain! Prétendrais-tu par hasard te mettre à notre niveau? Mais ta vie, c'est ce qu'il y a de meilleur marché sur terre. Nous autres, la pierre, le fer, l'acier, l'or, l'argent, nous sommes ce qui se paye cher et ce qui dure."

– Mais la vie, la vie d'un homme, insista Emmanuel.

"La vie, la vie d'un homme! On n'a jamais calculé ça encore. C'est une chose si petite, si éphémère, si docile, la vie d'un homme." (322)

Desire, like happiness, always involves an excess in relation to the satisfaction of needs. (We remember Lear's angry response to his daughter Regan: "O, reason not the need! Our basest beggars / Are in the poorest things superfluous. / Allow not nature more than nature needs, / Man's life is cheap as beast's.") But desire itself is polarized along lines of possession (economic) and communion (symbolic).[12] On the economic plane, consumer society reinforces class distinctions by multiplying the possibilities of semiotic discrimination (the designer labels of yuppie culture are a good example) while at the same time creating a class (the poor, the unemployed) excluded from the benefits of this social logic. On the symbolic plane, consumer society offers few possibilities for communion, since it isolates and alienates its chosen ones while crushing the others under the weight of a desire it keeps constantly alive and never satisfies. In this respect Daniel's fate is symptomatic, for Rose-Anna's tragedy is that she satisfies neither the needs nor the desires of her son. Daniel not only suffers from malnutrition, he dies in hospital surrounded by toys – amongst them a tin flute – provided by the charity of the rich. The poor do not consume, they are consumed.[13]

WHEN Hannah Josephson translated *Bonheur d'occasion* into English in 1947, she chose to call it *The Tin Flute,* a title which was retained by Alan Brown for his 1980 version. This title has often been criticized. John O'Connor, for example, complains in 1981 about Brown's failure to find something better: "The strong emphasis on happiness in Roy's title and novel demands some acknowledgment in the English title. Moreover, the 'tin flute' is but one symbol of happiness, and then only for a secondary character. Such a title therefore deflects attention both from Roy's central theme and from her two main characters, Rose-Anna and Florentine" (O'Connor 1981, 94). Whatever the shortcomings of Josephson's and Brown's translations, it seems to me that their instinct served them well when it came to the choice of a title. *The Tin Flute* takes us right to the heart of the book, which is, I would suggest, structured around an opposition between need and desire that mediates the various relations between characters, themes, and objects; as well, the title reflects the historical transition to an urban economy of consumer capitalism portrayed in the novel.[14] Far from deflecting the reader's attention "from Roy's central theme and from her two main characters, Rose-Anna and Florentine," it directs us to the centrally important ninth chapter in which these two characters play out their tragic dilemma. Moreover, the English title has the very substantial advantage of operating metonymically rather than metaphorically, thereby emphasizing the strengths rather than the weaknesses of Gabrielle Roy's style. The little tin flute comes to represent a residue of resistance to the new economic order, to the seduction of the sign and the compelling logic of consumer society.

The preference I have just indicated for Roy's use of metonymy over her use of metaphor calls for a word of explanation. It goes back to a comment made earlier concerning the descriptions of Emmanuel leaving Saint-Henri and Orwell leaving Wigan and of what they see from their respective train windows. I argued then that, because of his manifest presence in the text, Orwell's generalizations about what he sees are not received as interventions by the reader, whereas Roy's use of a closing metaphor to make her point is. Not trusting the reader to make the right connections and reach the correct conclusions from the metonymic chains of the narrative, she cannot resist the urge to intervene and spell it out in a different mode. (The French title does precisely this; the English translation does not.)

As Guy Laflèche points out, this kind of intervention is frequently proleptic in nature; it breaks the chronology of the particular narrative episode to anticipate later events or opinions. Thus, in the restaurant scene discussed earlier, Jean is mesmerised by a metonymic detail: "Elle jouait maintenant avec la carte, se donnant des airs de réfléchir. Jean ne voyait que le haut de sa figure et, ressortant sur le carton blanc, ses ongles où le vernis se fendillait et se détachait par plaques. Au petit doigt, il n'y avait presque plus de laque, et cet ongle nu, blanc, à côté d'un doigt teinté de carmin, le fascinait. Il ne pouvait en détacher son regard" (82). In itself, the detail of the nail stripped of its polish is eloquent and moving, the perfect image of Florentine caught, as I have argued, between the economies of need and desire. But the author does not trust us to get the point and adds, proleptically, "Et si longtemps, si longtemps par la suite, il devait, en pensant à Florentine, revoir cet ongle blanc, cet ongle du petit doigt, toujours il devait se rappeler ce petit ongle mis à nu, marqué de rainures et de taches blanches ... un ongle d'anémique."

The text is saturated with such examples.[15] In fact there is a fairly systematic recuperation of metonymy as metaphor in the novel, which reverses in a sense Peter Brooks' contention that narrative is the unpacking of metaphor as metonymy (Brooks 1984, 26). One conclusion that might be drawn from such an observation is that *Bonheur d'occasion* is, as Laflèche argues, an excellent popular novel which works extremely well on its own terms but which should not be confused with "works of literature," that is, in the critic's words, works which are "exceptional, original and subversive" (Laflèche 1977, 113). Now, while I am perfectly willing to admit that *Bonheur d'occasion* is a popular novel which comes directly out of Roy's journalistic writing of the early forties, I am not at all convinced that one can draw a hard and fast line between popular and literary novels along purely formal lines, as Laflèche tries to do. And as soon as one shifts perspective to examine this distinction from an institutional point of view, the ground looks very different indeed. One would certainly not be hard pressed to make a strong case for the novel's being "exceptional, original and subversive" in the context of the Quebec of the forties, not least on the basis of its very coherent critique of consumer capitalism.

To argue for or against *Bonheur d'occasion* as a "literary" novel, as many critics have felt obliged to do,[16] is probably to miss the point. In fact the distinction between popular and literary, when argued in this way, is just as spurious and misleading as the one between fact and fiction – or between documentary and imaginary – discussed at the beginning of this chapter. Such distinctions are extraneous to the central problem Gabrielle Roy faced, as had George Orwell before her: how does a "cultivated" man or woman go about describing the life of the man or woman in the street? This problem is, at once, one of social relationship and of literary form. Roy's solution is a complex one. In the first place, she opts not to participate directly, in her own persona, as Orwell had chosen to do in *The Road to Wigan Pier* or *Down and Out in Paris and London,* but rather to spread the observer/eavesdropper function around her different characters, thereby bestowing upon them both vision and voice. In addition, she grants special status to two of her characters, Rose-Anna and Emmanuel, who, in their different ways, allow Roy to retain a degree of ideological control over how what is seen and heard is received. But such measures are apparently insufficient; Roy feels obliged to generalize or globalize her intervention, she constantly transgresses the limits and restrictions that her chosen technique implies in order to ensure that the community of feeling and ideas between author, reader, and characters is not broken.

One of the frustrations she must have felt on publishing the novel, however, was an awareness of its failure to translate that community of feeling – based ultimately on moral indignation – into any kind of force for change. The crucial factor here is probably Emmanuel's ultimate insufficiency as the novel's political philosopher. His creed of international humanism is manifestly inadequate in the face of the kind of suffering that the novel portrays. (One is tempted to see in Emmanuel a surrogate for Gabrielle Roy: imperfectly integrated into the world of the novel, hovering on the margins of its society, he functions, in much the same way as some novel prefaces, as a kind of ideological brake. The author uses the character to recuperate story through discourse and to bring back under her control material which, through its own intrinsic power, threatens to escape her grasp.) It is interesting that just as Orwell, from the diary to the book of *Wigan Pier,* was careful to expunge all trace of organized *working-class* socialism (Williams 1984, 51–2), so Roy stops short of advocating a socialist remedy to the woes of the people of Saint-Henri by excluding any mention of organized political opposition and even going so far as to delete some of the more outspoken social criticisms from the second and subsequent editions (Shek 1977, 82–3, 110). Roy's "post-scriptural" solution, as we have seen, is to follow Orwell out of Wigan and back to "civilization" where, after sending her spokes-man – and presumably an important part of herself – off to die in a distant prison camp, she will plead the case of the oppressed in her own name and her own voice, but with all the weight of her flawed yet impressive creation behind her.

CHAPTER FOUR

Stopping the Kaleidoscope: Narrative Ambiguity in André Langevin's Poussière sur la ville

There is a temper wont to twist the past into a theaterpiece, mistake the reasonable for the historical.   John Barth, *The Sot-Weed Factor*

Because we cannot describe the totality of the dance, which is incessant and infinite, we must stop the kaleidoscope in our imaginations, calling each slice-of-time configuration a "pattern." But by stopping the kaleidoscope we have lost the dynamic essence of the dance, for the static "patterns" never in fact existed as discrete entities.   N. Katherine Hayles, *The Cosmic Web*

André Langevin's *Poussière sur la ville* was first published in 1953, eight years after the first edition of *Bonheur d'occasion* and sixteen years after *Menaud, maître-draveur*. The distances separating these three novels, in terms both of the worlds they represent and of the techniques they use to do so, attest to the accelerated evolution of the Quebec novel during the period 1937–53. At the same time, the gap between the literary production of France and that of Quebec seems to narrow rapidly: with *Poussière sur la ville* we step into the postwar mainstream of existentialist humanism, into the intellectual world of Sartre and Camus.

At the end of Langevin's novel, the central character, Alain Dubois, affirms his resolution to stay on as doctor in the inhospitable mining town of Macklin, where his wife Madeleine has recently committed suicide after wounding the man who had loved and left her. Beyond the melodramatic elements – which, as we shall see, are quite deliberate and have an important thematic as well as structural function – the novel invites us to consider the hero's existentialist commitment, presented here in terms of an ideological opposition between Christianity and secular humanism: "Je resterai. Je resterai, contre toute la ville. Je les forcerai à m'aimer. La pitié qui m'a si mal réussi avec Madeleine, je les en inonderai. J'ai un beau métier où la pitié peut sourdre sans cesse sans qu'on l'appelle. Je continue mon combat. Dieu et moi, nous ne sommes pas quittes encore. Et peut-être avons-nous les mêmes armes: l'amour et la pitié. Mais moi je travaille à l'échelon de l'homme. Je ne brasse pas des mondes et des espèces. Je panse des hommes. Forcément, nous n'avons pas le même point de vue" (*Poussière,* 213). The question is clear, the decision apparently unequivocal: Dubois, like other existentialist heroes before him, has chosen his weapons and his ground in the struggle against the absurd. (One is reminded paradoxically of Sartre's Orestes who, at the end of *The Flies,* decides not to stay in Argos but to leave, Pied Piper fashion, with the Furies in tow.) And yet we are haunted by a vague uneasiness, by the suggestion in this final sentence of something unresolved. "Forcément, nous n'avons pas le même point de vue." Seemingly innocent at first, the words take on resonance when we recall that Dubois is not only the hero of the novel but also its sole narrator; indeed, in the context of the Quebec novel, *Poussière sur la ville* is innovative not only for its introduction of the existentialist preoccupations of Langevin's French contemporaries but also for its violent break with the convention of the omniscient narrator. In neither the moral nor the formal sense is it possible for the humanist Dubois, who is bound by the limits of his own vision, of his own subjective consciousness, to share God's point of view.

This is not in itself, however, sufficient cause for concern and does not explain our feeling of dissatisfaction with Dubois's profession of existentialist faith at the end of the novel. After all, there is a consistency of thought and practice in Langevin's refusal of the Judaeo-Christian worldview and his uncompromising rejection of the literary device of the omniscient narrator. The problem must rest elsewhere. Looking more closely at Alain Dubois and at his three distinct roles or functions in the novel, those of doctor, husband, and narrator, the first thing we note is an obvious dissymmetry in this tri-partite distinction; for while the roles of husband and doctor are played out on the same level, in the same world so to speak, the role of narrator belongs inevitably to a different level, to a universe of discourse which embraces the world of Alain and Madeleine. There is the Dubois who loves, marries, and loses Madeleine, but there is also the Dubois who tells the story of that love. There is the Dubois who ministers to the sick, but there is also the Dubois who says (or writes?), "Je panse des hommes." I shall try to show that the relation between the two levels – that of the narrated "I" and that of the narrating "I" – is the main source of our uneasiness as readers.[1]

The first level, as in any narrative, is entirely dependent on the second: the reader's knowledge of plot and character derives solely

from what the narrator tells and how he tells it. (Narration, etymologically, implies both knowing and telling.) When, at the end of
the novel, Alain Dubois announces his decision, he does so in the
most anodyne terms, in the context of his professional commitment
to mankind. That this commitment is, however, suspect – or at least
less straightforward than Dubois would like us to think – is clear
from the fact that it is inextricably bound up with his highly unsat-
isfactory relationship with Madeleine and his far from simple commitment in his role as husband: "La pitié qui m'a si mal réussi avec
Madeleine, je les en inonderai." It is significant that there is no place
here for Dubois's third role, that of narrator: in the history of the
Quebec novel, we have not yet arrived at the age of the self-conscious
narrator, where the narrative act itself becomes problematic and
charged with significance. Alain Dubois is a self-conscious *hero:* his
existential crisis does not, explicitly at least, embrace the act of
narration.

And yet the ambiguity persists. Dubois and God do not share the
same point of view: "Forcément, nous n'avons pas le même point
de vue." As stylistic commentary, the observation is too fine, too
satisfying, to be gratuitous. It strengthens the reader's suspicion that
all is not quite what it seems, that the narrative is not, after all,
altogether innocent. "Je ne brasse pas des mondes et des espèces,"
disclaims Dubois. "Je panse des hommes." Very well, that is his
choice. But, of a man obsessed with the problem of knowledge,
we might legitimately ask some concern for the equally important
problem of telling. The absence of any explicit reflection or comment
on the narrative activity in which he is engaged is, at best, ambiguous.
If Dubois's commitment as a doctor cannot be separated from his
failed marital commitment, it is equally certain that his relationship
with Madeleine can be evaluated and understood only in terms of
his commitment as a narrator, in terms of his narrative *project.* Since
Dubois does not tell us what that project is, we shall have to ask
whether his ambiguities stem from aesthetic paradox or from personal
duplicity.

THE DOCTOR

It is not by chance that Langevin makes his hero a doctor. Camus
had set the example in his 1947 novel *The Plague* with his hero-
narrator Bernard Rieux. For both novelists the choice of a doctor
as protagonist is dictated by their perception of sickness and death
as manifestations of the absurd; more importantly, such a choice
allows the possibility of non-collaboration, of active, meaningful

revolt against the absurd. Rieux's principal focus is of course the plague that seals off the city of Oran, isolating it from the outside world. For Dubois the fight against the absurd takes the less dramatic form of general practice in the hostile, snow-bound mining town of Macklin, a town equally isolated and isolating. (The dust of the title is asbestos dust, interestingly enough.[2] Falling incessantly over the town, it suggests a broader canvas: Hiroshima, with all its implications for the human condition, is still a recent memory, and Macklin, like Oran, is to be seen as a microcosm of human society.)

As a doctor, Dubois has a model in the novel: old Dr Lafleur, who has spent most of his life in the community and is now close to retirement. Unlike his younger colleague Lafleur is a believer, but his faith does not bring peace of mind: "Croyant, sans phrases et sans belles attitudes, le docteur Lafleur s'incline avec une humilité réelle devant l'absurde parce que sa foi l'éclaire sans lui permettre de voir, mais son humilité n'exclut pas la tristesse et, peut-être, l'indignation" (48). For Dubois it is inconceivable that a doctor, of all men, could accept, in the face of so much evidence to the contrary, the notion of a just God – "On ne parle plus du ciel à un enfant tordu par une méningite cérébro-spinale" – and he remains fascinated but sceptical before Lafleur's religion, offering an ultimately humanistic explanation of his colleague's evident goodness: "La paix doit lui venir davantage de sa pitié et de sa commisération proprement humaines" (48).

We have already seen that pity is at the root of Dubois's humanism and is the motivating force in his commitment against the absurd. Here again, in his judgment of Lafleur, pity is seen as the ultimate virtue, the measure of the man. What is interesting is that, for Dubois, pity is an exclusively human sentiment, incompatible with the idea of a Creator who has abandoned his creatures to a life of pain and suffering that culminates in the ultimate absurdity of death. It comes as no surprise to find that the only priest in the novel is, according to the doctor, a man without pity, "cruel pour les faibles" (165). And yet even the priest has no certainty when faced with death: "Je ne donne l'extrême-onction qu'en tremblant. Chaque mort me fait tout remettre en question" (163). In this he resembles Lafleur, who is confronted rather brutally by a distraught Dubois on the question of divine justice:

- Au chevet du malade je n'accepte jamais. Je lutte. Je lutte aussi dans la vie chaque fois qu'il m'est possible. Je suis toujours battu.

Il regarde dans la fenêtre et fait de la main un geste d'impuissance.

- Mais je continuerai jusqu'à la mort. Ma foi ne m'empêche pas d'aimer assez les hommes pour les soustraire quand je peux à ce que vous considérez comme l'injustice de Dieu. Vous voyez, nous sommes deux à lutter contre Lui. Il n'y a pas d'autres solutions que de faire notre métier d'homme. (127–8)

And Dubois comments: "Lui aussi doit tout ramener sur le plan de l'homme." Ideological differences aside, Lafleur, like the priest in his own limited fashion, does his job. Dubois, who is in the throes of an existential crisis brought on by a rapidly failing marriage, does not.

This is made apparent by two episodes in particular. The first involves a sixty-five-year-old widow, mother of seven children (three of them under twenty!) who consults Dubois in his office about the difficulty she has in breathing. The doctor quickly diagnoses an imminent heart attack and orders complete rest, forbidding her to go back to her work as a cleaning woman. Even as he is talking to her he knows that she will not follow his advice, that her children will not allow her to stop working. Indeed, when Dubois is called to the home that same evening, he finds her dead, while her astonished offspring wonder aloud how she could have been ill when she had worked as usual in the afternoon. However, Dubois's moral indignation has been somewhat undercut by his behaviour during the initial consultation earlier in the day, when, distracted by the sound of Madeleine's laughter on the stairs, he leaves his patient and walks through the waiting-room to confront his wife, who is on her way out. The brief, sullen exchange that follows can be heard by all. Dubois returns to find, to his dismay, that he has left the door to his office open, exposing his half-dressed patient to the stares of those in the waiting-room: "J'avais laissé la porte de mon bureau ouverte et le dos de ma malade fait une tache grise devant ma table, une tache que les deux personnes qui sont dans la salle ont pu regarder tout ce temps. La cardiaque, elle, n'a pas bougé. Pour fermer la porte il eût fallu montrer sa poitrine. Elle a courbé le dos et supporté patiemment cette atteinte à la pudeur" (55).

Quite apart from the extraordinary lack of professional consideration shown by the doctor in this episode, what is remarkable in his account of the incident is the depersonalizing effect of his own vision: seen through the open door, his patient is transformed into "une tache grise," as though she were a splash of grey paint on a canvas. Nor is this an isolated occurrence. Something very similar takes place in exactly the same surroundings in the opening pages of the novel: "Par la porte entrouverte de mon bureau je vois briller sur ma table le stéthoscope que j'avais oublié. Et ce simple objet, qui m'identifie aussi sûrement que le marteau le charpentier, ne m'est plus familier" (16). In this instance Dubois's alienating vision is turned, via the stethoscope, against himself, against his own professional identity. Gratuitous, contingent, the stethoscope is no longer a stethoscope but an unfamiliar object, without context and without meaning. In the space of that vision, a whole world of definitions and responsibilities and of plans and possibilities has fallen away.

More often, however, the doctor's reifying gaze is directed towards others, as a necessary part of his work. On the operating table, for example, a patient is no longer a human being with a life of her own, but a machine which is in need of repair: "L'activité minutieuse et diverse au-dessus de la table m'enlève toute émotion, et je suis plus attentif aux rouages du corps humain qu'au corps lui-même" (47). Of course, without this kind of professional depersonalization, the surgeon could not function efficiently; it is inescapable. It is also quite acceptable so long as, once off the operating table, the patient regains in the eyes of the doctor her identity as a human being with a past and a future of her own. Such a way of looking at others becomes less acceptable when, in the final stages of a dying marriage, it is turned against the doctor's own wife: "Ce n'est plus de la pitié que j'ai pour elle, c'est le regard froid du clinicien. Je surveille l'incubation" (181). It might have been reasonable to examine the marriage itself with the clinical eye of the pathologist; but for Dubois to look at his wife in this way seems symptomatic of a bad case of professional deformation.

The second incident leading us to question Dubois's commitment as a doctor involves a night-call to an isolated house in the country to deliver a baby. On this occasion his professional conduct is, ironically, much less exceptionable; ironically, because he happens, for reasons of marital strife, to be quite drunk and reeking of whisky – scarcely a state to inspire confidence in one's physician. However, he soon sobers up as the full horror of the labour unfolds: the child is hydrocephalic and cannot be delivered. To save the mother Dubois is obliged, under the close scrutiny of a tyrannical grand-mother, to puncture the baby's head, thereby sacrificing the child and offering, to the morbid fascination of the onlookers, a spectacular display of spurting fluids. The entire episode is profoundly depressing, revolting both in the cruel absurdity of the child's deformity and death and in the circumstances and attitudes that turn a traumatic event into a sickening fiasco. Once again, Dubois's marital distress has interfered with the performance of his professional duties, with disastrous results.

The conflict between Dubois's marriage and his profession makes itself felt in other ways too. As a doctor in a small mining town, he belongs inevitably to a certain social elite, as he is well aware. His membership in the club entails tacit prohibitions, such as not drinking at the hotel (which he does) and not eating at the restaurant (which his wife does): "Les notables de Macklin, et même sans le sou j'en étais, ne dînent pas au restaurant, surtout pas en compagnie de leurs épouses. Mais Madeleine ignorait d'instinct les différences de classe" (31). And so, on their first day in Macklin, they find themselves at Madeleine's insistence in the town's only restaurant, run by the Syrian, Kouri. The restaurant is full of miners who avidly feast their eyes on the doctor's wife. Dubois's reaction is curious: "En somme j'étais venu chercher leur argent; cela leur donnait presque le droit de déshabiller ma femme. J'évitais de les regarder" (32). The more one thinks about it, the more astonishing this statement becomes. Why, for example, does Dubois assume that his presence in the community will be seen by the miners primarily in terms of money? Is it perhaps because that is how he sees it? And why should he imagine that what he is selling, if indeed it is the selling that is important, is not so much his services as a doctor as the right to undress his wife? Why indeed should he see the miners' casual sexual interest in Madeleine as a function of his own professional ambition? It is as though Madeleine had become the object of some kind of primitive social or economic exchange, the price of his establishing himself professionally in the town. One is obliged to wonder seriously if there is not a certain predisposition in Alain Dubois to the condition of deceived husband, if his wife's eventual infidelity is not in some way foreseen or even invited by the doctor as a necessary corollary of his position in the community. "J'aurais déjà des instincts de victime!" he says at the very beginning of the novel (14), as he stands outside in the snow staring up at the window of their bedroom.

What is already clear is that Dubois will remain essentially passive and make no attempt to forestall what he apparently sees as inevitable. In the restaurant he does not try to talk to his wife but accepts her teasing and, though quite unable to forget the presence of the staring miners, keeps his own eyes carefully averted. This position becomes more difficult to maintain when Jim, the taxi-driver, tries to get a better look: "Il ne se contenta pas de regarder Madeleine à distance. À deux reprises il traversa toute la salle dans le seul but de passer lentement à côté de nous et de lorgner ostensiblement Madeleine" (33). But if Dubois will not react, his wife will and does, by sticking out her tongue, to the raucous delight of everyone present. Everyone, that is, but her husband, who is ready to die of embarrassment: "Quant à moi je ne savais où regarder. La femme du docteur Dubois ne pouvait tirer la langue dans le restaurant de Kouri" (33). His passivity by now has become, in his own eyes at least, a frank admission of impotence: "En ne faisant rien moi-même pour la défendre, je leur cédais le terrain sur le seul plan qui les intéressait vraiment, celui de la virilité" (33). However, the day is saved at least partially by Madeleine's gesture as they leave the restaurant; it lends a little dignity to an otherwise ignominious retreat: "En quittant le restaurant, elle me donna le bras et se pressa contre moi avec l'air d'annoncer au monde entier qu'elle était mienne. Je lui pardonnais tout" (35).

Dubois clearly interprets the gesture as a public one, intended less for him than for the others, the spectators of their little drama. This distinction between public and private is important, since it underscores the mutual interference of Dubois's two roles as doctor and husband. At the beginning of the novel, he can still say, "Cela ne concerne que Madeleine et moi" (13). Later, his attitude will change: "Au fond je ne veux qu'empêcher qu'elle ne nourrisse la rumeur publique. Ce n'est pas entre elle et moi, mais entre nous et les autres" (66).

THE HUSBAND

If Dubois's commitment as a doctor is essentially a problem of action, his commitment as a husband is defined largely in terms of the problems of knowledge, communication, and freedom. He had fallen in love with Madeleine's physical beauty without ever really getting to know her: "J'en vins à l'aimer peu à peu, mais en adolescent, sans trop chercher à la connaître, sans rien analyser. Je crois que j'aimai une image plutôt qu'elle-même" (18). Once the honeymoon is over, he finds himself married to a puzzling creature, one who is inconsistent and irresponsible, "qui ne vit que dans l'instant, au point de manifester dans tous ses actes un illogisme déconcertant" (20). Dubois tries to explain this behaviour in terms of his wife's working-class origins: "Elle a conservé de son milieu ouvrier un étonnant instinct d'imprudence, la liberté de jouer son va-tout à l'instant, parce que possédant peu ou rien. C'est un terrain où je ne peux la suivre avec naturel. D'une famille de petits bourgeois, je n'ai pas d'inclination pour les départs subits, les mains vides, et sans but" (62). He, on the other hand, prides himself on his middle-class sense of proportion, a virtue which, to the spirited Madeleine, looks suspiciously like avarice: "L'animal en liberté n'amasse pas, ne tient à rien qu'à sa nourriture du moment. Madeleine de même. Pour employer un mot qui amènerait un sourire dédaigneux sur ses lèvres, elle sera toujours prolétaire. C'est à l'instant même qu'il lui importe d'être satisfaite, non pas dans un avenir problématique" (63). The problem for Dubois is how to reconcile his own perfectly conventional view of marriage with the untamed creature he has chosen for a partner. How far is it possible to carry one's respect for the other's freedom within the institution of marriage in the Quebec of the 1950s?

One response – and the temptation is certainly present in Alain – is to try to tame the animal, to yield to the instinct of domination she arouses: "Elle agace comme le cheval sauvage en liberté. Elle ne séduit pas tant qu'elle ne donne le désir de lui passer le licol. Sa façon d'être libre est proprement irritante" (17). It is clear that he considers her as his possession and that her refusal of all constraint, her defiant affirmation of independence, irritates him profoundly: "Je suis un homme et à côté de moi dort une femme qui m'appartient, comme un jouet qui se remonte seul et quand il le veut bien" (39). However, he knows he would find no satisfaction in simply taking Madeleine; more than mere possession, he wants submission, possession with consent: "Oh! non, je ne lui passerai pas le licol! C'est en liberté qu'il me faut la posséder" (64). At the same time he realizes that, with someone like Madeleine, this kind of possession does not necessarily come with the marriage contract: "De droits sur elle, je n'ai que ceux qu'elle accepte. Un pacte pour la vie? Madeleine ne signe pas de pactes, ne se donne pas en contrat" (64). If he is to avoid her bitterness and resentment, that of the prisoner despising her jailor, he will have to find another way of coming to terms with his wife's fiercely defended autonomy.

Curiously, it is only as a last resort, when his suspicions of Madeleine's infidelity have apparently been confirmed, that he stumbles on the idea of *talking* to her. Words, he now thinks, might take some of the pain out of the situation: "Le langage a encore des possibilités. Nous expliquer. Quand on met des mots sur les choses, elles s'édulcorent un peu, elles deviennent plus familières et, peut-être, s'abolissent à la fin. On peut se laisser prendre aux mots, accepter leur écran" (99). But Madeleine, for whatever reason, will not take the bait, and Alain is left literally waiting in the dark: "J'attends dans le noir, j'attends qu'elle me parle. Le silence persiste, stupide et ridicule. Je m'assois sur son lit, sans la toucher, et je tourne dans ma tête des mots que je repousse, des mots piteux qui ne seraient que des sons sans signification" (102).

Words, then, have lost their meaning, are neither a means of

communication nor a way of getting at the truth, but, at best, one
more screen[3] to be placed between oneself and the world. It is
hardly surprising that Madeleine will have none of Alain's words.
She prefers a more direct language to give vent to her feelings:
"Elle s'abandonne de nouveau et, cette fois, en frappant son oreiller
de ses poings fermés. C'est un langage que je n'avais pas prévu,
qu'il me faut comprendre. Veut-il signifier qu'il n'y a rien à dire,
qu'elle souffre de ne rien pouvoir pour moi, qu'elle n'a pas désiré
ce qui arrive, qu'elle est victime elle aussi? Ou qu'elle ne comprend
pas, qu'elle se débat dans une situation insoutenable, où elle a glissé
et d'où elle ne peut s'échapper?" (102–3). Clearly, it means all of
these things and none of them. The great advantage of non-verbal
or pre-verbal language lies in its semantic power, its ability to convey
an undifferentiated totality of emotion. The price of that power is
ambiguity; without the syntactic distinctions of verbal language, the
message has meaning but no signification and cannot be resolved
into a single unequivocal statement. Madeleine, it would appear,
lives her life on this level, but for Alain this kind of communication
is inadequate; he wants to *know,* not to *understand:* "Moi, je n'ai
plus ni sagesse, ni compassion ni envie de comprendre; je n'ai que
le désir forcené de la vaincre, de l'humilier, de la briser. Je la prends
aux poignets et la retourne sur le dos. – Tu ne t'en tireras pas
ainsi, Madeleine. J'ai le droit de savoir, j'ai le droit tu entends!" (104).
Incapable of understanding and denied the unambiguous knowledge
he desires, he resorts to a body language of his own and takes
revenge in rape. Later he will say: "Il n'y a pas eu d'explication.
Tout demeure en suspens. Et j'avoue que je me satisfais assez bien
de cet état de choses. Tant qu'il n'y a rien d'expliqué, rien n'est
définitif" (130). The failure, whether definitive or not, has been more
than one of words.

Alain's way of dealing with the situation and with Madeleine's
evident suffering is to abandon the role of husband as defined by
the social conventions of the time – "Je vais cesser de couper les
cheveux en quatre et lui parler en mari" (86) – in an attempt to
help her: "Je ne peux rendre Madeleine heureuse, mais je n'ajouterai
pas à son malheur. Je ne suis plus son mari, je suis son allié contre
l'absurde cruauté" (153). A husband, it is implied, can be only a
collaborator with the absurd; if Alain is to be Madeleine's friend
and ally, he must break with the role of husband and the social
expectations that go with it. Such an ambition, while it may seem
unremarkable today, is nothing short of astonishing in small-town
Quebec in the middle of the "great darkness" of the Duplessis era.

Curiously, Dubois sees in Madeleine's condition another manifestation of God's injustice: "Cette femme pantelante n'est plus la mienne, je ne me reconnais plus aucun droit sur elle. Je ne veux que la consoler, la soustraire à l'injustice divine, ainsi que disait le docteur Lafleur" (152). His choice of words becomes even more transparent after a heated conversation with the priest, who is mortified by Alain's refusal to intervene in Madeleine's affair and put an end to the public scandal. Is it by irony alone that the doctor seems to adopt a religious vocabulary, which echoes and transposes the words of the priest: "Moi aussi j'ai charge d'âme. Je me tiens responsable de Madeleine, non pas de son salut, mais de son bonheur" (173)? By this point, Madeleine has started receiving her lover, Richard Hétu, on a regular basis in the Dubois's apartment, and Alain's "understanding" is sorely tried by this knowledge: "Hé oui! il faut du courage pour maintenir la pitié, pour continuer à porter l'âme de Madeleine, à veiller à son bonheur. C'est un entraînement aussi difficile que celui de n'importe quelle vertu" (174). To keep his pity alive, he has started to drink heavily: "Autrement, je renoncerais peut-être à l'apprentissage de la sainteté" (174).

From husband (or man – the connotations of the two words are equally negative in the novel[4]) to saint – Dubois seems to be following the path described by Camus's character Tarrou in *The Plague*: "All I maintain is that on this earth there are pestilences and there are victims, and it's up to us, so far as possible, not to join forces with the pestilences" (*The Plague*, 236). The problem for the humanist who sides with the victim is how to become a saint, a "saint without God," to use Tarrou's formulation of the problem. Tarrou, however, acknowledges a third category of men, "that of the true healers. But it's a fact one doesn't come across many of them, and anyhow it must be a hard vocation" (*The Plague*, 236). Dubois's tragedy is that he discounts this third possibility without ever really examining it. Blinded by the polarization of the role of husband into pestilence or victim, he loses sight of the possibility of being a healer, a real doctor – not one who will passively watch the last stages of Madeleine's illness with the cold eye of the clinician but one who will try to be her active ally against the absurd cruelty of the world. Opting for sainthood, Dubois ceases to be a doctor in *any* sense of the word.[5]

But if the doctor will not act the priest will, swiftly and brutally as his conscience dictates. Richard Hétu is duly engaged to the niece of a local businessman, and Madeleine finds herself powerless to combat this alliance of church and trade. Telling Alain that she is leaving for her mother's, she takes a taxi to her lover's house where, after shooting vaguely in his direction, she turns the gun on herself.

Alain's reaction to the news of her death, which he had evoked relatively early in the novel as the logical end of their marriage (73, 88, 100), is typically self-centred: "C'est une machination de la ville. On porte le grand coup. On veut m'assassiner" (190). He, rather than Madeleine, is the true victim. It is, after all, the role he has chosen.

Once the news has sunk in, Alain is allowed to lose himself again in speculation – speculation as to the significance of the jewellery Madeleine was wearing when she died, speculation also as to the reasons for her death: "J'ai toute la vie pour essayer de comprendre pourquoi Madeleine n'a pas vécu sa vie. Au fond, c'est peut-être tout simple. Madeleine n'a peut-être jamais cru réellement au révolver. Ce n'est qu'en voyant tomber Richard qu'elle a su qu'elle venait de jouer à la grande personne et a fait ce que les grandes personnes font dans ces occasions-là, un acte définitif. On ne saura jamais, jamais" (196). There have been no explanations and there will be none. No words. No knowledge. Nothing definitive. Nothing, that is, except the death of his wife.

THE NARRATOR

Once Madeleine is dead, Dubois has to decide whether or not he is going to stay on in Macklin. As we have seen, he tries to resolve this question in terms of his commitment as a doctor to a community which does not want him. That this commitment is, at best, problematic is evident from a cursory examination of his behaviour as a doctor in the novel. It is equally evident that there is considerable interference between Dubois's role as a doctor and his role as a husband and that, if we look closely at what he says, the whole question of commitment is displaced from the sphere of action, where it is explicitly formulated, to the sphere of knowledge, where it is actually lived.[6] This observation is borne out by a passage at the end of the book, in which Dubois gives another reason for not wanting to leave: "Partir. Mais je ne puis pas quitter tout cela sans avoir vu clair. J'émerge de ma stupeur enfin, je cesse de vivre au ralenti, mais tout se confond, se mêle. Arrêtez le kaléidoscope. Je veux voir les images une à une, leur donner un sens. Pour m'assurer de ma qualité de vivant, il me faut la logique de la vie" (212). Clearly, the project of stopping the kaleidoscope is utopian. As Katherine Hayles points out in a discussion of scientific field models of reality, such a metaphor exposes not only the problems endemic to synchronic analyses in general but also the limitations deriving from the lack of an exterior, objective point from which to observe.

In fact, the observer cannot be abstracted from what is being observed: "No matter where we stand we are within the kaleidoscope, turning with it, so that what we see depends on where we stand. To change positions does not solve the problem, because the patterns are constantly changing: what we see when we change positions is not what we would have seen, for in the intervening time the patterns will have changed, and our shift in position will be part of that change. Moreover, there will always be one place we can never see at all – the spot we are standing on" (Hayles 1984, 20). These reservations notwithstanding, if we are to grasp the nature and the implications of Dubois's decision not to leave Macklin, we must try to determine what exactly he means by the "logic of life" that he hopes will be revealed when the kaleidoscope is stopped, thereby giving meaning to the chaotic images of the past, enabling him to see things clearly and to understand the events he has just recounted.

The novel ends in much the same way as it begins – with the problem of interpretation. At the origin of Dubois's narrative is Kouri's enigmatic warning about Madeleine's frequent presence in his restaurant. The early stages of the narrative represent an attempt to understand what lies behind the warning: "j'essaie de trouver un sens aux paroles de Kouri" (12); "Kouri a mis en branle dans mon cerveau un mécanisme" (24). Gilles Marcotte has spoken of the "mission of deciphering reality" and "the desire to understand," (Marcotte 1977, 82) which characterize Langevin's hero. However, Dubois's first reaction is an apparently healthy refusal of idle speculation, of brooding over what he calls "le jeu des images": "Je n'ai ni la force ni la lucidité nécessaires pour relier entre elles ces images d'un passé tout neuf. Elles sont séparées, sans signification commune. Il y aurait le fil fragile de l'avertissement de Kouri, mais les images ne se laissent pas joindre par un lien si ténu" (38). The metaphor he finds for his own intellectual impotence in this regard is revealing: "Comme si l'arme était chargée et qu'il ne manquât que la gâchette. Une telle arme ne peut faire feu, et il n'appartient pas à la victime de fournir la pièce perdue" (38). More important than the obvious Freudian linking of sexuality and knowledge are the Chekhovian overtones of this metaphorical pistol, which will be used in act 3 of the play.

The image also gives a clear indication of where Dubois will look for the "logic of life" that so eludes him. His preoccupation with the theatre and things theatrical begins with a simple observation about his ability to detach himself from his own life and actions: "Je trouve curieuse cette facilité que j'ai maintenant de prendre du

recul devant les spectacles de la vie et d'y assister en spectateur"
(135–6). This splitting of the self will be exacerbated by the effects
of the whisky that he starts to consume in alarming quantities: "Tous
les soirs, je bois et peux ainsi assister à ma propre vie en témoin
de l'extérieur" (174). But it is only after Madeleine has told him that
she loves Richard, after he has abandoned the role of husband for
that of friend and ally against the absurd, that the dissociation
becomes explicitly theatrical.

Thus it is that the only real dialogue in the entire novel between
Alain and Madeleine, a dialogue which culminates in at least a
temporary physical reconciliation, is undercut by Alain's sense of the
betrayal of words, of the impossibility of any communication beyond
the ritual exchanges of the stage: "Dire cela sur la scène et entendre
rire dans la salle" (154). "Il ne nous reste plus qu'à tomber dans les
bras l'un de l'autre, ce que nous faisons. Où sont les spectateurs
de cette belle scène? Il faudrait que la ville voie cela!" (155). "Nous
avons joué la scène jusqu'au bout et je crois qu'elle a trahi l'autre.
Je n'en ai aucune joie. Il y a demain ... et tous les autres jours"
(156). Later, after Madeleine's death, Alain will contemplate this same
stage, with the same decor, and look back on the second act of
their play, of which these exchanges constitute the last scene: "Les
habitants de Macklin attendent eux aussi. Ils ne seraient pas étonnés
d'apprendre demain qu'on a relevé le rideau durant la nuit, qu'un
acteur avait oublié une réplique ... un jeu de scène" (196). Later
still, three months after the curtain has fallen, we find him still
unsure of his own part in the drama. Was he an actor or simply a
spectator in Madeleine's life? "Je me sens semblable au spectateur
dont la bouche forme encore le dernier mot prononcé par le
comédien alors que la salle a cessé d'applaudir. Je reste seul en
scène, le survivant dont on ne se demande jamais ce qu'il deviendra"
(204). Play, audience, and characters have all forgotten him. The
curtain is down and the lights are out. But he remains on stage,
waiting for some piece of business – a phone call perhaps – to get
him off and into the safety of the wings.

The theatrical images of the novel's last pages might conceivably
be explained "psychologically," in terms of Alain's bereavement, as
a natural part of the grieving process. His incomprehension, his
self-reproach over his failure to act, his profound sense of unreality
and dissociation – all these things are surely not unusual in the
circumstances. If we accept this reading, however, we are left with
a problem; as we have seen, the theatre motif is introduced well
before Madeleine's death, as are the various images of splitting and
alienation that are associated with it. This fact in itself does not

weaken the psychological interpretation, but it does displace it, especially when taken in conjunction with the several passages which seem to "predict," in various ways, Madeleine's death. We are left wondering whether Alain's predisposition to the role of victim ought not to embrace, beyond the part of deceived husband, that of widower.[7]

The problem is compounded when we take into account the fact that, as critics have pointed out, the novel is constructed like a tragedy in three acts (Bérubé 1969, Beaver 1973). This, of course, would not be a problem at all if we were dealing with an omniscient narrator, or even a first-person narrator telling his story after the fact. In *The Plague,* for example, we learn at the end of the novel that what we have just read has been narrated, in the third person and the past tense, by Dr Rieux himself, as a kind of testimony to the human knowledge gained during the plague through the experience of injustice and violence: "None the less, he knew that the tale he had to tell could not be one of a final victory. It could be only the record of what had had to be done, and what assuredly would have to be done again in the never-ending fight against terror and its relentless onslaughts, despite their personal afflictions, by all who, while unable to be saints but refusing to bow down to pestilences, strive their utmost to be healers" (*The Plague,* 284). Not only is this technique consonant with Rieux's avowed project, it allows the narrator considerable latitude in his constructions. In *Poussière sur la ville,* however, there is no such link between Dubois's narrative project – which is nowhere made explicit – and his profession of humanist faith at the end of the novel. Instead, what we have is a first-person narrative in the present tense, each chapter representing something akin to an undated diary entry for that day, with occasional flashbacks to the narrator's recent past. It is not clear whether the narrative is written (using the present tense as a rhetorical device), spoken, or simply thought aloud as a kind of interior monologue.[8] What is certain is that the technique requires that the narrator have access only to past and present events and that he have no knowledge of what is to come later in the story – he cannot anticipate. The form implies, to a greater or lesser degree, a subordination of "story" to "life."

Sartre's hero-narrator, Antoine Roquentin, had confronted this problem in the 1938 novel *Nausea.* Roquentin realizes one day to his chagrin that he has never had any adventures, that adventures belong in books and not in life. Of course, he tells himself, everything that happens in books can happen in life, too, but not in the same way – and that is what matters. Adventures, he decides, are told, not lived. Anyone who thinks he has adventures is trying to live his

life as though he were telling it. "But you have to choose: live or
tell" (*Nausea,* 39). One has to choose, because the two activities are
incompatible. In life nothing ever happens, there are no beginnings:
"But everything changes when you tell about life; it's a change no
one notices: the proof is that people talk about true stories. As if
there could possibly be true stories; things happen one way and
we tell about them in the opposite sense. You seem to start at the
beginning: 'It was a fine autumn evening in 1922. I was a notary's
clerk in Marommes.' And in reality you have started at the end"
(*Nausea,* 39–40). Stories, then, are teleological: the end is always
there, shaping and transforming the material of life, creating beginnings where there are none, giving form to the formless, direction
to that which is without. There are no "true" stories, because all
stories are fictions, all stories are *made.*

What then of *Poussière sur la ville?* At first sight Langevin seems
to have taken Roquentin's lesson to heart; there is, for example, no
beginning in the traditional sense of the word: "Une grosse femme,
l'oeil mi-clos dans la neige me dévisage froidement. Je la regarde
moi aussi, sans la voir vraiment, comme si mon regard la transperçait
et portait plus loin, très loin derrière elle. Je la reconnais vaguement.
Une mère de plusieurs enfants qui habite dans le voisinage. Cela
dure une demi-minute au moins, j'en jurerais. Puis elle s'en va d'un
pas lent et lourd qui troue silencieusement la neige. J'écrase ma
cigarette sur le mur contre lequel je suis adossé et je comprends
tout à coup. La bonne femme a dû me croire fou ou ivre. Il est
presque minuit. Un vent violent fait tournoyer une neige fine dans
la rue déserte. Et, tête nue, sans pardessus, je contemple ma maison"
(11). The technique is simple: using the first person and the present
tense, the narrator presents an act of consciousness in two stages
– first he registers an impression, then he ventures an explanation
of what he sees ("je comprends tout à coup"). Clearly, there is no
danger of Dubois's falling into the trap denounced by Roquentin:
"I wanted the moments of my life to follow and order themselves
like those of a life remembered. You might as well try and catch
time by the tail" (*Nausea,* 40).

The same device of delayed comprehension is used to great effect
in the opening paragraph of part 3 of the novel, where Dubois is
stopped in his car at a red light: "Je suis arrêté par le feu rouge
devant l'église. Sur le trottoir, le curé me salue. Je lui rends son
salut, mais il continue à agiter la main et je le regarde sans comprendre. Mon air d'étonnement doit lui paraître hostile. Pour qu'il
n'interprète pas mal mon visage je salue de nouveau. Il agite encore
le bras, puis, penaud, détourne son regard vers les voitures qui sont

derrière moi. Je comprends tout à coup. La chaleur me monte au visage. Le curé me demandait de monter dans ma voiture. Je corne et l'invite de la main" (159). As Alexandre Amprimoz has pointed out, the misunderstanding on the level of gesture foreshadows a more serious misunderstanding on the level of language: living in different worlds, as they do, the doctor and the priest can have nothing meaningful to say to one another. One can surmise that the source of this episode is once again to be found in Camus, in a meditation on the absurd in *The Myth of Sisyphus:* "A man is talking on the telephone behind a glass partition; you cannot hear him, but you see his incomprehensible dumb show: you wonder why he is alive" (*Sisyphus,* 11). But what is perhaps even more interesting from our point of view is the intratextual symmetry that is established between Langevin's passage (the first paragraph of part 3) and the opening paragraph of *Poussière sur la ville,* a symmetry which reminds the reader that this is indeed a story with its formal divisions into parts and chapters, with its beginning and, therefore, its end. This would seem to be what Gilles Marcotte has in mind with his suggestion that *"Poussière sur la ville* can be defined as a novel of the sentence – of the complete sentence, organizing its meaning from start to finish, leading it step by step through the meanderings of syntax" (Marcotte 1977, 88). The technique of delayed comprehension, with its implication of a lived rather than a narrative attitude to time, is thus subtly undermined by the formal symmetry of its repetition, of its measured insertion into the syntax of story. Beneath Dubois's dress of life, we catch a glimpse of Langevin's artistic slip.

There is, in the novel, a clear conflict between two ways of looking at events, between "the logic of life" and "the logic of story" (of which the theatre motif is a variant). All that remains is to determine whether Dubois, in looking desperately for the "logic of life," is not in fact imposing on the events of his existence another quite different logic – that of story. Why, for instance, does he say in part 1 of the novel that Madeleinc's death is the "logical end" of their marriage: "Cette idée de sa mort, et c'est la fin logique de notre mariage, donne à mes paroles et à mes actes les plus anodins une impressionnante gravité" (73)? Partly, no doubt, because there is nothing like the fear of death for intensifying the experience of the present moment, for giving meaning to the apparently insignificant events of daily life. But partly, too, because, as Walter Benjamin points out, "death is the sanction of everything the storyteller can tell," since an individual's life first assumes transmissible form at the moment of his or her death (Benjamin 1969, 94). Alain's secret hope is that Madeleine's death will complete the narrative sentence, will break through the shapeless muddle of life and release him from his hopeless search for understanding by putting an end to what David Miller has called the "narratable": "the instances of disequilibrium, suspense, and general insufficiency from which a given narrative appears to arise" (Miller 1981, ix).[9] This reading is confirmed some fifteen pages further on in the novel by a passage in which the verbal echo is unmistakable: "Je suis las de poursuivre, las de chercher une signification aux gestes et aux mots les plus anodins, las de tourner sur mon pieu. Qu'on profite de mon engourdissement pour me détacher de Madeleine, qu'on m'assure lorsque je rouvrirai les yeux, que tout est rompu, que je peux me remettre à vivre, que je n'ai plus de soeur siamoise!" (88). It is clear that he cannot "get on with life" while he is still attached to Madeleine. However, the end of part 1 of the novel finds him still tied to his stake, starting yet another circle: "Cela finit par faire une vie" (91).

This, then, is the logic of life, the sum of human wisdom – the understanding that there is no logic, "qu'il n'y a rien à comprendre, que la mort n'a pas plus de sens qu'une pierre, que mieux vaut continuer de vivre en fermant les yeux" (196). Life is not an adventure, not a story; life has no "beginning" and no finality to give it form and sense. Its only end is death and death is, from an existential humanist point of view, senseless. Alain and Madeleine have no shared project which might have enabled them to *make* sense of their lives. Alain's project is his career, in which his wife plays no part. Madeleine, like some latter-day Emma Bovary, is left to find distractions and meaning where she can: in the songs she plays on the juke-box at Kouri's restaurant, in the movies she sees at the local cinema, in her sad passion for a truck-driver. Looking for her own logic of life, she exchanges one mediocrity for another. "Oh! Madeleine," Alain cries out at the end of the novel, "que ne sommes-nous demeurés médiocres, loin l'un de l'autre dans le même lit sans le savoir!" There would have been children and, with them, a home – drab and uncertain, perhaps, but held together nevertheless by force of habit, by the logic of life. "C'eût été la vie, Madeleine, chaude et pacifiante, sans exaltation, mais sans danger aussi" (212).[10] Instead, Dubois gets a story with a violent death and the sense of an ending. And the problem of life after the story: "Et il me faut te chercher sur le divan rose!"

Poussière sur la ville has sometimes been described as a novel of failure.[11] Bearing in mind that the *Grand Jury des Lettres* voted it the best French-Canadian novel to appear between 1945 and 1960, we are now obliged to ask, in light of our analysis, whether it is also a failed novel, the flawed work of a young author. If we are to answer this question, we shall have to distinguish several different reading strategies, all of which are possible but some of which are, it seems to me, better than others. It is possible, for example, to read *Poussière sur la ville* as a straightforward existentialist novel, in which the protagonist, at the end of a very distressing period in his private and professional life, reaffirms his commitment to humanity and declares his intention to carry on the good fight against the various manifestations of the absurd. The problem with this reading (and with its negative variant – that *Poussière sur la ville* is a straightforward psychological portrait of failure) is that it takes no account of the fact that the protagonist is also the narrator and that the relation between the two roles is far from innocent and trans-parent.

Another reading would allow us to account for some of the problems we have raised by laying them fairly and squarely at the door of the author. Thus, for example, the apparent contradictions between Dubois's phenomenological narrative (as instanced in the technique of delayed comprehension) and the theatrical structure of the novel as a whole (which implies a certain teleological shaping of events) might be explained in terms of a lack of technical consistency on the part of Langevin. This interpretation would have the effect of splitting the two terms of Roquentin's dilemma: Dubois does the living while Langevin does the telling. This would, inci-dentally, provide us with an answer to one of Dubois's many questions: "Depuis mon mariage, c'est une histoire bizarre. Je vois bien que je n'ai pas tiré moi-même toutes les ficelles. Plusieurs me sont tombés des mains. Madeleine n'avait qu'une faible partie de celles-là. Qui actionnait les autres?" (174). The answer would then be clear: Why! God himself, in the guise of the author, Langevin. And the novel would indeed be flawed.[12]

A more interesting reading would assume that Langevin is, on the contrary, aware of the implications of the narrative form he has adopted and of the apparent inconsistencies or ambiguities we have noted. We could then suppose that the psychological portrait of Dubois embraces his activity as a narrator and that his inability to make a clear choice between living and telling is indicative of a fundamental bad faith or self-deception that runs throughout the novel. Each reader would then be free to condemn or to sympathize according to his or her own experience and personal morality. Such a reading would not make Dubois a monster; he would simply be depressingly familiar: half pestilence, half victim, one of life's survivors and, more distressingly, one of life's failed healers.

The principal merit of this last reading is that it enables us to account for the narrative technique without being ungenerous to the author[13] and to interpret the form of the novel and the ambiguities to which it gives rise in terms of the novel's psychological content. There is, however, another possible reading which, though more elusive and less easy to justify, would frankly displace the burden of interpretation from content to form, from the psychology of the narrator to the narrative act *per se*. According to this reading, the ambiguities engendered by the narrative act would not be explained in terms of faulty technique, nor would they be resolved under the umbrella of a coherent psychological interpretation, rather they would be seen as intrinsic to the sub-genre "first-person, present-tense novel of consciousness." Such a view would focus attention on the uneasy relation between "life" and "story," between the represented world of the novel – which here includes the narrator's perception of events – and the way in which that world (and the narrator's perception of it) is ordered and presented by the narrative. Far from resolving the tensions and ambiguities created by the form, this kind of reading would maintain them as integral parts of the novel's structure, would drive a wedge between form and content, freeing form from its position of servitude, giving it a measure of autonomy and the capacity to resist the reader's inevitable attempts to integrate it into a harmonious whole according to the dictates of the novel's "content." In this light, *Poussière sur la ville* could be seen not only as reacting against the "omniscient" narrative of novels like *Bonheur d'occasion,* but also as announcing, through its ultimate incoherence – "on ne saura jamais, jamais" – the narrative schizophrenia of the novels of the sixties, when "life" and "story" will be forced explicitly and violently apart.[14] Such a reading would echo David Miller's claim that "the problematic of closure thus posed has nothing to do with the frequently evoked conflict between the closed form of art (as Henry James said, 'all discrimination and selection') and the openness of life ('all inclusion and confusion'). The conflict that interests me here occurs not between the novel and its referent but, within the novel, between the principles of production and the claims of closure to a resolved meaning" (Miller 1981, xi).[15]

It should be stressed that the difference between these last two "readings" is not really a difference between interpretations. The first of them, it is true, allows an interpretation insofar as it permits a coherent reading of the novel in terms of the narrator-hero's psychology – a reading which enables us to integrate form and content in a satisfactory manner without pointing to lapses of technique on the part of the author. The second does not really involve interpretation as such and is better thought of as a reading strategy, a way of looking at the novel from a particular vantage-point. As such it recalls André Belleau's remarks on *Poussière sur la ville,* which the critic reads in terms of a conflict of codes. According to Belleau, Dubois's existentialism is important not only as a textual generator but also as a signal of the novel's status as a "serious" literary text as defined by the (French) codes of the day. In this sense it is possible to speak of the inscription in the novel of an imported literary code which functions both "as a text-producing model and as a signal of the text's legitimacy" (Belleau 1983, 22). However, this tone of high seriousness is somewhat undermined by the novel's simplified topography, which substitutes for the complex social stratification of the modern urban novel the single street of the western. The imported literary code is thus undercut by a more primitive ideology imposed through the novel's use of space, an ideology which Belleau assimilates to the dominant socio-cultural code of Quebec in the 1950s. Small wonder that Alain Dubois is confused!

If I have chosen to privilege this last reading by placing it at the end of the chapter, it is not so much that I think it is necessarily the "best" reading as that it serves as a link with the subject matter of the chapters to come. Here, too, ordering and shaping make their demands, and the reader should be aware of how they are met.

CHAPTER FIVE

The Politics of Incoherence: Narrative Failure and the Invention of History in Hubert Aquin's Prochain épisode

All history is contemporary history ... the consciousness of one's own activity as one actually performs it. History is thus the self-knowledge of the living mind.
John Berger, *G.*

Mythology is much better stuff than history. It has form; logic; a message.
Penelope Lively, *Moon Tiger*

In Canada the only history is writing history.   George Bowering, *A Short Sad Book*

Hubert Aquin's *Prochain épisode,* published in 1965 in the middle of the Quiet Revolution, is a novel within a novel. Its narrator, who is never named, is confined to a Montreal psychiatric hospital, where he is awaiting trial on charges related to his underground political activities as a revolutionary separatist. Ostensibly to help pass the time, he tries to write a spy novel, which is set in Switzerland and narrated in the first person. Its hero, an equally nameless Quebec separatist, is involved in a series of adventures typical of the genre they parody (car chases, love trysts, kidnappings, secret codes, attempted murders, and so on); he then flies back to Montreal where he is arrested and curiously assimilated to the incarcerated narrator of the story he has just "lived." The structure of *Prochain épisode* is thus ideally suited to an explicit exploration of the problematic relationship between the logic of life and the logic of story, the relationship which, as we have seen in the previous chapter, implicitly informs Langevin's *Poussière sur la ville.*

And indeed, such a confrontation of life and story is very much at the centre of *Prochain épisode,* a fact which is at once underscored and further complicated when we recall that the narrator's situation is an essentially accurate reflection of the circumstances in which Aquin himself wrote the novel. However, while the critical relation between the logic of life and the logic of story is explicit in Aquin's novel (and therefore, in principle, accessible), it is mediated and set

in motion by the introduction of a third term – the logic of history
– which interferes at every level with the apparently simple mechanism of binary oscillation, thus complicating the issues and shifting
the values associated with the two poles of life and story. (André
Brochu points out, in *L'Évasion tragique* (173), that Langevin never
goes beyond a metaphysical view of the absurd, that history is
missing from his work. In other novels of the early sixties, written
in an atmosphere of turbulent nationalism, history makes an explosive
comeback.) From this point of view *Prochain épisode* is a difficult
and often frustrating text; it is best read in close conjunction with
the various essays and articles that Aquin published between 1961
and 1965, which provide a historical context for the interpretation of
the novel.[1]

(I should point out that, in this respect, my reading of *Prochain
épisode* goes against the flow of Aquin criticism in the eighties, the
dominant tendency of which has been to shake the novels loose –
in various ways, some more subtle than others – from the Quebec
national socio-text of the 1960s and 1970s.[2] This tendency will
undoubtedly be reflected in the multi-volume critical edition now
being prepared by the ÉDAQ team [Édition critique de l'oeuvre d'Hubert
Aquin]. Though this deliberate shift away from the historical context
of the work's production is usually seen by the second generation
of Aquin scholars as a liberation of the literary text from an outmoded
and overly constraining nationalist thematics, and hence as part of
a progression toward the more complex "truth" of the text, I am
more inclined to mix metaphors and see it as a perfectly natural
swing of the critical pendulum, as it keeps time with the evolution
of Quebec society and culture in the 1980s. If the movement proves
to be sufficiently dialectic, we can hope that the inevitable "coming
home" will be to an enriched, more intelligently textualized referentiality. In the meantime I believe there are some basic things about
Prochain épisode that have either not been said or not been said
clearly enough.)

A PEOPLE WITHOUT HISTORY

Much of Aquin's thinking during the early 1960s seems to have been
informed by his meditation on Lord Durham's statement of 1839 that
the French Canadians were a people without literature and without
history. More than any other writer of his generation, Aquin appears
to have taken this statement to heart and to have brooded on its
implications. Thus, in "The Cultural Fatigue of French Canada," published in 1962, he allows that Durham had been right and that,

indeed, little has changed in the intervening years: "Lord Durham was right, in this sense, when he wrote that French Canadians were a people without history! (History obviously belonged to English Canadians, and all we could do was to take it as one takes a train.) If we agree to play a role, however noble, it has to be in a history written by others" (*Writing Quebec,* 48). Wrested from the French-Canadian people by an initial act of conquest, history has remained ever since in the hands of English Canada.

One of the most striking features of this and other essays written by Aquin during the period is the conception of history as narrative that they embody and illustrate in varying degrees. One is reminded, in this respect, of Jean Pierre Faye's statement in his *Théorie du récit* that history is, first and foremost, an act of narration (Faye 1972, 15). The critique of history, then, becomes a problem of narrative: "Because history is made only in its telling, a critique of history can be effected only by telling how, through narrative, history is produced" (9). From this point of view, playing on the double meaning of the French word *histoire,* Aquin can say that French Canada has no history because it suffers from a chronic disability to tell its own story. Thus, in responding in "The Cultural Fatigue of French Canada" to Pierre Trudeau's claim that French Canadians would best serve their own interests by making themselves indispensable to the destiny of Confederation, Aquin states that this would inevitably imply a form of assimilation; French Canada, while playing a part on the federal stage, would remain caught in a structure not of its own invention: "In this scenario, French Canada would play a role, sometimes even a starring role, in a story it could never write itself" (*Writing Quebec,* 38). So long as it stays within Confederation, Aquin writes in "The Politics of Existence" (1962), French Canada is destined to rehearse its role of conquered people according to a script that never varies and that allows no scope for improvisation: "We are beaten before we have started. Confederation has institutionalized this inequality and, even if we go along with the system, we shall wear ourselves out in defence of our status as a conquered people. If we remain in Confederation, our history is written in advance and allows no possibility of starting afresh" (*Writing Quebec,* 9).

This insistence on history as a story which is created and told, shaping political attitudes and actions in the process, underlines the fact that nationalism, for Aquin, is ultimately an existential matter of political will. The main thrust of "The Politics of Existence" lies precisely in the belief that a people is defined by its project and not by its past. While using the memory of past humiliations as a goad to political action, French Canadians should not allow themselves to be paralysed by the plot of the past, with its history of failure and defeat. The passage from a historically determined, emotional nationalism to a lucid plan of action defined in political terms must begin with a clear understanding that separatism is not to be confused with the various forms of autonomism preached during different periods of Quebec's history and that true nationalism has nothing to do with going cap in hand to Ottawa to negotiate a "better deal." It must also be understood that faith cannot replace works and that nationalist rhetoric, no matter how stirring the sermons, must be accompanied by concrete, explicitly formulated political programs if it is to lead to something.

The same distinction between historical causes and political remedies underlies Aquin's consistent use of the terms *French Canada* and *French-Canadian* during this period, a usage which may seem surprising today, accustomed as we are to hearing the terms *Québec* and *québécois* in a nationalist context. In Aquin's case, the choice of words cannot be explained away simply by reference to the period in which he was writing. His use of the term *French Canada* is quite deliberate and in no way compromises his separatist position; on the contrary, it is essential to his formulation of the historical problem and is closely connected with his conception of dialectic fatigue. As he makes clear in "The Cultural Fatigue of French Canada," dialectical tension, which he describes as a source of lucidity and logic, has a very positive value – especially in the realm of politics – insofar as it prevents thought from degenerating into the intellectual sclerosis of preconceived systems: "In other words, the real dialectic is in dialogue, and not in two parallel monologues" (*Writing Quebec,* 20). True thought is still possible, and dialectic is seen as a guarantee against the temptations of a facile causality. For example, Trudeau's attempt to establish an invariable causal link between nationalism and war is dismissed by Aquin as an act of *lèse-dialectique.* It leads to a doctrine of transcendental pacifism which has the effect of blocking all serious thought on the issues involved: "In the name of a peace plan whose failure would be fatal for the world, we are incited to fear such a failure, the philosophic opposite of which is a detachment from everyday reality" (*Writing Quebec,* 27). Clearly, the kind of Armageddon logic that Aquin is denouncing here goes back farther than Hiroshima. The canonic French example is Pascal's wager, which subverts dialectical argument by the introduction of an overwhelmingly transcendent term, giving rise to the doctrine of the machine – the mechanical performance of ritual actions – as sole remedy for the existential anxiety induced by the prospect of eternal damnation.

According to Aquin, Trudeau's anti-nationalism is dangerous precisely in that it refuses to recognize that, historically at least, Canada is the site of a dialectical confrontation between two cultures. Instead, the dialectic is displaced by shifting the context of definition and denying the totality of French Canada by comparing it to a much larger entity or concept. French Canada's nationalist aspirations are thus easily crushed by placing them in "dialectical" opposition to any number of transcendent terms, of which nuclear warfare is merely the most dramatic and all-embracing. Similarly, the dialectical reality of the two Canadian cultures is denied by placing it in the political context of federal-provincial relations: "The political portrait of Canada masks the real confrontation between two cultures and glosses over this confrontation in a disguised monolithic regime which legalistically considers French Canada to be one province out of ten" (*Writing Quebec,* 45).

The weight attributed to the term *French Canada* in Aquin's view of things should now be apparent. Whereas *Quebec* is the name of a political entity defined by its (minority) position within Confederation, *French Canada* represents a cultural group which defines itself historically in relation to another cultural group – that of English Canada. To realize the Canadian dialectic is to work toward the politicization of that historical confrontation. By the same token, to confine French Canada to the province of Quebec is to depoliticize the notion of culture, reducing it to its least offensive, "regionalist" manifestations – preferably those which are recognized as legitimate and worthy of encouragement by federal agencies such as the Canada Council. (The terminological question can be thrown into stark relief by asking what the effects would be of changing the title of Aquin's essay from "The Cultural Fatigue of French Canada" to "The Cultural Fatigue of Quebec." Clearly, a large part of the argument would simply disappear.)

One result of the subversion of the Canadian dialectic by the federal system is the ontological insecurity of French Canada, which in turn gives rise to a collective guilt complex as nationalists are condemned for their acts of profanation and quasi-adolescent sacrilege. Caught in the vicious circle of dialectic fatigue, French-Canadian culture grows weary, as it succumbs to the psychological side-effects of its minority position: "self-punishment, masochism, a sense of unworthiness, 'depression,' the lack of enthusiasm and vigour – all the underlying reactions to dispossession that anthropologists refer to as 'cultural fatigue'" (*Writing Quebec,* 35). Already ridden by guilt and self-doubt, French-Canadian nationalism is further emasculated[3] by the paternalistic tolerance with which it is received and which reduces it to the status of a cathartic psychodrama, an adolescent crisis: "Its very toleration is an effective form of subordination whereby nationalism is made into a kind of sinful excess built into the system it is incoherently trying to overthrow, but which it never really disturbs" (*Writing Quebec,* 36). Any nationalist impulse, any movement of revolt, is thus anticipated and recuperated before the fact by the highly efficient mechanism of dialectic fatigue embodied in the political structure of confederation, a system which in no way threatens the continued existence of the French fact in Canada but which assures its total domestication.

Depoliticized, the minority culture undergoes a process that Aquin, in "Occupation: Writer" (1964), calls "folklorization": "The domination of one human group by another places an exaggerated importance on those powers of the inferior group which are harmless: sex, artistic proclivities, natural talent for music or creation, and so on. Are we not, as French Canadians, interested in Eskimo art and in the mythology of the Indians we keep on reservations?" (*Writing Quebec,* 51–2). In a colonial context, culture in general and literature in particular have a compensatory function in the overall dynamics of the society, which is why colonized countries inevitably produce excessive quantities of literature: "For want of realities, there is an overproduction of symbols" (53). This explains why for a long time Aquin felt it necessary to refuse the path of "art" – precisely because of a cultural conditioning that had placed special emphasis on artistic talents. "As an artist, I would be playing a part that had been assigned to me: that of a talented underling. Well, I refuse this talent, uncertainly perhaps, because I refuse everything that has to do with my domination" (52). In French Canada, as Aquin would say in an interview given to Jean Bouthillette in 1967, one is a writer only because one cannot be a banker – writing is a compensation for the lack of any real power, be it political or economic. Aquin's refusal to write in the early sixties was thus a refusal of the compensatory and "therapeutic" status of literature in a social situation he defined as colonial and paternalistic. Yet write he did, and much of the interest of *Prochain épisode* stems precisely from the way in which Aquin attempts to reconcile the incontrovertible fact of writing a novel with his repeated rejection of literature and the mechanism of compensation it inevitably implies for a colonized people.

THE NARRATIVE PROJECT

Aquin wrote *Prochain épisode* in the Institut Albert-Prévost, a Montreal psychiatric clinic where he was being held pending trial on a weapons charge. The novel's narrator finds himself in a similar situation: "Je suis soumis à une expertise psychiatrique avant d'être envoyé à mon procès. Mais je sais que cette expertise même contient un postulat informulé qui confère sa légitimité au régime que je combats et une connotation pathologique à mon entreprise. La psychiatrie est la science du déséquilibre individuel encadré dans une société impeccable. Elle valorise le conformiste, celui qui s'intègre et non celui qui refuse; elle glorifie tous les comportements d'obéissance civile et d'acceptation. Ce n'est pas seulement la solitude que je combats ici, mais cet emprisonnement clinique qui conteste ma validité révolutionnaire" (*Prochain épisode*, 15–16). The logic is clear: the novel's narrative situation is to serve as an analogy for the status of the French-Canadian nationalist within Canadian society; his politics are merely symptoms of a "disturbed" adolescence, of a difficult stage which, with a little professional help, he will be able to negotiate successfully. Once over the inevitable personality problems associated with his psychological age, he will be able to take his rightful place in society and look back with amused tolerance on his juvenile excesses. For the time being, he needs therapy and some kind of compensatory activity into which he can channel his potentially destructive energy.

These, then, are the circumstances in which he decides to write a novel, for what better therapy is there than writing? But what kind of novel? "Au fond, un seul problème me préoccupe vraiment, c'est le suivant: de quelle façon dois-je m'y prendre pour écrire un roman d'espionnage?" (7). Here again, he runs into the problem of implicit laws and unwritten rules which recall the "postulat informulé" of psychiatry: "Cela se complique du fait que je rêve de faire original dans un genre qui comporte un grand nombre de règles et de lois non-écrites" (7). However, his laziness – or his cultural fatigue – gets the better of him and he soon renounces any claim to originality, any desire to innovate within the genre. He settles down to write a spy story according to the canon of the day: "J'éprouve une grande sécurité, aussi bien l'avouer, à me pelotonner mollement dans le creuset d'un genre littéraire aussi bien défini. Sans plus tarder, je décide donc d'insérer le roman qui vient dans le sens majeur de la tradition du roman d'espionnage" (8). To understand the ideological implications of this decision, it is important that we have a clear idea of the unwritten laws of the mainstream spy novel in ·1964.

THE LAWS OF THE GENRE

The spy novel, as it had evolved in the 1950s and early 1960s, was dominated by the James Bond novels of Ian Fleming. In an interesting essay on "Narrative Structures in Fleming," published in his book *The Role of the Reader,* Umberto Eco points out that, unlike his predecessor Mickey Spillane, Fleming deliberately excludes neurosis from the genre's narrative possibilities and that, unlike his successor John Le Carré, he eliminates all moral ambiguity from the world in which Bond, a "magnificent machine," functions. In fact, from the last pages of *Casino Royale,* the first novel in the 007 series, Fleming "renounces all psychology as the motive of narrative and decides to transfer characters and situations to the level of an objective structural strategy" (Eco 1984, 146). Such a decision allows the semiotician to see, as early as the first novel, "all the elements for the building of a machine that functions basically on a set of precise units governed by rigorous combinational rules" (146).

According to Eco, the 007 novels are constructed on a series of fourteen oppositions which allow a limited number of permutations and which constitute invariant features governing the appearance of minor dichotomies as free variants. The first four of these oppositions involve four basic characters, who enter into the following fixed combinations: (1) Bond – M; (2) Bond – Villain; (3) Villain – Woman; (4) Woman – Bond. The remaining oppositions represent pairs of opposing values, variously embodied in the basic characters and grouped around two ideological and ethnic divisions: (5) Free World – Soviet Union; (6) Great Britain – Non-Anglo-Saxon countries.

The relationship between Bond and his chief is one of power and dominance, the main criterion for domination being M's omniscience.[4] This is made particularly clear on those occasions when M sends his agent off on adventures, the outcome of which he has foreseen from the start. There exists between the two characters a certain ambivalence of attitude and a repressed tension, which surfaces in *The Man with the Golden Gun,* where Bond is led to attempt a kind of ritual parricide. Fleming's villains, on the other hand, represent a whole menagerie of monsters, frequently of indeterminate sexuality and ethnic origin, who contrast with Bond's virile good looks and racial purity. Exploited and dominated in various ways by these villains are the women of the Bond novels: "The general scheme is (i) the girl is beautiful and good; (ii) she has been made frigid and unhappy by severe trials suffered in adolescence; (iii) this has conditioned her to the service of the Villain; (iv) through meeting Bond she appreciates her positive human chances; (v) Bond possesses her but in the end loses her" (Eco 1984, 154).

The six basic oppositions along with the pairs of values that they embody can thus be seen as the "elements of an *ars combinatoria* with fairly elementary rules" (155). This narrative scheme does not determine the order of the permutations but, before the end of the book, "the algebra has to follow a prearranged pattern." (The 1966 French version of this text uses an even more telling expression for our purposes, one which recalls Aquin's formulation of the problem of history for a colonized people: "l'algèbre doit se dérouler *selon un code fixé d'avance.*"[5]) A Bond novel is thus conceived as a kind of game revolving round certain archetypal play situations such as the meal and the journey (for example, the chase through the Swiss countryside in *On Her Majesty's Secret Service*). Such standard game situations constitute formalized miniatures of the general play situation of the novel itself:

The novel, given the rules of combination of oppositional couples, is fixed as a sequence of "moves" inspired by the code and constituted according to a perfectly prearranged scheme. The invariable scheme is the following:
A M moves and gives a task to Bond;
B Villain moves and appears to Bond (perhaps in vicarious forms);
C Bond moves and gives a first check to Villain or Villain gives first check to Bond;
D Woman moves and shows herself to Bond;
E Bond takes Woman (possesses her or begins her seduction);
F Villain captures Bond (with or without Woman, or at different moments);
G Villain tortures Bond (with or without Woman);
H Bond beats Villain (kills him, or kills his representative or helps at their killing);
I Bond, convalescing, enjoys Woman, whom he then loses. (Eco 1984, 156)

It should be pointed out that while this scheme is, according to Eco, invariable in the sense that all the elements are always present in every novel, it is not essential that the moves always be in the same sequence. The basic scheme can also generate quite complicated variants involving the multiple repetition of one or more "moves."

However, despite the possibility of local complications, the Bond novels do not testify to any great powers of narrative invention on Fleming's part. In fact they fall into the more general category of detective stories as a whole: "Under the guise of a machine that produces information, the criminal novel produces redundancy; pretending to rouse the reader, it in fact reconfirms him in a sort of imaginative laziness and creates escape by narrating, not the

Unknown, but the Already Known" (160). The ideological positions implied by such perfectly functioning narrative machines derive not so much from the content of the stories as from the way in which that content is structured. In this respect Fleming's racial and political stereotypes do not embody seriously held ideological opinions; they are there for purely rhetorical purposes and testify not to their author's own beliefs but rather to his cynical use of the basic tools of his trade, that of storytelling. If Fleming is reactionary, it is not because his villains are Russians or Jews or halfbreeds; it is because he creates a Manichean world of stereotypes and fixed dichotomies, a static universe of absolute oppositions which allow no ambiguities, contradictions, or critical distinctions. His conservatism is that of myths, fairy-tales, and fables: "If Fleming is a 'Fascist,'" Eco concludes, "he is so because of his inability to pass from mythology to reason" (162).

THE NARRATIVE PROJECT REVISITED

In choosing to write a spy story to fill the long hours of his incarceration, the narrator of *Prochain épisode* would seem to have opted for mythology rather than reason. Accepting the comfort and security of a narrative machine "qui comporte un grand nombre de règles et de lois non-écrites" (7), he adopts a mode of writing that conforms perfectly to the state of cultural and dialectic fatigue in which he finds himself. His novel is, in a sense, written in advance; the laws of the genre allow for no improvisation, and the author quickly discovers that he is, to use an expression coined by Aquin in "The Cultural Fatigue of French Canada" to describe the French-Canadian people, "held within the confines of a structure [he] never invented" (*Writing Quebec,* 38). The pieces of the game are rapidly assembled, and the rules take over as the novel, with its projected hero Hamidou Diop, is put on automatic pilot: "Et le tour est joué. Moyennant l'addition de quelques espionnes désirables et la facture algébrique de l'intrigue, je tiens mon affaire. Hamidou s'impatiente, je le sens prêt à faire des folies: somme toute, il est déjà lancé. Mon roman futur est déjà en orbite, tellement d'ailleurs, que je ne peux plus le rattraper" (9).

However Aquin's cynicism is evidently no match for Fleming's, as becomes clear when the therapeutic and compensatory value of story-telling is immediately called into question and measured against the depth of cultural and psychological fatigue of the narrator's "real" situation: "Je reste ici figé, bien planté dans mon alphabet qui m'enchaîne; et je me pose des questions. Écrire un roman d'espionnage comme on en lit, ce n'est pas loyal: c'est d'ailleurs impossible. Écrire une histoire n'est rien, si cela ne devient pas la ponctuation quotidienne et détaillée de mon immobilité interminable et de ma chute ralentie dans cette fosse liquide" (9). The projected tale of the Senegalese agent's adventures in Switzerland turns irresistibly to parody, as the dose of required distraction increases in direct proportion to the narrator's deepening depression: "Pour peupler mon vide, je vais amonceler les cadavres sur sa route, multiplier les attentats sur sa vie, l'affoler par des appels anonymes et des poignards plantés dans la porte de sa chambre; je tuerai tous ceux à qui il aura adressé la parole, même le caissier de l'hôtel, si poli au demeurant. Hamidou en verra de toutes les couleurs, sinon je n'aurai plus le coeur de vivre. Je poserai des bombes dans son entourage et, pour compliquer irrémédiablement le tout, je lui mettrai les Chinois dans les pattes, plusieurs Chinois mais tous pareils: dans toutes les rues de Lausanne, il y aura des Chinois, des hordes de Chinois souriants qui regarderont Hamidou dans le blanc des yeux" (9–10). But irony proves an inadequate support and the logic of fiction, no matter how parodic, fails in face of the growing desperation of the narrator's condition. Drugged and defeated, his mind wanders back to the woman he loves, back to Quebec, to his own "lived" past, to roads and places which are charged with memories and emotion.

Disoriented by these disconcerting fragments of his past and depressed by the hopelessness of his present situation, the narrator finds it difficult to hold on to any clear plan for the novel he is writing. On the one hand, his own incoherence seems to preclude the all too predictable narrative algebra of the spy story: "Je laisse les vrais romans aux vrais romanciers. Pour ma part, je refuse illico d'introduire l'algèbre dans mon invention. Condamné à une certaine incohérence ontologique, j'en prends mon parti" (14). On the other hand, he cannot quite bring himself to relinquish the dream of a Balzacian hero like the conspirator Ferragus: "Je veux m'identifier à Ferragus, vivre magiquement l'histoire d'un homme condamné par la société et pourtant capable, à lui seul, de tenir tête à l'étreinte policière et de conjurer toute capture par ses mimétismes, ses dédoublements et ses déplacements continuels" (16). He is, however, perfectly aware of the deception involved in the elaboration of such a romantic mythology and of the compensatory mechanism it implies: "Plus j'avance dans le désenchantement, plus je découvre le sol aride sur lequel, pendant des années, j'ai cru voir jaillir une végétation mythique, véritable débauche hallucinatoire, inflorescence de mensonge et de style pour masquer la plaine rase, atterrée, brûlée

vive par le soleil de la lucidité et de l'ennui: moi!" (16). Unlike
Fleming, the narrator of *Prochain épisode* seems able and willing
to make the transition from mythology to reason; but such awareness
is achieved at great psychological cost, since reason allows no escape,
whether it be into a past spun from romantic lies or into a future
compromised by past failures.

In the second chapter, the narrator returns to his novel, but
Hamidou Diop seems to have been demoted to secondary status as
the third-person narrative gives way to a first-person account of the
narrator's fictional activities in Switzerland. This passage from a
projected third-person narrative to the first person marks the first
stage in the failure or abandonment of the initial narrative project
and in the assimilation of the hero to the narrator. In his essay on
André Langevin, Brochu proposes a Derridean formula for what he
calls the "false" narrator of *Poussière sur la ville* and Camus's *The
Outsider*: "One might then speak of a character-narrator" (Brochu
1985, 113). While I cannot, for the reasons given in chapter 4, wholly
accept this view, it does seem to me that a displaced version of
the formula would be appropriate in the case of *Prochain épisode,*
where one might reasonably speak of "a narrator-character." The
hero would then have the same referential or ontological status as
the reptiles in Escher's famous lithograph, climbing out of the page
only to return again to it. This textual circularity is reflected paratextu-
ally on the covers of the original edition of the novel, which carry
photographs of, on the front, part of a page of Aquin's handwritten
manuscript and, on the back, Aquin-as-writer seated at a desk,
apparently producing what we are invited to believe is the text we
have just read.[6]

The polarization of the two worlds is, however, no less marked;
it takes the form of an opposition between murder and suicide. In
his Swiss incarnation, the narrator, acting under orders transmitted
to him by his lover κ, who is a member of the same terrorist
organization, determines to pursue and kill a mysterious enemy,
while for the writer in Montreal romantic dreams of revolutionary
violence dissolve in the underlying suicidal reality: "Chef national
d'un peuple inédit! Je suis le symbole fracturé de la révolution du
Québec, mais aussi son reflet désordonné et son incarnation suicidaire
… Me suicider partout et sans relâche, c'est là ma mission. En moi,
déprimé explosif, toute une nation s'aplatit historiquement et raconte
son enfance perdue, par bouffées de mots bégayés et de délires
scripturaires et, sous le choc noir de la lucidité, se met soudain à
pleurer devant l'immensité du désordre et l'envergure quasi sublime
de son échec" (25). It is in this state of depression and suicidal

identification with a history of collective failure that the narrator conceives a second narrative project, very different from the compensatory formulae of the spy novel: "Arrive un moment, après deux siècles de conquêtes et 34 ans de tristesse confusionnelle, où l'on n'a plus la force d'aller au-delà de l'abominable vision. Encastré dans les murs de l'Institut et muni d'un dossier de terroriste à phases maniaco-spectrales, je cède au vertige d'écrire mes mémoires et j'entreprends de dresser un procès-verbal précis et minutieux d'un suicide qui n'en finit plus" (25–6).

The narrative schizophrenia that is apparent in these passages bears witness to the painful transition from mythology to reason of which the Bond novels had been, according to Eco, incapable. The narrator's ontological incoherence introduces a dialectical struggle at the very source of the narrative project, and the proposed spy story is rendered profoundly ambiguous from the outset by the irreparable fault in its foundations. On the one hand, the narrator would like to write a straightforward spy novel, compensatory, predictable and cathartically therapeutic. On the other hand, he is well aware that such a novel, no matter how "revolutionary" its content, is necessarily recuperated *in advance* by the system it claims to contest. No matter how successful its celebration of the mythical exploits of the FLQ or the FLN, such a novel remains a product of cultural fatigue, a mere distraction from the historical reality of French Canada, of which the incarcerated narrator is a much truer reflection than his adventurous *alter ego* in the world of international espionage.

This, then, is the context in which the spy story proper finally gets underway. Hamidou is soon forgotten, and the story centres round the attempts of the novel's hero – the narrator's "délégué de pouvoir" – to kill his adversary, the mysterious H. de Heutz, a professor of Roman history at the University of Basel. Before taking up this story, a short digression is in order to look briefly at an essay which Aquin published at the beginning of 1965 and which provides the basis for an interpretation of the plot of *Prochain épisode*.

THE ART OF DEFEAT

Chapter 2 opens with a discussion of Harold Rosenberg's account of Braddock's Defeat, an event which serves as a parable of the failure of a cultural group to improvise a style appropriate to its changing historical and geographical circumstances. There is a close parallel to be drawn between Rosenberg's analysis and an essay first published by Aquin in the January-April 1965 issue of the journal

Liberté. In "The Art of Defeat," Aquin offers a "stylistic" commentary on the failure of the Rebellion of 1837–38 and lays bare what might be called a founding *mythos*[7] which sets the pattern for all subsequent historical events in Quebec: "Everything was foreseeable – everything! And everything was foreseen; nothing was left to chance ... The rebellion of 1837–1838 is incontrovertible evidence that French Canadians are capable of anything, even of conspiring in their own defeat" (*Writing Quebec,* 67). But why should the *Patriotes* have fought as though their rebellion were a lost cause? Why should they have conspired in their own defeat? Aquin sees a first clue in Groulx's account of the surprising victory of the *Patriotes* in the first battle at St Denis. Why, asks Groulx, did they not press home their advantage and give chase to Gore's companies which were in total disarray? How does one explain this "strange and mysterious lapsus"? Might it be, as Aquin suggests, a case of temporary memory loss, a kind of collective amnesia? "It was like being at a performance of a classical tragedy during which the chorus, all at once and in the most unlikely unanimity, forgets its lines. A deathly silence ensues" (*Writing Quebec,* 69). Perhaps a more likely, if no less theatrical, hypothesis would be that the *Patriotes,* rather than forgetting their lines, had been upset by a cue to which they were unable to respond: "The chorus, dumbstruck, cannot say its lines if what has just happened on stage was not in the script; the *Patriotes* did not forget their lines at St Denis, but were thrown by an event which was not part of the play: their own victory!" (69). Whatever the explanation, the *Patriotes* seem to have fallen victim to what Rosenberg might have called a form of inverted Redcoatism, of adopting the codes of the enemy when it was clear that some new improvisation was needed to meet the challenge of unforeseen circumstances.

Contrasting the "stylistics" of the Rebellion of 1837 with the careful planning of the invasion of 1838, dwelling on the "suicidal style" of the *Patriotes'* military strategies, comparing their rebellion to the "poetic undertaking" of a man grown indifferent to the forms of his own failure, Aquin insists in various ways on the literary nature of the events which took place at St Denis. The defeat of 1837 is thus seen primarily as a *narrative* failure: the *Patriotes* were incapable of winning because they were unable to tell the unlikely story of their victory – a story which would have broken all the rules of the genre. As Lord Durham would say in 1839, the French Canadians are a people without literature and without history; in Aquin's words they were a people caught in a history of which they would never be the author, a history made by others. Incapable of telling its *own* story, of controlling the narration of its *own* history, French Canada sits back and waits to have its destiny dictated to it by the historical Other.[8]

By the date of publication (Jan.-April 1965) as well as by their subject matter, these reflections on the defeat of the *Patriotes* might well be read as a preface to the novel that Aquin would publish in November of the same year. As I have already indicated, the spy story in *Prochain épisode* turns around the various attempts made by the hero to assassinate the historian H. de Heutz (alias Carl von Ryndt, a respectable Swiss banker). These attempts give rise to three confrontations, which constitute a kind of ritualized combat between the young revolutionary and the professor of history − a combat which is presented as a transparent analogy for the frustrated efforts of a people to tell its own story and live its own history.

The first confrontation takes place somewhere between Geneva and Lausanne in the castle of Échandens. The hero of the spy story, who has been knocked unconscious and abducted by enemy agents, comes to his senses in the castle and finds himself face to face with his mysterious adversary. Groping for words in his still stupefied state, he has to rely on his wits and his powers of invention to get himself out of a tricky situation: "Il me fallait élaborer une riposte-éclair et puisque je n'avais plus d'arme à dégainer, vider mon chargeur dialectique sur cet inconnu dressé entre le jour et moi" (58). As has been pointed out by Marta Dvorak (1975, 376), his only weapon is his narrative competence, his ability to invent and tell a story. This fact is underlined by an immediate return to the narrative situation and to the narrator's sense of impotence: he is unable to prompt his double, who seems to have dried up on stage. Both narrator and hero are for the moment incapable of improvising the script that would break the spell. Finally, the hero manages to spin a half-hearted and unconvincing tale about his state of depression, his money problems, and the wife and two children he has abandoned. Taking advantage of the moment of doubt which his story creates, he is able to disarm his enemy and so win a first, surprising victory.

However, his success does little to improve his state of mind and he feels himself falling prey to depression and fatigue: "J'éprouve une grande lassitude: un vague désir de suicide me revient. Je suis fatigué à la fin" (67). His problem is how to go on with his story: "Une seule chose me préoccupait alors, à savoir la méthode que je devais utiliser pour tuer H. de Heutz" (67). The verbal echo of the novel's first page − "Au fond, un seul problème me préoccupe vraiment, c'est le suivant: de quelle façon dois-je m'y prendre pour

écrire un roman d'espionnage?" – removes any trace of doubt as to
the nature of the hero's dilemma, which is one of narrative: the
narrator does not know how to tell the story of his double's victory.
Instead, he starts thinking about the road from Papineauville to La
Nation and about his imminent appearance before the Court of
Queen's Bench, which is suddenly invested with historical significance: "Devant le juge, je devrai répondre et me disculper de
l'obscuration suicidaire de tout un peuple; répondre de mes frères
qui se sont donné la mort après la défaite de Saint-Eustache et de
ceux qui n'en finissent plus de les imiter, tandis qu'un écran de
mélancolie les empêche de voir le soleil qui éclaire La Nation en
ce moment même" (79). He wants to have done with H. de Heutz
"et toute cette histoire" (75) just as the *Patriotes* had wanted to have
done with the humiliation which still haunts French Canada. However,
like the "bons colonisés" of 1837, he behaves like a perfect gentleman,
allowing the enemy time to compose himself and regroup his forces:
"No low blows, no French frenzy; no tricks (or none worth writing
home about), nothing untoward in their table manners. One eats
like one's host" (*Writing Quebec*, 70).

And indeed, in the second confrontation between the two, it is
the enemy rather than the hero who resorts to dirty tricks. In the
woods at Coppet where he has been taken by the hero in the trunk
of his car, H. de Heutz plagiarizes the hero's own improbable story,
creating the character of François-Marc de Saugy in an attempt to
regain control of the narrative. This unexpected mirroring has the
desired effect of plunging the hero once again into a state of
mesmerized fatigue, in which all he can do is admire the diabolical
art of his adversary: "Cet homme possède un don diabolique pour
falsifier la vraisemblance; si je n'étais pas sur mes gardes, il m'aurait
à coup sûr et pourrait me convaincre qu'il est mon frère, que nous
étions nés pour nous rencontrer et pour nous comprendre. J'ai
vraiment affaire au diable" (84–5). Devil or brother, the historian
manages to cast his spell over the paralysed hero, thereby under-
mining the dialectical confrontation and creating an overwhelming
sense of unreality.

The echoes of Sartre's *Lucifer and the Lord* are unmistakable
throughout this highly theatrical scene. In fact, the following exchange
between Heinrich and Goetz seems to rehearse the confrontation in
Prochain épisode:

HEINRICH: Your words are dead before they reach my ears, your face is not
like those a man can meet in daylight. I know everything you will say, I
can foresee all your movements. You are my own creation, and your

thoughts come only at my bidding. I am dreaming, the world is dead, and
the very air is full of sleep.

GOETZ: In that case, I am dreaming too. I can see your future so clearly,
your present bores me. All we need to know now is which one of the
two is living in the dream of the other. (*Lucifer and the Lord*, 32)

Like Aquin's *Patriotes* at St Denis, Heinrich has great difficulty remembering his lines when he attempts to confront Goetz: "Wait: it is a
blank in my memory.[9] I am subject to these absences; it will soon
come back. (*He walks up and down in agitation*.) Yet I had taken
every precaution; this morning I went over everything in my head
... it is your fault; you aren't at all as you ought to be" (128).[10] It
is interesting, too, that the image of the double agent, so central to
Aquin's work and to the universe of the spy novel, is used by
Goetz to explain to Heinrich the meaning of betrayal: to be a
bastard, he says, is to be a double agent by birth.[11]

The most interesting feature of the confrontation scenes as stage-
managed by Aquin is that H. de Heutz's strategy is essentially literary
or poetic. His story is totally lacking in verisimilitude and makes no
real attempt to create a referential illusion; it works its enchantment
through its formal properties alone, holding the hero spellbound by
its vertiginous mirroring, not of any supposed reality, but of his own
desperately absurd fiction. Defying and subverting any notion of
dialectical reason, the historian's tale recuperates the revolutionary
initiative launched by the hero's initial, unexpected victory, assimilating it to the pattern established by the founding *mythos* of a
conquered people.[12] All too predictably, the hero falls victim to the
strange paralysis that had afflicted the victors of St Denis and had
introduced an abyss of hesitation between the first battle of 1837
and all the defeats which followed. Once again the narrative nature
of the failure is underscored by a return to the narrator and by his
confession of impotence in face of a plot that constantly escapes
from his control and is apparently determined to conform – against
all his efforts to the contrary – to an historical, atavistic model which
makes nonsense of any notion of invention: "Je n'écris pas, je suis
écrit. Le geste futur me connaît depuis longtemps. Le roman incréé
me dicte le mot à mot que je m'approprie, au fur et à mesure,
selon la convention de Genève régissant la propriété littéraire. Je
crée ce qui me devance et pose devant moi l'empreinte de mes
pas imprévisibles. L'imaginaire est une cicatrice" (89–90). Like the
character he has created, and true to his conditioning as a member
of a minority, the narrator must apparently resign himself to living
a novel written in advance.

After an ignominious flight, provoked by the appearance of a mysterious blonde woman, and followed by a copious meal at the *Auberge des Émigrés,* the hero returns to the castle, where the third encounter is to take place. He decides to rely on surprise and uses the historian's car as a Trojan horse to smuggle himself into the enemy's stronghold: "Moi, agent révolutionnaire par deux fois pris au dépourvu, j'étais en quelque sorte déguisé en H. de Heutz, revêtu de sa cuirasse bleue, muni de ses fausses identités et porteur de ses clés héraldiques" (115). Once again the theatrical nature of his adventure is emphasized; the hero, we learn, suffers from stage fright: "En fait, j'avais le trac. Avant d'entrer en scène, j'étais soudain la proie d'une agitation incontrôlable" (116–17).

Once in the theatre, the would-be assassin finds that history is again on the other side: "The mistake made by the *Patriotes* of 1838 cannot be explained in terms of a failure of their will to win or by the use of outmoded tactics; their mistake was to underestimate the enemy and to make the implicit assumption that it would be the same kind of enemy as in 1837" (*Writing Quebec,* 73). During his long wait in the wings, the actor falls deeper and deeper under the spell of the atmosphere of history and culture that surrounds his enemy. H. de Heutz, in his absence, seems to take on almost mystical powers and the intended dialectic runs the risk of once more being subverted by the introduction of a transcendent term: "H. de Heutz ne m'a jamais paru aussi mystérieux qu'en ce moment même, dans ce château qu'il hante élégamment ... l'homme qui demeure ici transcende avec éclat l'image que je me suis faite de ma victime ... Je suis aux prises avec un homme qui me dépasse" (129). The hero acknowledges that he is not privy to the code or alphabet in which the narrator has imprisoned him and that, in fact, it is the historian – absent yet omniscient – who controls the algebraic formulae of the novel they are living.

Succumbing to cultural and dialectic fatigue, the young nationalist is lost in an adolescent sense of awe. He is paralysed by the contemplation of his adversary's overwhelming superiority, a superiority which now takes on mystical overtones: "Ce que je perçois de lui ne sera toujours qu'une infime portion de sa puissance. Ses épiphanies me déconcertent et me prennent au dépourvu. L'impression qu'il produit sur moi neutralise ma capacité de riposter. Pétri d'invraisemblance, H. de Heutz se meut dans la sorcellerie et le mystère" (134). Trapped in a magnificent prison, the hero's situation comes to resemble the narrator's own, which in turn is inseparable from the historical being-for-defeat of the *Patriotes:* "J'agonise sans style, comme mes frères anciens de Saint-Eustache ... je suis sur le

point de céder à la fatigue historique … J'ai besoin de H. de Heutz.
S'il n'arrive pas, que vais-je devenir? Quand il n'est pas devant moi,
en personne, j'oublie que je veux le tuer et je ne ressens plus la
nécessité aveuglante de notre entreprise" (139–40). The failure, once
again, is essentially a narrative one, an inability to control and
organize the story: "Les coordonnées de l'intrigue se sont emmêlées.
J'ai perdu le fil de mon histoire, et me voici rendu au milieu d'un
chapitre que je ne sais plus comment finir" (142).

When H. de Heutz finally makes his entrance, it is a foregone
conclusion that the attempted assassination will be botched by a
hero who cannot perform what his narrator cannot write. The young
revolutionary remains trapped in the narrator's indecipherable alphabet, caught in a story of which he will never be the author. His
return to Montreal, his failed rendezvous with M and his subsequent
arrest, his total assimilation to the imprisoned narrator – all flow
inevitably from the *mythos* of defeat which has informed his every
move. "The narrative that leads out of prison," writes Ross Chambers,
"leads back into prison, and no more economical way could be
imagined of embodying in story form the thesis of this book concerning the identity (or at least inseparability) of story and situation"
(Chambers 1984, 210). (I cannot – for obvious reasons, given my
argument so far – accept Chambers' conclusion: "The narrative of
Prochain épisode presents itself, then, as an attempt to gain authority,
the authority of authorship, as compensation for loss of power" (210).
As I have tried to show, and as I shall continue to maintain in the
remainder of this chapter, the temptation of authorship as compensation for loss of power is consistently refused by Aquin. His analysis
of the role of literature in a colonial situation renders highly problematic Chambers' claim that narrative seduction, "producing authority
where there is no power, is a means of converting (historical)
weakness into (discursive) strength. As such, it appears as a major
weapon against alienation, an instrument of self-assertion, and an
'oppositional practice' of considerable significance" (212). If *Prochain
épisode* has a single message to convey, it is surely that any attempt
to attain a position of discursive strength through narrative seduction
is doomed to failure, precisely because such attempts are pre-programmed by the system they strive to disrupt.)

INTERPRETING FAILURE

To what extent, then, does the spy story told in *Prochain épisode*
conform to the laws of the genre as formulated by Eco? In the first
place, we can say that all the surface elements of the 007 novels

are to be found in Aquin's story. The four basic characters are the same – hero, chief, villain, and woman – though the role of M is greatly reduced (he appears only at the end of the novel, where he is apparently arrested along with the hero). In the absence of an all-powerful chief, it is the villain, H. de Heutz, who usurps the role of omniscient father-figure, becoming in the process an altogether more complex and ambivalent character than in the Bond novels. The woman K – who is strongly identified with the country (*Kébec*) which she represents – retains the ambiguous status she had in the world of Ian Fleming, but it is an ambiguity which the dénouement of *Prochain épisode* does nothing to resolve. In this she reflects not only the merging of the functions and attributes of chief and villain, but also the ontological insecurity of the hero, who swings uncomfortably between the roles of Bond and Hamlet. As far as the two ideological and ethnic divisions go, a straightforward substitution of "Colonized countries – Imperialist countries" for Free World – Soviet Union and "French Canada – English Canada" for Great Britain – Non-Anglo-Saxon countries captures the substance of the new polarities but does nothing to explain their modalities; here again we have to remember that, in *Prochain épisode,* the oppositions are far from unequivocal and, indeed, are most often fraught with moral ambiguity, since it is the enemy within who is always the most dangerous.[13]

We have seen that, for Eco, these elements combine in the Bond novels according to elementary rules to generate plots or game sequences, the algebra of which follows a prearranged pattern or code. In this respect Aquin's story again contains all the elements – including the same archetypal play situations such as the meal and the car chase – that are found in Fleming. The sequence of "moves," too, is very similar, involving no major changes until we come to the last two, in which the hero kills the villain and enjoys the woman. However, as we have seen, the fact that these last two moves are never made is indicative of the profound transformation undergone by a narrative machine which, instead of running its appointed course along the lines laid down by the laws of the genre, breaks down repeatedly and ends up on a different course, programmed by a different code, that of the historical *mythos* of conquest and humiliation. Fleming's *ars combinatoria* is thus transformed by Aquin into an art of defeat.

But what, we must ask, has been defeated in *Prochain épisode?* What has failed? Is it, as some critics have suggested, the very possibility of revolutionary action that perishes in the hero's repeated failure to kill his enemy? Or are such critics falling into an elementary trap of reading, implicitly accepting a referential illusion that is explicitly denounced in the novel itself? After all, the spy story in *Prochain épisode* is quite clearly a fiction; its fictional status is an integral part of the novel's structure and, presumably, of its intended meaning. Thus, while it is necessary to read Aquin's novel as a historical allegory of collective guilt and failure, it is not sufficient to do so. The overall structure of *Prochain épisode* is characterized by what might be called a narrative schizophrenia, an explicit splitting of the narrative subject into the "I" of the narrator and the "I" of the hero and of the narrative impulse into discourse (the narrative situation) and story (the world of the spy novel).[14] To interpret the failure of the spy story as a simple allegory for the failure of the revolutionary nationalism it claims to portray is to ignore the critical, dialectical relationship that exists between the two levels of the text. In this respect, Aquin – the least naïve of novelists – has been the victim of a surprising number of "naïve" readings of one kind or another. It is perhaps useful to stress the fact that the failure of the spy story must be read *in context* and that this context is both historical and literary.[15]

The failure of the spy story is the failure of a narrative machine to function according to the rules with which it has been programmed; it is the failure of a text to generate a referential illusion which recognizes neither psychological complexity nor moral ambiguity; it is the failure of a form of therapy which depends on a mechanism of escape and compensation and implies that the narrator's politics are but the symptoms of an illness; it is the failure of a genre which prefers the comfortable stereotypes of myth to the disturbing realities of life and which achieves coherence through redundancy. In this respect, *Prochain épisode* is neither a revolutionary novel (in the sense that it sets out to portray a revolutionary episode) nor, as has been claimed, a counter-revolutionary novel (in the sense that it portrays the inevitable failure and recuperation of revolutionary activity). It is rather, as its title would indicate, a pre-revolutionary novel – a novel which, while exorcizing the myths and compensatory temptations of a colonized people, presents a lucid account of dialectic fatigue and its historical determinants.

FORM AND (DIS-)CONTENT: A STYLISTIC ONTOLOGY

Can we then speak of Aquin as a committed novelist, "un romancier engagé"? Aquin himself addresses the question in "Occupation: Writer," where he makes it clear that he prefers to think of himself as an "écrivain enraciné," in order to avoid the restrictive connotations that the term "committed" can take on, particularly in moments of political crisis: "The problem is not one of being a member of the PSQ or the RIN or the PRQ, or of stuffing envelopes in a typically disorganized party office. The problem for the writer is to live in his country, to die and be resurrected with it" (*Writing Quebec,* 57). Aquin's commitment as a writer is a matter of ontology, of personal and collective identity, rather than of party politics. However, it should be stressed that this identification with the nation is the very opposite of the process of folklorization at work in the stereotyped productions of a domesticated and largely compensatory literary regionalism: "It is sterile to use one's land only in slices of life which, through their anthological status, clearly establish the writer's lack of roots" (*Writing Quebec,* 57).

This rejection of local colour recalls an earlier statement by Aquin who, in "The Cultural Fatigue of French Canada," had indicated the kind of "enracinement" that the French-Canadian writer should assume: "The problem is not to write stories that take place in Canada, but to assume all the difficulties of one's identity fully and painfully. French Canada, like Fontenelle on his deathbed, feels 'a certain difficulty of being'" (*Writing Quebec,* 41). But how can this "difficulty of being" be translated into literary terms without being immediately recuperated by the mechanism of cultural and dialectic fatigue? The question is one that will haunt Aquin even after the publication of *Prochain épisode.* In a 1969 article, "The Death of the Accursed Writer," he proposes a "stylistic" solution to the problem: "Whatever the message of a Quebec writer, whatever the contents of a book or a piece of writing, he finds himself faced, in spite of himself, with the following problem: how to invent a new way of being Québécois through the writing of books. Not that he should take it into his head to represent or reflect the Quebec society that he sees around him (we are not mirrors); but by virtue of his Quebec roots, he will probably have no choice but to be blatantly Québécois, to create his personal mode of revelation and invent the style of his own epiphany, in order to be (in his books) so Québécois that it will make you want to throw up" (*Writing Quebec,* 93). In advocating a stylistic assumption of his country's difficulty of being, Aquin is returning to a notion he had formulated as early as 1961, when he coined the term "le malheur d'expression" to describe a style which, in its very infelicity, would embody the profound unhappiness of a dispossessed and alienated people.[16]

The first target of Aquin's stylistic terrorism is his own language: "I am prey to destructive impulses against this wretched French language which, for all its majesty, still comes second" (*Writing Quebec,* 50). The problem is not to write stories about revolutionaries, but to produce texts which, in their "malheur d'expression," enact the ontological crisis of the society whose form they embody: "Syntax, form, the meaning of words – all are subject to explosion" (*Writing Quebec*, 57). If literature is capable of being revolutionary, it is not by what it says but by what it is. The literary text must embody, in its own difficulty of being, the collective ontology of the French-Canadian people: "the writer who attempts to breathe life into what is killing him will not write a Stendhalian tale of French-Canadian *carbonari*, but a work as uncertain and formally unwholesome as the one taking place in him and in his country" (57). Buffon's "The style is the man" becomes, for Aquin, "The style is the country." The writer should break with the transcendent coherence and inevitability of dialectic fatigue by choosing, like Hamlet, the incoherence and unpredictability of the monologue: "During this period of troubles, how could the writer finish his sentence the way he had planned?" (*Writing Quebec*, 58). He must reject the transcendent structures of literature and language to create forms which embody the passion and daily agony of French Canada: "It is a waste of time to write novels unsullied by the intolerable realities of our collective daily life, in an antiseptic French untouched by the spasms which shake the ground we walk on" (58).

It is this "enracinement," this commitment to the painful reality of what it is to be French Canadian, that constitutes the true opposition to historical fatigue and to the collective *mythos* of defeat. It is what permits the transition, in *Prochain épisode*, from the "invisible coherence" of history as story (or anti-dialectical *mythos*) to the open, uncertain future of history as discourse (or *logos*). As Aquin says in *Point de fuite*, his book is neither depressive nor suicidal, since the "next episode" is the revolution yet to come (16–17). Which is why, in spite of the fact that *Prochain épisode* is a book of failure and despair – "ce livre défait" as the narrator himself styles it (92) – I find it hard to accept the interpretation of critics like André Berthiaume, who want to see in the novel a kind of historical closure in which the future is determined by the past (Berthiaume 1973, 148). Such a judgment clearly flies in the face of Aquin's own existentialism, an aspect of his thought which has frequently been neglected: "Why, in the name of a past which is held to be determining, would we refuse a future which we still have the power to shape, at least according to the philosophies of Aquinas and Sartre?" (*Writing Quebec*, 8). As Aquin says in "The Cultural Fatigue of French Canada," a people is not subject to ontological determination and this lack of determination is the very basis of its freedom: "The future history of a human group is not fixed; it is unforeseeable.

'A man is defined by his plans,' said Jean-Paul Sartre. The same is true for a people" (*Writing Quebec,* 28). Indeed, the comparison with Sartre could be taken further to embrace a shared attitude toward the role of despair, as exemplified in the exchange between Zeus and Orestes in act 3 of the wartime play, *The Flies:*

ZEUS: What do you propose to do?
ORESTES: The folk of Argos are my folk. I must open their eyes.
ZEUS: Poor people! Your gift to them will be a sad one; of loneliness and shame. You will tear from their eyes the veils I had laid on them, and they will see their lives as they are, foul and futile, a barren boon.
ORESTES: Why, since it is their lot, should I deny them the despair I have in me?
ZEUS: What will they make of it?
ORESTES: What they choose. They're free; and human life begins on the far side of despair. (*The Flies,* 159–60)

In demystifying the mental structures of the French-Canadian people, in dismantling the mechanism of historical fatigue with its cultural and psychological corollaries, *Prochain épisode* embodies this liberating despair. This refusal to lie or to engage in compensatory fictions, this written despair, is all the book is capable of. The rest, the "désespoir agi" (94), belongs to a history as yet untold, a collective *mythos* of uncertain future.

NEXT EPISODE

I have suggested that a kind of code switching takes place in *Prochain épisode,* as the generic conventions of the spy story, with their particular ideological freight, break down when faced with a superior truth or reality: the logic of life wins out over the logic of story because it has, in this instance, history on its side. ("History is disorder, I wanted to scream at them – death and muddle and waste," says the protagonist of Penelope Lively's *Moon Tiger.*) This abandonment of one code for another is particularly apparent in the novel's failure to generate certain narrative sequences – especially the killing of the villain – which are called for by the 007 model. And yet closer examination reveals that the sequence in question is not in fact missing, it is simply narrated in another mode on the novel's last page:

Quand les combats seront terminés, la révolution continuera de s'opérer; alors seulement, je trouverai peut-être le temps de mettre un point final à ce livre et de tuer H. de Heutz une fois pour toutes. L'événement se déroulera comme je l'avais prévu. H. de Heutz reviendra au château funèbre où j'ai perdu ma jeunesse. Mais, cette fois, je serai bien préparé à sa résurgence. Je ferai le guet accoudé au larmier. Lorsque la 300 SL, gris fer à indicatif du canton de Zurich fera son apparition, elle me frappera comme une évidence et me conditionnera à l'action. D'abord je franchirai, sur la pointe des pieds, la distance entre le jour et la crédence Henri II, tout en dégageant le cran d'arrêt du revolver. Et aussitôt que j'aurai perçu le mouvement du pène dans la serrure, H. de Heutz entrera en scène et se placera, sans le savoir, en plein dans ma mire. Je l'abattrai avant même qu'il atteigne le téléphone; il mourra dans l'intuition fulgurante de son empiègement. Je me pencherai sur son cadavre pour savoir l'heure exacte à sa montre-bracelet et apprendre, du coup, qu'il me reste assez de temps pour me rendre d'Échandens à Ouchy. Voilà comment j'arriverai à ma conclusion. Oui, je sortirai vainqueur de mon intrigue, tuant H. de Heutz avec placidité pour me précipiter vers toi, mon amour, et clore mon récit par une apothéose. Tout finira dans la splendeur secrète de ton ventre peuplé d'Alpes muqueuses et de neiges éternelles. Oui, voilà le dénouement de l'histoire: puisque tout a une fin, j'irai retrouver la femme qui m'attend toujours à la terrasse de l'hôtel d'Angleterre. C'est ce que je dirai dans la dernière phrase du roman. Et, quelques lignes plus bas, j'inscrirai en lettres majuscules le mot:

FIN.

The use of the future[17] here will not fool the reader who has read the rest of the book: rather than expressing something that *will* happen, it serves to generate an unrealized sequence strongly reminiscent of the shift into the past conditional which we examined, in chapter 2, near the end of *Menaud, maître-draveur:*

Il s'était représenté cent fois la scène: la sommation d'abord, ensuite, sa réponse droite et fière. Puis, la pourchasse de l'intrus jusqu'au bas de la montagne, quelque chose comme une débâcle de toutes les colères que le pays avait sur le coeur depuis les années de servitude.

Triomphant, il aurait ensuite regagné ses chasses, les sanctuaires profonds de son domaine, les aires étincelantes de ses lacs; il aurait bu le coup de la liberté à même l'air frais et vierge des monts.

Le soir, il se serait enfin reposé en tête à tête avec ses morts consolés. (*Menaud,* 181–2)

In these passages we are dealing with instances of the "disnarrated" or "alternarrated," a category I borrowed from Gerald Prince (in chapter 1) to discuss the conflict of codes in certain nineteenth-century novel prefaces.[18] In both *Menaud* and *Prochain épisode,* the alternarrated is used to generate a sequence according to a generic code (nationalist epic, revolutionary spy story) which has already been abandoned in the text as not corresponding to any real (i.e., lived) historical context (or, in John Berger's phrase, to the "self-knowledge of the living mind"). However, the function of the alternarrated changes dramatically from one novel to the other as we pass from pathos to parody: in *Menaud* the alternarrated is the last expression of what might have been, the final stage of an old man's quixotic delusion as he descends into madness; in *Prochain épisode* it functions as an exorcism, reinforcing the ironic critique of a particular set of narrative conventions and their ideological implications. In *Menaud* the alternarrated conveys a profound sense of loss and regret, as it mourns the passing of a world in which heroic deeds were still possible; in *Prochain épisode* it performs a quite different task, one which Prince refers to as *discounting:* "It insists upon the ability to conceive and manipulate hypothetical worlds or states of affairs and the freedom to reject various models of intelligibility, of coherence and significance, various norms, conventions or codes for world- and fiction-making" (Prince 1988, 6).

In fact, the fictional author of the spy novel is no more free to end his story according to the narrative code he has chosen than the writer is able, in times of revolutionary change, to "finish his sentence the way he had planned" (*Writing Quebec,* 58). By placing the word "FIN" on the last page at the end of an alternarrated passage, Aquin wryly ensures that closure is postponed indefinitely, as the reader is drawn into what Douglas Hofstadter would call a "strange loop," a phenomenon which "occurs whenever, by moving upwards (or downwards) through the levels of some hierarchical system, we unexpectedly find ourselves right back where we started" (Hofstadter 1980, 10).[19] (The best visual analogue for the kind of loop we see in Aquin's novel is to be found in Escher's lithographs *Waterfall* and *Ascending and Descending.*) In this sense, *Prochain épisode,* the archetypal novel of *différance,* constitutes a "tangled hierarchy" and the reader is well aware that, just as Zeno's arrow will never reach its target, so the hero of the spy story will never kill his double or keep his rendezvous with κ on the terrace of the Hôtel d'Angleterre. And it is only in the eternally unrealized mode of the alternarrated next episode that the fictional author will be able to write, in capitals, a few lines below his last sentence, the word:

END.

CHAPTER SIX

An Archaeology of the Self: Narrative Ventriloquism in Anne Hébert's Kamouraska

What is Guilt? A stain upon the soul.   Nathaniel Hawthorne, "Fancy's Show Box"

He do the Police in different voices.   Charles Dickens, *Our Mutual Friend*

FRAMING THE WORLD / FRAMING THE SELF

In chapter 49[1] of *Kamouraska,* we find the novel's central character, Elisabeth, on watch at her window, scraping away the frost with her fingernails, clearing a space – doubly framed – in which to observe the drama being played outside in the street. What she sees – or, to be more precise, the telling of what she sees – is strongly reminiscent of Dubois' encounter with the priest in the third part of *Poussière sur la ville,* which I discussed in chapter 4 as an example of Langevin's "phenomenological" narrative. As Elisabeth watches, "Aurélie Caron trottine sur la neige, son ombre légère et dansante devant elle. Un homme vêtu d'un manteau de chat sauvage vient à sa rencontre sur la route, dans le grand froid de l'hiver. Il agite le bras au-dessus de sa tête. Fait de grands signaux à Aurélie. Les voici l'un près de l'autre: Aurélie et cet homme dont la silhouette, alourdie par le manteau de fourrure, fait battre mon coeur soudainement. Je les vois très bien, tous les deux. La fumée de leurs haleines s'échappe en nuages pressés. Aurélie baisse la tête" (*Kamouraska* 185). As in the Langevin passage, a momentary confusion is created while the reader waits for Elisabeth to interpret what she sees. The man, we understand by the sudden beating of Elisabeth's heart, is George Nelson, her lover. But what is he saying to Aurélie Caron? What secret and criminal words are being exchanged there in the street before our eyes? Elisabeth can only imagine the conversation, project her own subtitles onto the silent screen,[2] script the dialogue she can see but not hear: "Derrière la vitre, j'en suis réduite à imaginer la conversation précise de George Nelson et d'Aurélie Caron. À reconstituer le son des voix que je n'arrive pas à retrouver justes et qui détonnent désagréablement" (185).

Dubois in his car, Elisabeth in her room – insulated from the outside world they wait and watch. And yet there is a crucial difference between Elisabeth's efforts to supply the words that go with the pictures and Alain's attempts to make sense of the priest's dumb show. This difference has to do primarily with time. For Dubois the interpretation is delayed, but only by a few seconds; he soon realizes that the priest is simply asking for a ride. In Elisabeth's case, however, the conversation between George and Aurélie has to be imaginatively *reconstituted,* and even then the sound of their voices is distorted.

For a conversation to be reconstituted implies that the conversation is over at the time of reconstitution. It also implies some basis for the reconstitution, some support for the act of interpretation. The explanation, though not apparent to anyone opening *Kamouraska* at chapter 49, lies in the novel's narrative structure and in the fact that the "I" of this chapter, as of most of the others, is double. It refers, on the one hand, to the young Elisabeth Tassy (née d'Aulnières) whom we see here looking out of the window of her house on the rue Augusta in Sorel; but it has its source in the Elisabeth of twenty-odd years later, who lives in a house on the rue du Parloir in Quebec City where her second husband, Jérôme Rolland, is dying. Distressed and sedated, Elisabeth is reliving in a tormented sleep the events leading up to the violent death of her first husband, Antoine Tassy. If Elisabeth is able to reconstitute the conversation taking place between George and Aurélie, it is because she has information about that conversation acquired sometime between the seeing and the re-membering. Similarly, the distortion of the voices of which she complains is due not to the glass which separates George and Aurélie from the watching Elisabeth, but to the more than twenty years which separate them from the dreaming Madame Rolland and to the blurring effects of the dream itself.

Thus, while the first-person, present-tense narrative of the passage quoted from *Kamouraska* is stylistically indistinguishable from that of the Langevin passage, it derives from a very different narrative logic. In *Poussière sur la ville* the narrative is driven by Dubois' efforts to interpret the images and events of his daily life. One might speak in this sense of a hermeneutic narrative, of a logic of interpretation. In *Kamouraska,* on the other hand, the narrative motor is one of dream and memory, and the central question is not one of meaning but of saying, not of how to *read* the events but whether or not they can be *told.* It is in this sense that one can speak of a logic of reconstitution, of re-membering, or of restoration. And what is at stake in this work of restoration is not just the fresco of past events but the narrator's own sense of self, the possibility of resurrecting and restoring a psyche that had been buried along with her memories all those years ago by an act of denial and repression.

What remains unclear is the degree of control exercized by Madame Rolland over the re-membering of past events in her dream. In chapter 49, Elisabeth is reduced to the role of spectator, unable to hear what is being said outside in the "real world" and equally unable to make herself heard when she tries to intervene to influence the course of events: "J'ai beau m'époumoner, elle ne m'entend plus. Ni elle ni personne, d'ailleurs. Ma vie entière doit se dérouler à nouveau, sans que je puisse intervenir. Ni changer quoi que ce soit. Il ne me sera fait grâce d'aucun détail. Autant ménager mes forces. Ne pas appeler en vain, dans ma cage de verre, ouvrir et refermer la bouche comme les poissons rouges dans leur aquarium" (186). This haunting image of impotence and alienation is less reminiscent of Alain Dubois's vain search for meaning (though the image of the fish in their tank is not unlike Camus's image of the man in the telephone booth) than it is of the anguished immobility of Aquin's sequestered narrator in *Prochain épisode* and of his failure to tell the story he would like to tell. In Hébert's novel, as in Aquin's, the problem of narrative is not one of knowledge – "Je suis Mme Rolland et je sais tout," says Elisabeth (126) – but one of competence (can this story be told?) and of ontology (what will I be when I have told it?). But whereas in *Prochain épisode* the context in which these questions are asked is profoundly political, in *Kamouraska* it remains essentially private, an archaeology of the self rather than a prospecting of history.[3]

IN MY COMPARISON of the two "plays without words" in Hébert and Langevin, I have deliberately omitted a crucial detail. It concerns the relationship between the observer and the communication which is being observed. In *Poussière sur la ville* Dubois is not only the observer but also the intended receiver of the priest's increasingly frantic attempts to communicate. In *Kamouraska,* Elisabeth stands outside the circuit of communication in the position, much exploited by the nineteenth-century novel, of eavesdropper.[4] But this is eavesdropping with a difference, since Elisabeth hears nothing but is obliged to reconstruct, after the fact, the conversation taking place before her eyes. In fact if eavesdropping serves, in the nineteenth century, as an image in miniature of realist fiction, creating the illusion of an objective world not intended for us but artlessly laid bare, stumbled upon by accident and therefore authenticated, then the silent eavesdropping of Elisabeth constitutes a *mise en abyme* of the hybrid narrative structure which characterizes *Kamouraska*. For, unlike Langevin, who makes an apparently clean break with the omniscient narrator of the realist novel, Hébert retains a *simulacrum* of traditional third-person narrative in keeping with her nineteenth-century setting. This difference can be seen most clearly by comparing the opening paragraphs of the two novels:

Une grosse femme, l'oeil mi-clos dans la neige, me dévisage froidement. Je la regarde moi aussi, sans la voir vraiment, comme si mon regard la transperçait et portait plus loin, très loin derrière elle. Je la reconnais vaguement. Une mère de plusieurs enfants qui habite dans le voisinage. Cela dure une demi-minute au moins, j'en jurerais. Puis elle s'en va d'un pas lent et lourd qui troue silencieusement la neige. J'écrase ma cigarette sur le mur contre lequel je suis adossé et je comprends tout à coup. La bonne femme a dû me croire fou ou ivre. Il est presque minuit. Un vent violent fait tournoyer une neige fine dans la rue déserte. Et, tête nue, sans pardessus, je contemple ma maison. (*Poussière sur la ville,* 11)

L'été passa en entier. Mme Rolland, contre son habitude, ne quitta pas sa maison de la rue du Parloir. Il fit très beau et très chaud. Mais ni Mme Rolland, ni les enfants n'allèrent à la campagne, cet été-là. (*Kamouraska,* 7)

From a stylistic point of view, the two passages could almost be used as textbook illustrations of opposite poles of French narrative prose. On the one hand, Alain Dubois' first-person, present-tense narrative seems to register events phenomenologically as they happen, taking the reader inside the narrator's consciousness, inside the kaleidoscope of perception where disjointed images can be related only after the fact by an effort of interpretation. The logic of story, the search for meaning in an absurd world, comes *after* the logic of life – or so it would seem. In the opening lines of *Kamouraska,* on the other hand, any sign of a registering consciousness, of events being filtered through perception, has been carefully ironed out by a third-person narrative which transforms events in time into a purely verbal configuration, an ordered grammatical space of pure relation.

The novel's opening lines might have been written with Roland Barthes's famous description of the French simple or historic past in mind.

For Barthes the simple past is the cornerstone of story, not so much a tense as an ordering principle, a sign of hierarchical relations which transform process into system. Its function is "to reduce reality to a point of time, and to abstract, from the depth of a multiplicity of experiences, a pure verbal act, freed from the existential roots of knowledge, and directed towards a logical link with other acts, other processes, a general movement of the world: it aims at maintaining a hierarchy in the realm of facts" (Barthes 1968, 30). Emptied of any existential content, Anne Hébert's sentences construct a fortress of pure negativity, a barricade of style to hold at bay the disturbing events of immediate reality. Madame Rolland, her home, and her children are relegated to the timeless past of story, where they exist only differentially in relation to other elements of their narrative world. Langevin's space is full, overcrowded with objects and images jostling to be given meaning, to be interpreted, but at the same time resisting interpretation. Hébert's space is here empty, hollow, pure form, pure sign, already interpreted, already significant. But it is the closed significance of story – life already shaped into narrative, into relation.

It would be naïve, however, to try to fix the differences between these two styles as an opposition between life and story. As I tried to show in chapter 4, the apparent innocence of Langevin's phenomenological narrative conceals an art which betrays itself in the structuring of the novel as a whole; the conflict between the logic of life and the logic of story is problematic because it is impossible to identify with certainty the source and intention of the interference. We do not know whether the structuring agent is Dubois or Langevin and cannot therefore say whether or not the logic of story belongs to the same level of narrative consciousness as the logic of life. In *Kamouraska* we have a similar duality of structure but with the terms reversed: the constructed order of the beginning is pure surface, a façade erected by the narrator to conceal the disorder and confusion of her "real" life. Moreover, the novel is, despite certain appearances to the contrary, considerably less problematic than either *Poussière sur la ville* or *Prochain épisode,* precisely because, after an initial hesitation on the part of the reader, the source and intention of the interference receive a psychological interpretation which leaves little room for doubt: life and story are but symptoms of a kind of narrative schizophrenia, they are two facets or narrative modes of a personality at war with itself.

The slipping from one mode to another, which occurs throughout the novel, is apparent from the first page. After the impeccable narrative absence of the first paragraph, the prose slides imperceptibly towards the full presence of narrative consciousness: "Son mari allait mourir et elle éprouvait une grande paix. Cet homme s'en allait tout doucement, sans trop souffrir, avec une discrétion louable. Mme Rolland attendait, soumise et irréprochable" (7). The use of the imperfect is already bringing us a step closer to the central character's state of mind, but more important still are the expressions "avec une discrétion louable" and "soumise et irréprochable," which constitute the first indications of a subjective narrative voice and of the overwhelming sense of guilt which is about to emerge. We learn too, in the same paragraph, that Madame Rolland is waiting not only for the death of her husband but also for some revelation that is to come in the wake of that event: "Tout semblait vouloir se passer comme si le sens même de son attente réelle allait lui être bientôt révélé. Au-delà de la mort de l'homme qui était son mari depuis bientôt dix-huit ans" (7). But Madame Rolland revolts against the uneasy serenity engendered by the anticipation of meaning revealed, preferring to cling to the anguish that wells up inside her as a defence against this disturbing calm: "Mais déjà l'angoisse exerçait ses défenses protectrices. Elle s'y raccrocha comme à une rampe de secours. Tout plutôt que cette paix mauvaise" (7).

This statement raises a number of questions. What, for example, is the nature of the meaning which is about to be revealed and which threatens to fill her with an unwanted serenity? Why should she seek a refuge against peace in her own anguish? For the moment, I would simply like to suggest that the meaning that Madame Rolland expects to be revealed on the death of her husband is of the same kind as that which, according to Barthes, makes it possible to tell stories in the simple past: "The narrative past is therefore a part of a security system for Belles-Lettres. Being the image of an order, it is one of those numerous formal pacts made between the writer and society for the justification of the former and the serenity of the latter. The preterite *signifies* a creation: that is, it proclaims and imposes it. Even from the depth of the most sombre realism, it has a reassuring effect because, thanks to it, the verb expresses a closed, well-defined, substantival act, the Novel has a name, it escapes the terror of an expression without laws: reality becomes slighter and more familiar, it fits within a style, it does not outrun language" (Barthes 1968, 32). If we accept this hypothesis we are left with a paradox, for it would appear that Elisabeth – if indeed it is her voice that we detect in the opening sentences of the novel – is

playing a double game, attempting to control a wayward and excessive reality by means of linguistic or stylistic closure, while at the
same time seeking refuge against that narrative order in her own
inner turmoil.

This is a paradox we must accept and attempt to explain, for our
hypothesis concerning the narrative voice of the first two paragraphs
would seem to be borne out by the fact that, no sooner has Madame
Rolland's anguish been invoked as a possible defence against an
unwanted peace, than we see a transition, in the third paragraph,
to a first-person, present-tense narrative: "Il n'y a plus personne que
je connaisse en ville. Si je sors, on me regarde comme une bête
curieuse" (7). We are presented, then, with a kind of double bind
as the narrator tries to use reality or life (as represented by the
first-person, present-tense narrative mode) as a defence against a
particular kind of narrative closure (represented by the third-person,
simple past narrative mode) which itself is being used as a defence
against reality. Thus, the oscillating rhythm of what I have called
narrative schizophrenia is established from the very first page, and
the novel's principal interest will lie precisely in the various manifestations of this schizophrenia and the different attempts to resolve
the narrative and psychological double bind which is its apparent
cause.

The first clear indication of an emotional disturbance comes at
the bottom of the highly charged first page, when Elisabeth complains
of being watched and followed: "On m'observe. On m'épie. On me
suit. On me serre de près. On marche derrière moi" (7). The
impersonal, ubiquitous "on" of these sentences would seem to represent the collective consciousness of the community as perceived
(or imagined) by Elisabeth. The insistence with which it is presented
here suggests a certain paranoia and provides a further clue for the
interpretation (or diagnosis) of the narrative disturbance already noted.
Seen in this light, the third-person, simple past narrative of the
opening lines combines with the expressions "avec une discrétion
louable" and "soumise et irréprochable" to create an illusion – the
illusion of the voice of the community as Elisabeth would like to
hear it.[5] The distance between this anonymous, impersonal voice of
the first lines and the obsessively repeated "on" of three paragraphs
later is the distance between serenity and anguish, between acceptance and rejection, between order and excess. It is between these
poles that the novel's narrator and heroine will oscillate as she
attempts to discover her "real life." (In chapter 30, for example,
Elisabeth will lament the lack of "reality" of her past: "La vraie vie
est ailleurs; rue du Parloir, au chevet de mon mari" [133], whereas

in chapter 63 she will refuse the claims of the present as being less "real" than the past: "Les prières des agonisants résonnent trop fort, dans mon oreille. Risquent de m'attirer hors de ma vraie vie, de me ramener incessamment dans ma maison de la rue du Parloir" [238].)

Interestingly enough, the first explicit evocation of Elisabeth's "real life" is presented in the context of a world splitting in two: "C'est cela ma vraie vie. Sentir le monde se diviser en deux haies pour me voir passer. La mer Rouge qui se fend en deux pour que l'armée sainte traverse. C'est ça la terre, la vie de la terre, ma vie à moi" (8). It is this image of the narrator as the centre of attention of a world divided by her own presence that triggers Madame Rolland's first descent into her past, which is the first fragment of the story that is to be told: "Un jour, c'est entre deux policiers que j'ai dû affronter cette terre maudite" (8). And with this first foray into the past, this first departure from the novel's (not so reassuring) frame, comes the question of identity, defined here as a layering of social and legal designations that were imposed or adopted in virtue of the character's changing marital status: "Moi, moi, Élisabeth d'Aulnières, veuve d'Antoine Tassy, épouse en secondes noces de Jérôme Rolland" (8).

There follows a series of apparently random images and narrative details which, without explaining everything, create a vivid picture of events, all of which are intimately related to the question of identity: a sleigh ride from Lavaltrie to Montreal; the narrator's arrest by two policemen smelling of beer; an apologetic prison warden; a black door, four mouldy walls; the smell of latrines, the cold; her appearance, in September 1840, in Court of King's Bench; the charges, the questions, the witnesses; her return home, after two months in prison, for health and family reasons. There are also allusions to a lover, whose extradition (from Burlington in the United States) apparently did not take place. And then, after two years, marriage to Jérôme Rolland – a marriage, the sole object of which was to give her new respectability. But at the first mention of respectability, the narrator cannot conceal her disdain and veers to the opposite pole of passionate defiance and escape to the (figurative) other end of the world: "C'est cela une honnête femme: une dinde qui marche, fascinée par l'idée qu'elle se fait de son honneur. Rêver, m'échapper, perdre de vue l'idée fixe. Relever mon voile de deuil. Regarder tous les hommes, dans la rue. Tous. Un par un. Etre regardé par eux. Fuir la rue du Parloir. Rejoindre mon amour, à l'autre bout du monde. À Burlington. À Burlington" (9).

We learn of a journey undertaken by this lover, alone, in winter, to Kamouraska – a round-trip of some four hundred miles. We learn how, his hands covered with blood after "le malheur de Kamouraska," he had left her in Sorel one February evening. We learn, too, something of her eighteen years of marriage to Jérôme Rolland, of the mechanical rhythms of "marital relations" and relentless procreation: "Pourquoi faire tant de simagrées. Je n'ai été qu'un ventre fidèle, une matrice à faire des enfants. Huit enfants de celui-ci. Et les trois petits d'avant celui-ci, du temps que j'étais l'épouse d'Antoine Tassy, seigneur de Kamouraska" (10). Her third son, Nicolas, we are given to understand, is her only child of love: "Mon petit Nicolas à qui ressembles-tu? Tes yeux? Ce sont les yeux de l'amour perdu. J'en suis sûre" (10). The chapter closes with a further reference to Kamouraska and a cryptic allusion to a sacrifice: "Le sacrifice célébré sur la neige. Dans l'anse de Kamouraska gelée comme un champ sec et poudreux. L'amour meurtrier. L'amour infâme. L'amour funeste. Amour. Amour. Unique vie de ce monde. La folie de l'amour" (11).

In the space of less than five pages we have passed from an initial impression of serene, meaningful order to an anguished evocation of love and death, madness and sacrifice. We have gone back in time some twenty years, travelling from the safety of the house in the rue du Parloir in Quebec City to the snowy wastes of Kamouraska. We have been given almost all the essential elements (characters, events, locations, themes) of a story which remains to be told, enough of the key pieces of the jigsaw puzzle to afford us at least a glimpse of both the novel's frame (the imminent death of Jérôme Rolland in the house in the rue du Parloir) and the picture it contains (the violent events of Elisabeth's passionate past).

Kamouraska cannot, however, be described as a traditional framed novel in which frame and story constitute two quite distinct narrative levels, two narrative worlds linked by the act of narration. As we have seen, Hébert chooses to multiply the interferences between the two worlds, past and present, story and frame, and to set up a kind of double bind. The frame is no longer the reassuring home base of the traditional *roman à cadre,* representing the familiar, comfortable order of an everyday life impervious to the excesses of fiction. The frame is itself the site of a traumatic event (the imminent death of Jérôme Rolland) which is fraught with perceived danger for the narrator, Elisabeth. In these circumstances, the latter's entry into story is highly ambiguous. For one thing, the "story" receives no external expression: "story" here refers to remembered events from the narrator's own past life which are relived (rather than written down or recounted orally to some listener) in an uneasy state of hallucinatory fatigue somewhere between waking and dream.[6] (It is worth pointing out that, as we shall see, these events are relived by

Madame Rolland through language, as narrative; the story remains
very much a story, despite the closed circuit of its telling.) As is
suggested by one of the novel's main narrative metaphors, a key
question is whether the story, as it is relived by Elisabeth, will
contain the truth, the whole truth, and nothing but the truth, or
whether, on the contrary, it will serve merely as an escape mechanism,
a means of evading the moral and emotional problems raised by
the situation of the frame – whether it will be therapeutic or merely
compensatory.

Another key question concerns the relation between frame and
story. Since both are highly charged emotionally for the narrator,
there is a constant danger that each will be pressed into service as
a refuge against the other. Thus, as we have seen, the function of
the simple past is to give the story a name, to set linguistic limits
capable of containing reality: "the Novel has a name, it escapes the
terror of an expression without laws: reality becomes slighter and
more familiar, it fits within a style, it does not outrun language"
(Barthes 1968, 32).[7] In the same way, the frame must contain the
chaotic lived experience of the story, must prevent it from overflowing
the limits of psychological and emotional acceptability. (Hébert's
image for the interplay of raw sexual energy and society's attempts
to contain it is appropriately Victorian. When ministering to the dying
Monsieur Rolland, Elisabeth is described as leaning over him, "ses
seins rebondis, sous l'étoffe du corsage étroit" (17); a short time
later, alone in the sad little room of Léontine Mélançon, the children's
governess, Elisabeth seems to come apart at the seams, her hair
falling down over her eyes as she bends down to unlace her boots,
and almost chokes on a hairpin she is holding in her mouth. "Un
sein déborde du corset" (31) we are told, in much the same way
as reality, for Barthes, threatens to overflow (déborder) the constraining forms of language.[8] But the frame itself is not stable. Like the
picture frame in Escher's *Picture Gallery,* it starts to lose its contours,
to oscillate wildly between the third and first persons, between the
strategies of containment and denial epitomized by the simple past
and the existential fullness of the present. Frame and picture flow
back and forth, blurring distinctions and transgressing limits according
to a delirious logic of dream and hallucination, a rhetoric of entrances
and exits, of shifting scenes and metonymic substitutions.

SON ET LUMIÈRE

By chapter 8 the novel's frame is established and Elisabeth locks
herself into Léontine Mélançon's bedroom, where she prepares herself

for sleep and for the battle ahead: "Désarmer le génie malfaisant des sons et des images, lui consentir quelques concessions minimes. Tricher avec lui. Choisir mes propres divagations" (40). Elisabeth's words, as she lies there on the threshold of dream, do not bode well for the cause of truth. Her intention is clear: the world of dream will be an escape from the present, a world in which she will have control, in which she can cheat and manipulate and tell the story she wants to hear and needs to hear. As readers though, we are sceptical of so much confidence, for we have seen this "evil spirit of sounds and visions" already at work and know the terror it induces in even the conscious Elisabeth, know its ability to resurrect the most disturbing scenes from her past. In chapter 2 the sound of a horse and cart echoing through the empty night streets had conjured up images of flight in a sleigh, of her desperate attempt to reach the American border and her arrest at Lavaltrie. In chapter 6 it had been the voice of her daughter Anne-Marie commenting on her mother's flushed face: "Ta petite voix d'enfant tire au jour une autre voix enfouie dans la nuit des temps. Une longue racine sonore s'arrache et vient avec la terre même de ma mémoire. L'accent rude et effrayé de Justine Latour qui témoigne devant le juge de paix" (34–5).

In chapter 8 it is not a sound but a trick of the light which allows characters from her past – Justine Latour, Sophie Langlade, and Aurélie Caron – to invade the present. The image of the root reappears, this time provoking a violent reaction from Elisabeth: "Ces images monstrueuses, aiguës comme des aiguilles. C'est dans ma tête qu'elles veulent s'installer. Me tourner de côté, ouvrir les yeux. Ne pas leur permettre de prendre racine, les arracher de mes yeux, ainsi qu'on extirpe une poussière" (41). But she is fighting a losing battle. The three phantom serving-girls go about their business, rearranging the furniture, transforming the little room in the house on the rue du Parloir into the familiar surroundings of her aunts' home on the rue Augusta in Sorel. Elisabeth is once again transported back into the nightmare of her first marriage, a nightmare punctuated by snatches of testimony from her trial. By the end of the chapter, the evil spirit clearly has the upper hand and, as the trial becomes a circus, Elisabeth's struggle for control has become a struggle for survival. Tossing and turning in Léontine's narrow bed, Madame Rolland tries desperately to get her younger self out of the ring, where she is forced to stand with her hands tied behind her back, her breasts uncovered, as an unseen knife-thrower takes aim at her heart: "Mme Rolland se débat sur le lit de Léontine Mélançon. Elle tente de sortir de ce cauchemar. Voit venir l'éclair métallique du

couteau s'abattant en plein coeur de la femme condamnée. Parvient
à fermer les yeux. Dans le noir cherche éperdument l'issue cachée
pour sortir de ce cirque" (49). In another remarkable confluence of
frame and picture, Elisabeth finds a staircase leading from past to
present and climbs, Alice-like, back up to consciousness: "Réussit à
remonter un escalier dans l'obscurité. Croit enfin se réveiller. Entrevoit
le papier à fleurs de la chambre de Léontine et porte la main à son
sein. Éprouve une vive douleur." The pain of the past is resurrected;
it penetrates even the safe, sterile confines of Léontine's room.

The next section (chapter 9) is the first to open directly into the
world of dream. The passage is no longer subterranean (the image
of the root), nor is it effected within the confined spaces of domestic
interiors (via doors and staircases); instead we find ourselves outdoors,
our exact location in time and space as yet unfixed, as we hover
over the deserted city of Sorel, bathed in a gentle light which induces
in Elisabeth a voluptuous feeling of well-being. The impression is
one of freedom from constraint, of detachment and control, of
distance achieved this time through movement in space rather than
through the grammatical displacements of the novel's opening pages.
But the calm is not to last; the quality of the light changes suddenly,
as the town is plunged into darkness, leaving only a single house
at the corner of Philippe and Augusta picked out against the night.
This light is brutal, it floods the façade of the house, illuminating
the smallest detail. Elisabeth's only recourse is in flight, away from
the shuttered house on the rue Augusta, from the gothic madness
that lies within, back to the rue Georges, to the house where she
was born, and beyond to her mother's womb. For the space of a
chapter she had found refuge in her early childhood. But, at the
age of seven, she is back again, standing with her mother on the
steps of her aunts' house as a deathly hush settles on the lit scene:
"Une seule maison demeure tout illuminée. Pareille à un tréteau. La
moindre poussière vole avec la précision d'une phalène, autour d'une
lampe. L'air, lui, ressemble à la lumière, clair, et sonore. On entendrait
respirer une souris" (54).

At the beginning of chapter 10, the stage is once again plunged
into darkness as the spot is turned off: "Le soleil s'est éteint au-dessus
de la maison. Comme une lampe qu'on souffle. Il fait brusquement
très noir" (56). The three aunts scurry about outside the house
gathering up the pots of geraniums before disappearing from view
inside the house. A door slams, echoing loud and long as if in an
empty, unfurnished and uncurtained house. We hear a voice off,
identified by Elisabeth as that of her Aunt Luce-Gertrude, uttering
commonplaces about flowers and frost. Again trying to flee, Elisabeth

refuses to cross the threshold, hiding this time behind her new identity in another world: "Non, non! Je ne veux pas. Je ne franchirai jamais plus le seuil de la maison. Vous vous trompez, je ne suis pas celle que vous croyez. J'ai un alibi irréfutable, un sauf-conduit bien en règle. Laissez-moi m'échapper, je suis Mme Rolland, épouse de Jérôme Rolland, notaire exerçant dans la ville de Québec" (56–7). But this time her protestations of respectability and responsibility are not enough to take her out of the dream and back to Léontine's room in the house on the rue du Parloir where her second husband is dying. Instead she is drawn irresistibly into the past, into the house on the rue Augusta where the story of her first marriage, to Antoine Tassy, has its beginnings.

THE TOPOGRAPHY OF TIME

First is the courtship, short and bittersweet. The sixteen-year-old Elisabeth realizes she does not love Tassy, but she will marry him anyway, out of ignorance; out of desire and curiosity; out of the jealousy and sheer lust her drunken, sentimental, whoring husband-to-be provokes in her; out of the need to kick over the traces, to escape from the Victorian straitjacket of life with her mother and maiden aunts. But once the wedding has taken place and the bride and groom are ready to leave on their honeymoon, the narrative consciousness is once again split as Elisabeth comments graphically on the inadequacy of the frame to contain what is about to be portrayed: "Que Mme Rolland ne se rassure pas si vite. Ne se réveille pas en toute hâte, dans la petite chambre de Léontine Mélançon. Pour classer ses souvenirs de mariage et les accrocher au mur, les contempler à loisir. Rien n'est moins inoffensif que l'histoire du premier mariage d'Elisabeth d'Aulnières" (70). Despite this evident disdain for her own psychological manipulations, her defences are still kept high and all contact is eluded, as once again the visual or spatial distance of these sequences finds a grammatical correlative: "Ce n'est pas que la lumière soit particulièrement insistante. Mais c'est cette terrifiante immobilité. Cette distance même qui devrait me rassurer est pire que tout. Penser à soi à la troisième personne. Feindre le détachement. Ne pas s'identifier à la jeune mariée, toute habillée de velours bleu" (70–1). Transformed under Elisabeth's gaze into painted wooden figures with mechanical gestures, bride and groom embark on their long journey to Kamouraska. "Quant à moi," says Elisabeth, "je suis Mme Rolland, et je referai mon premier voyage de noces, comme on raconte une histoire, sans trop y croire, avec un sourire amusé" (71).

The arrival at Kamouraska, recounted in chapter 14, is the occasion for a curious prolepsis; the repetition of the word "manoir" gives rise to a telescoping of two other "récits de voyage" which have Kamouraska as their destination:

Le manoir, quelqu'un demande où se trouve le manoir. Une voix d'homme, avec une pointe d'accent américain. C'est l'hiver. Il gèle à pierre fendre. On lui indique d'un geste lent de paysan le bout du village, un cap solitaire qui s'avance dans le fleuve.

À l'auberge Dionne, une fille aux cheveux crépus (qui n'est pas du village) demande le manoir. Elle pose sa main sur la vitre gelée et gratte avec ses ongles, pour faire fondre le givre. Longtemps elle regarde dans la nuit, en direction du manoir. (75)

The archaeological nature of the narrative is seen here at its clearest. The site-specific layering of events in time is underscored by the paradigmatic gesture of the girl as she scrapes away the frost on the windowpane in order to look towards Kamouraska; as we saw earlier, Elisabeth will do the same thing, more than a hundred pages later, in order to watch George Nelson and Aurélie Caron talking in the snow before the latter's journey to Kamouraska, a journey which will take Aurélie, "comme une mariée qui part en voyage de noces" (186), to the auberge Dionne where she will scrape away the frost on the windowpane …

Of course time in the novel is not really circular. The events in question can be laid out in chronological sequence on a line: first, Elisabeth's own arrival at Kamouraska with Antoine Tassy (A); next, Elisabeth watching from the window of the house on the rue Augusta, as George Nelson and Aurélie Caron discuss the latter's departure for Kamouraska (B); then, Aurélie Caron watching from the window of the inn just before *her* arrival at Kamouraska (C); and finally, the arrival of George Nelson at Kamouraska (D). The impression of circularity or *déjà vu* is created by a combination of the internal mirroring of motifs ("the woman at the window," "the honeymoon," and "all roads lead to Kamouraska") and the transformation of the story sequence ABCD into the narrative sequence ADCB.[9] Within the grand analepsis of the dream are framed a number of prolepses, of which C and D are particularly striking examples and to which we should add another event (E) – the burning of the manor – located somewhere in the limbo between D and the narrative present of the rue du Parloir: "Le manoir. Vous ne risquez pas grand-chose d'y retourner, madame Rolland. Vous savez bien qu'il n'y a plus rien. Tout a brûlé en 18 … Rasé, nu comme la main. Qui peut se vanter de pouvoir ainsi effacer sa vie passée, d'un seul coup? Quelques flammes, beaucoup de fumée, puis plus rien. La mémoire se cultive comme une terre. Il faut y mettre le feu parfois. Brûler les mauvaises herbes jusqu'à la racine. Y planter un champ de roses imaginaires, à la place" (75). Here again, time and memory are presented both topographically and archaeologically: as a series of lines converging in space (the manor as site) and as a vertical pattern of layers in the ground (the root as conduit between two worlds[10] – the subterranean world of the past as revealed in dream and the surface world of the present, of the controlling narrative consciousness, which can burn the weeds and in their stead plant roses). Time in *Kamouraska,* whether past, present, or future, is always local: the images that haunt Elisabeth can all be plotted along the axes of time and space.

Another proleptic image which haunts these pages is that of Antoine Tassy, risen from the dead, his head swathed in bandages. From his resting place under the family pew, he makes his way underground as far as the ruins of the manor where, ensconced in his armchair, he summons the servants: "Le voici qui commande en rêve ... Supplie qu'on lui envoie sa femme, immédiatement. Croit qu'il vient de hurler un ordre sans réplique. Alors qu'il chuchote, derrière sa main gantée de noir. Proclame que tout est prêt pour la reconstitution" (81). Elisabeth is ushered in by Aurélie Caron but is herself disturbed by the anachronism: "Pourquoi garde-t-il sa tête enveloppée de linge? Cela ne fait que quelques mois que nous sommes mariés? Personne encore, en mon nom, n'a tenté d'assassiner mon mari?" (82). She is forced to watch, terrified, as Antoine unwinds the bandage. But the horror she expects – bullet holes, brains flowing out of his ears – does not materialize. Instead Antoine is restored to his unmarked self as the story is picked up a few months after the wedding. It is as though the act of unwinding the bandage had been a filmic metaphor for turning back the hands of the clock or rewinding the reel, a metaphor preparing us for the reenactment that is to follow.

As for Aurélie, her function in this reconstruction of the events would seem to be to keep reinserting Elisabeth into the action, using her own knowledge of the script (both past and future – like Madame Rolland, she is "omniscient") to ensure that her mistress does not attempt to circumvent the truth or avoid the painful parts (96, 103).[11] At times Elisabeth seems capable of stopping the kaleidoscope herself and organizing the chaotic images in time: "Je frappe dans mes mains. (Je ne sais quelle réserve de force, quel sursaut d'énergie.) Chasser les fantômes. Dissiper l'effroi. Organiser le songe.

Conserver un certain équilibre. Le passé raisonnable, revécu à fleur de peau. Respecter l'ordre chronologique. Ne pas tenter de parcourir toute sa vie d'un coup" (97). More often than not Elisabeth needs to be prompted, and the most frequently heard voices, including that of Aurélie, come from the trial, which, in the second half of the novel, combines with the theatre motif to become the main narrative device within the dream.

THE TRIAL

"Rétablissons les faits et les jours aussi exactement que possible," announces a voice at the beginning of chapter 23. Elisabeth's failure to recognize the voice is symptomatic of her ambivalent attitude toward this part of her story, for the testimony recalled from the trial coincides with the entry of George Nelson into her life: Elisabeth's feelings are polarized between desire (desire to relive the episodes of her love affair) and guilt (the need to repress the truth about her role in the murder of Antoine). Although the trial becomes the dominant narrative structure, through organizing and focusing the dream and acting as a metaphor for the act of reading, it will still contain elements of interference which succeed in blurring the truth. One such element had been identified relatively early in the book when Aunt Adélaïde's character testimony had been denounced, presumably by Elisabeth, as a "petit morceau de roman" (46). In chapters 24 and 25, the interference is described not in terms of fiction, but in terms of theatre: "Tout recommence. Je ne puis fuir. Il faut continuer, reprendre le fil. Jouer la deuxième scène du médecin. Impossible de me dérober, de prétexter la fatigue. Ils sont déjà là, les témoins. Les voici qui entrent un à un, solennels et guindés. Ils reprennent la pose" (110). But it is a theatricality which, despite an unidentified dissenting voice, is apparently sanctioned by the court: "Quelqu'un dit que c'est absurde et que ces sortes de reconstitutions n'ont jamais rien apporté pour l'avancement d'une affaire." Absurd or not, the device of the theatre, previously denounced by Antoine's mother as a form of excess and emotional disorder (78), has a liberating or galvanizing effect on Elisabeth:

"Tout ça c'est du théâtre," déclare la voix méprisante de ma belle-mère.
   Comme si je n'attendais plus que ce signal, j'entre en scène. Je dis "je" et je suis une autre. Foulée aux pieds la défroque de Mme Rolland. Aux orties le corset de Mme Rolland. Au musée son masque de plâtre. Je ris et je pleure, sans vergogne. J'ai des bas roses à jours, une large ceinture sous les seins. Je me déchaîne. J'habite la fièvre et la démence, comme mon pays natal. J'aime un autre homme que mon mari. (115)

This wholehearted acceptance of the trial (and hence of the story of her adulterous love affair) as theatre marks a turning point in Elisabeth's attitude to the past: she is willing now to turn her back on Madame Rolland and the defences she has created in her new life, to throw off the Victorian straitjacket ("le corset de Mme Rolland") and reaffirm the passion and the sheer excess of her relationship with George Nelson. The account of the various stages of this love affair will be characterized by an abandon reflected in the relative absence of censorship from the controlling narrative consciousness; for an unusually long stretch of text, interference between frame and story is reduced to a minimum.

The device of the trial is especially useful when Elisabeth has to recount those parts of the story which lie outside her personal experience, in particular the separate journeys of Aurélie Caron and George Nelson to Kamouraska. On watch at her frosted window, Elisabeth claims for herself clairvoyant powers, but acknowledges the help of the witnesses, who act as prompters: "Quoi qu'on dise et quoi qu'on fasse, je demeure le témoin principal de cette histoire de neige et de fureur. Les témoins secondaires viendront, en bon ordre, me rafraîchir la mémoire" (184). Her reconstruction will have all the immediacy of an eyewitness account, so vivid is her vision: "Les lieux eux-mêmes (de Sorel à Kamouraska et de Kamouraska à Sorel) me seront largement ouverts, afin que j'entre et sorte, au gré des événements" (184). Similarly, after the failure of Aurélie's attempt to poison Tassy, after Elisabeth has said farewell to Nelson through the same screen of glass and ice (189), Elisabeth will follow her lover's progress, from Sorel to Kamouraska, like an Indian scout with her ear to the ground (192). Reciting the names of the villages along the river as one recites a rosary, she can keep pace with George, aided in her pursuit by the words of witnesses like Michel-Eustache Letellier: "Je tente de prendre pied dans l'auberge de Saint-Vallier. D'apercevoir le jeune étranger. Déjà la voix de l'hôtelier enchaîne si rapidement que je suis précipitée dans le temps. À la vitesse même de la parole. Sans pouvoir m'accrocher à aucune image. Ni reconnaître aucun visage" (199). Sound travels faster than light here, and the spoken word becomes more and more important as we approach the scene of the crime.

As the story builds to a climax, Elisabeth's fear and guilt once more gain the upper hand. If she could, Elisabeth would conjure up the prattling voices of her aunts and mother to drown out the chorus of innkeepers and hold them at bay. She has taken to her bed with a fever after the birth of her third child, Nelson's child, but the witnesses are relentless; they transform her bedroom in the house on the rue Augusta into a courtroom and appear at the foot of her bed to take the stand.[12] Elisabeth's only defence is to counter language with language. Clinging to the sound of the names of the villages, she uses the material aspect of language, not to transport herself through time and space as the words of the witnesses had done, but to slow down the story, to put off the fateful moment of George Nelson's arrival at Kamouraska: "Rivière-Ouelle. Me raccrocher à ce nom de village, comme à une bouée. (Le dernier village avant Kamouraska.) Tenter de faire durer le temps (cinq ou six milles avant Kamouraska). Étirer le plus possible les premières syllabes fermées de ri-vi-, les laisser s'ouvrir en è-re. Essayer en vain de retenir Ouelle, ce nom liquide qui s'enroule et fuit, se perd dans la mousse, pareil à une source. Bientôt les sonorités rocailleuses et vertes de Kamouraska vont s'entrechoquer, les unes contre les autres. Ce vieux nom algonquin; il y a jonc au bord de l'eau. Kamouraska!" (206). Playing with the syllables (much as she had done with the grammatical categories of person and tense), she contrives to shut out the testimony from the trial: "Couvrir toutes les voix humaines qui pourraient monter et m'attaquer en foule. Dresser un fracas de syllabes rudes et sonores. M'en faire un bouclier de pierre" (206).

But the witnesses insist, filling the entire house on the rue Augusta, threatening to penetrate the barrier between the two worlds and find a way through to the house on the rue du Parloir, where they could entertain the dying Jérôme Rolland with stories about his wife's violent and adulterous past. Finally, in her half-way house in Sorel, Elisabeth can resist no longer. Abandoning both the rue du Parloir and the rue Augusta, she lets herself be dragged off to Kamouraska, to the inns and roads where the various witnesses had encountered George Nelson on his desperate mission. There she finds a strange gathering: "Ils sont tous là, dans l'auberge de James Wood. Échangeant leurs propos, à voix basse. Évitant de se voir les uns les autres. Regardant droit devant eux, sur le mur de bois nu, au-dessus de la planche, avec les bouteilles et les verres alignés. Comme s'ils voyaient (à mesure qu'ils parlent) passer sur ce mur une série de portraits esquissés à la hâte, effacés, puis redessinés à grands traits. Ils n'en finissent pas de comparer un homme, un cheval et un traîneau, sans cesse renaissants et reconnaissables, d'une fois à l'autre, sur le mur. Comme s'il s'agissait bel et bien d'un seul et même traîneau, d'un seul et même cheval, d'un seul et même homme, venu de Sorel pour ..." (228–9). Piecing together the jigsaw of images and events, arriving slowly but surely at an interpretation of what they have separately seen, the witnesses participate in a collective act which is part story-telling and part reading. As narrators, they are more like Alain Dubois than Elisabeth; they try to reconstruct, from their discrete and partial points of view, if not the logic of life, at least the logic of story.

SURFACING

There is, however, a gap in the testimony of the witnesses, a gap which Elisabeth is in no hurry to fill: "Il y a pourtant un trou dans l'emploi du temps de celui que je cherche. Moi-même complice de ce vide. Évitant avec soin une certaine heure, entre toutes capitale. Tous ces tours et détours pour éviter Kamouraska, l'anse de Kamouraska, vers neuf heures du soir, le 31 janvier 1839 ..." (224). This gap is partially filled by the report of the medical examiner, but his testimony is interrupted by the voice of Elisabeth's daughter Anne-Marie, pulling Elisabeth back to the rue du Parloir. Then the claims of the present are countered by another voice from the past, drawing her back into the dream: "La plus poignante et la plus prenante d'entre toutes les voix (son léger accent américain), tente pourtant de me retenir encore dans un pays de fièvre. Tu me supplies (tandis que ta voix s'altère, se gâte tout à fait, tombe en poussière, dans mon oreille) de bien vouloir écouter ton histoire jusqu'au bout" (233). Begging George to spare her the rest of his story, she paves the way for denial and betrayal, warning him that he can no longer count on her unfailing support.

The next voice she hears from the present is Léontine Mélançon's: "Me supplie de me lever de ce lit où je me prélasse dans un roman peu édifiant" (238). Florida proposes a cup of strong, black coffee, but Elisabeth is determined not to wake up at the very moment when she is expecting her lover's return. There will be no passionate reunion though, no happy ending, just a sense of mutual betrayal as George Nelson flees across the border and Elisabeth is arrested and tried. There is nothing left but to allow herself to be brought back to the surface, to be resuscitated and made presentable, ready to play another deathbed scene, head bowed, wiping a tear from her cheek, holding her husband's hand as Jérôme tells her he has received the last rites. Is this, after all, her true life? Or is this theatre? And what of the other Elisabeth, the one she has left behind? She, too, has surfaced, albeit in the third person:

Dans un champ aride, sous les pierres, on a déterré une femme noire, vivante, datant d'une époque reculée et sauvage. Étrangement conservée. On l'a lâchée dans la petite ville. Puis on s'est barricadé, chacun chez soi. Tant la peur qu'on a de cette femme est grande et profonde. Chacun se dit que la faim de vivre de cette femme, enterrée vive, il y a si longtemps,

doit être si féroce et entière, accumulée sous la terre, depuis des siècles!
On n'en a sans doute jamais connu de semblable. Lorsque la femme se
présente dans la ville, courant et implorant, le tocsin se met à sonner. Elle
ne trouve que des portes fermées et le désert de terre battue dont sont
faites les rues. Il ne lui reste sans doute plus qu'à mourir de faim et de
solitude. (250)

From the soil of memory uprooted, deprived of her other "real life,"
this creature of excess and abandon has no place in the orderly
world in which Jérôme Rolland is about to leave her to her own
devices. We remember her confession early in the novel: "Mon petit
Jérôme je puis bien te l'avouer maintenant, sans toi je serais morte
de terreur. Dévorée, déchiquetée par les cauchemars" (30). Stripped
of her roles and masks, she is now set free to wander the face of
the earth without hope and without purpose. "If I leave here," says
another pseudo-Victorian heroine, "I leave my shame. Then I am
lost."[13]

O F ALL Anne Hébert's works, *Kamouraska* has undoubtedly known
the greatest critical and popular success and now enjoys an
undisputed position in the canon of Quebec literature. While a good
number of critics seem to see no need to go beyond the novel's
themes or plot to explain its fascination, there are others who
unequivocally situate its chief interest in its narrative structure and/or
its style. Thus, for Grazia Merler, "the reader comes to be more
interested in the process of creation than in the unfolding of the
drama" (Merler 1971, 52), while for Robert Harvey "the particular
interest of *Kamouraska* lies in the *labour of writing* the past that
Elisabeth Rolland takes on in the course of her 'dream.' The narrative
structure of the whole novel bears witness to this predominance of
narration over story" (Harvey 1982, 8).[14] It is tempting to push this
critical dualism to a somewhat cynical conclusion and postulate that
the extraordinary success of *Kamouraska* stems, at least in part, from
its combination of familiar nineteenth-century subject matter (which
appeals to the general reader) with a twentieth-century form (which
makes it somehow critically "respectable"). I should like, in these
concluding remarks, to explore the implications of such a hypothesis.

I shall start from the assumption that *Kamouraska* is, in some
sense of the word, a text of *excess,* a point that is made by Janet
Paterson, for whom the confluence of hallucinations, dreams, reality,
and madness creates a text "qui déborde et qui fait jouir le lecteur
par l'excès même de ce débordement" (Paterson 1980, 71). However,

rather than simply accepting Paterson's claim that such excess is indicative of a radical questioning of traditional norms of literary representation, let us take up this notion of "overflowing" (*débordement*) and try to determine what exactly is at stake here.

"Un sein déborde du corset." The breast popping unexpectedly and disconcertingly out of the corset is an image I have already discussed briefly and which functions on several different levels. I have suggested that it figures the inability of the frame to contain the picture (or the story) and of language (or style) to contain reality. It is an image of transgression in Victorian society – "Aux orties le corset de Mme Rolland" – and of the resurfacing of repressed material from the unconscious. It has a certain erotic charge, associated with the sudden and incongruous appearance of what should be kept hidden, and can act as a voyeuristic equivalent of the eavesdropping motif, that tried and trusted nineteenth-century device for authenticating fiction, for creating an *effet de réel* – the illusion of a truth revealed by accident, outside of any framed or framing intention. In a word, the image acts as a complex representation in the text of Elisabeth's own narrative, as it struggles first of all to contain and control the protagonist's unruly emotions, then casts off the fetters of censorship in an affirmation of Elisabeth's sexuality, only to take refuge once again in authoritarian forms. All the while we are invited to stand in the shadows and enjoy the spectacle of Elisabeth's oneiric striptease, which is framed in the artfully lit window of the text. (It is in chapter 39 that George Nelson orders Elisabeth to strip in front of the well-lit window, so that anyone passing by outside in the night can see her naked.)

But does this make *Kamouraska* a text of bliss (*jouissance*)? Barthes's original distinction can help us here: "Text of pleasure: the text that contents, fills, grants euphoria; the text that comes from culture and does not break with it, is linked to a *comfortable* practice of reading. Text of bliss: the text that imposes a state of loss, the text that discomforts (perhaps to the point of a certain boredom), unsettles the reader's historical, cultural, psychological assumptions, the consistency of his tastes, values, memories, brings to a crisis his relation with language" (Barthes 1975, 14). I would suggest that, despite certain appearances to the contrary, *Kamouraska* is, in the terms of Barthes's definition, a text of pleasure rather than a text of bliss, a text which, far from disturbing the reader in any profound way, promises and delivers a "good read," a text which, to go back to an earlier distinction made by Barthes, is *readerly* rather than *writerly* (Barthes 1974, 4).[15]

Perhaps the best way of illustrating my point is to take up again the figure of breast and corset in the context of a question asked by Barthes in *The Pleasure of the Text:* "Is not the most erotic portion of a body *where the garment gapes?*" (Barthes 1975, 9). It is this kind of erotic intermittence, this "staging of an appearance-as-disappearance" (10), that Barthes contrasts with the pleasure associated with literal or figurative striptease: "The pleasure of the text is not the pleasure of the corporeal striptease or of narrative suspense. In these cases, there is no tear, no edges: a gradual unveiling: the entire excitation takes refuge in the *hope* of seeing the sexual organ (schoolboy's dream) or on knowing the end of the story (novelistic satisfaction)" (10). Now, while the image of the spontaneously over-flowing breast has in itself little in common with the carefully paced striptease of Barthes's text of pleasure, it does signal Elisabeth's inability to sustain the role (or the fiction) of Madame Rolland. It also heralds the spiritual striptease ("Foulée aux pieds la défroque de Mme Rolland") which will culminate, firstly, in the narration of the events of 31 January 1839 and, secondly, in the image of the disinterred woman let loose upon the town. In this respect, it is important to recognize the role played in Elisabeth's narrative by resistance (figured by the corset); far from being an obstacle to the reader's pleasure, Elisabeth's resistance is an integral part of the intellectual seduction of the reader for whom the whole picture is gradually reconstituted panel by panel. (This is particularly true of the reconstitution of George Nelson's journey to Kamouraska, during which Elisabeth has recourse, as we have seen, to a number of different devices in her attempt to put the brakes on a narrative which is going too fast for her taste and which threatens to escape her control. Narrative striptease is, above all, a matter of tempo, and the tempo is being controlled here by Elisabeth's resistance.) The glimpse of breast is the synecdochic promise of the whole, the fragment which speaks of *desire* rather than of *bliss* and of the desire to see and to know that which has been hidden, that which has been kept from us. This will keep us reading until we have found out, not so much what happened that 31 January 1839, but what will become of Elisabeth once she has relived the events in her own mind.[16]

The dialectic of abandon and constraint, which is figured by the image of the breast and the corset, gives rise in the text to a rhetoric of condensation and displacement. I have tried to show this in my discussion of the various phenomena of fusion and superposition, of diversion and substitution, phenomena which constitute what I have called the topography of time – the shifting of scenes on the stage of the unconscious to mirror the shifting of responsibility in

Elisabeth's mind and her various attempts to impose or elude censorship. A major element of this rhetoric is the process of fragmentation, which works on several different levels. Having already discussed the phenomenon of temporal dislocation which is so central to the novel, I shall confine my remarks here to questions of narrative voice.

Much of the literature on *Kamouraska* is either unhelpful or confusing when it comes to understanding the novel's narrative structure. Frequently failing to make basic distinctions between voice and focalization, or between narrative levels and temporal levels, critics have tended to compensate by multiplying the formal categories used to characterize the novel's narrative system, thereby distorting the subtle play of voices and missing the point of the fragmentation entirely. In such circumstances it becomes appropriate to invoke Ockham's razor – *entia non sunt multiplicanda praeter necessitatem* – and point out with Josette Féral that there is only one narrator in *Kamouraska,* and that is Elisabeth – one character but several personae.[17] Behind the shifting first, second and third person pronouns, there lies a single narrative consciousness; it is fragmented and dispersed through the text but traceable to a single source. In other words, we are dealing with a form of displacement or dislocation, a kind of narrative ventriloquism, which allows Elisabeth to project her desires and her anxieties into the simulated voices of others: "Vous entendez des voix, madame Rolland. Vous jouez à entendre des voix" (76).

The implications of such a reading are of considerable importance when we come to consider Janet Paterson's claim that *Kamouraska,* like Anne Hébert's other novels, participates in a postmodern aesthetic insofar as its referentiality is (partially) subverted by techniques of internal mirroring (Paterson 1985, 179). I have considerable difficulty with this notion and would suggest that self-reference in literature becomes *necessarily* subversive only when it appears in paradoxical or aporistic form, to borrow the terms suggested by Dällenbach to describe a particular kind of *mise en abyme* (Dällenbach 1977, 38, 51). The specularity that we find in *Kamouraska* is not, I would contend, of this kind. It involves no illicit crossing of narrative boundaries (as does that of *Prochain épisode* for example), nor does it raise the spectre of a narrator who tells more than he is supposed to know (Alain Dubois in *Poussière sur la ville*). The various forms and figures of self-reference which appear in Hébert's novel – metaphors of reading, intertextual fragments, the embroidery motif, the mirroring of motifs between temporal levels, the self-conscious theatricality of the *mise-en-scène* – can all be motivated by their topo-

graphical disposition within a single, "omniscient" narrative consciousness: "Je suis Mme Rolland et je sais tout" (126). In fact, Kamouraska
can be described in terms of what we might call classical or high
modernism, as it is defined by David Lodge:

First, it is experimental or innovatory in form, exhibiting marked deviations
from existing modes of discourse, literary and non-literary. Next, it is much
concerned with consciousness, and also with the subconscious or unconscious workings of the human mind. Hence the structure of external "objective" events essential to narrative art in traditional poetics is diminished in
scope and scale, or presented selectively and obliquely, in order to make
room for introspection, analysis, reflection and reverie. Frequently, therefore,
a modern novel has no real "beginning," since it plunges us into a flowing
stream of experience with which we gradually familiarize ourselves by a
process of inference and association; its ending is totally "open" or ambiguous, leaving the reader in doubt as to the characters' final destiny. By
way of compensation for the weakening of narrative structure and unity,
other modes of aesthetic ordering become more prominent – such as
allusion to or imitation of literary models, or mythical archetypes; or rep-
etition-with-variation of motifs, images, symbols, a technique often called
"rhythm," "leitmotif," or "spatial form." Lastly, modern fiction eschews the
straight chronological ordering of its material, and the use of a reliable,
omniscient and intrusive narrator. It employs, instead, either a single, limited
point of view, or multiple viewpoints, all more or less limited and fallible;
and it tends toward a complex or fluid handling of time, involving much
cross-reference back and forward across the temporal span of the action.
(Lodge 1976, 481)

Despite its insistence on formal innovation, the modernist text
does not represent the kind of definitive break with a totalizing
vision that Paterson ascribes to postmodern texts,[18] for while modernism may, in relation to its predecessors, propose a new (and
more fragmented) way of apprehending the world, it does so by
establishing its own codes and its own models of coherence and
intelligibility. Similarly, *Kamouraska* is a readable (coherent and intelligible) text in a way that *Prochain épisode* is not: the various forms
of fragmentation and dislocation – the projections of voice, the play
of tense and time, the stylization of reality[19] – can all be adequately
integrated into a total vision (can all be *recuperated*), for the very
simple reason that they can all be motivated as expressions of
Elisabeth's frame of mind.[20] (If we accept Brian McHale's view that
the change of dominant from modernist to postmodernist writing
involves a shift from epistemological concerns to ontological ones,

we can assert with a fair amount of confidence that *Poussière sur la ville* belongs to the former category and *Prochain épisode* to the latter. *Kamouraska,* on the other hand, is ultimately recuperable from *both* points of view, a fact which might lead us to believe that Hébert's novel is neither modernist nor postmodernist in any authentic sense but merely a simulacrum which partakes of some of the surface features of both.) Elisabeth's own resistance as a narrator is thus assimilated by the reader and interpreted as one of the codes according to which the novel is to be read; her frequent unwillingness to collaborate in the reconstitution of her past does nothing to detract from the readability of her story, but simply shifts the focus from the events themselves to the telling of them, to the theatre of Elisabeth's narrative consciousness. Far from being a postmodern novel, *Kamouraska* is supremely intelligible and perfectly coherent: modernist in its composition and Victorian gothic in its subject matter and setting, it combines its constituent codes in a seamless work of art. (John Fowles's enormously successful *The French Lieutenant's Woman,* which is roughly contemporaneous with *Kamouraska,* achieves similar effects. Clearly the formula is a winning one.) The only doubt it leaves in the reader's mind concerns the place of seamless works of art in the Quebec of 1970.

Afterword

Il n'y aura pas de récit
tout juste une voix plurielle
une voix carrefour
la parole immigrante.
  Régine Robin, *La Québécoite*

I indicated in my foreword to this book that it was not my intention
to define and defend any kind of unified position on narrative or
indeed on the Quebec novel. In retrospect, however, it does seem
desirable to make explicit certain similarities that exist between the
kinds of ontological and narrative uncertainty I have tried to explore
under the general heading of "a certain difficulty of being" and
André Belleau's sociocritical notion of the conflict of codes.

In a 1983 article, "Code social et code littéraire dans le roman
québécois," Belleau argues that a doubly marginalized literature like
that of Quebec (marginalized in relation to France as well as to
English-speaking North America) constitutes by definition a conflictual
space where rival demands and influences meet. The more closely
one studies the modern (post-1945) Quebec novel, says Belleau, the
more apparent it becomes that its very status as literature is defined
in large part by the conflict between social and literary codes of
which it is the scene: "The Quebec literary institution, understood
here in both its material and discursive aspects, finds itself embarrassed, hesitant, uncertain, especially when it comes to the selection
of literary codes. The constraints of the literary models themselves
are frequently ignored or circumvented or generally subsumed by
the social discourse of Quebec or, if you prefer, by its socio-cultural
codes" (Belleau 1983, 19).

I have argued in chapter 1 that the notion of a conflict of codes

can be extended back beyond the modern period to embrace the
literary institution of nineteenth-century Quebec. In the realm of the
novel, the literary codes, as such, of the nineteenth century were
imported: though predominantly French, they reflected the popularity
of certain English authors, most notably Sir Walter Scott. The socio-
cultural codes of the period, however, were resolutely indigenous,
and the pressure to conform to those norms, which was brought to
bear on would-be novelists, especially after 1860, by officially sanctioned public opinion (as opposed to popular taste and reading
habits), was considerable. In this respect a letter addressed in 1891
to Pierre Bédard, the editor of *Le Recueil littéraire,* would appear
symptomatic of the climate of self-censorship induced among French-
Canadian authors by the moral and political authority of the Church.
Le Recueil littéraire had announced the publication in its pages of
a new novel by J. de Lorde, but, as he explains in his letter, the
author has had second thoughts:

You had invited me to publish my Canadian novel, *Un Amour,* and I had
been pleased to acquiesce.
    ... But when I saw the first printed sheets of *Un Amour,* I had scruples,
fearing that certain passages in the novel were too light and, consequently,
somewhat unorthodox for the Canadian public.
    To see if my fears were justified, I submitted my work to a friend ...
And what was the verdict of this model of integrity? "It is a very interesting
novel, but one which, from a moral point of view, will do more harm
than good ..."
    I accepted this judgment and the work was burned. Which is why ...
Un Amour will appear neither in *Le Recueil littéraire* nor anywhere else.
(*Le Recueil littéraire,* t. II, 1891, 180; quoted in Dostaler 1977, 144)

Thus, while the novel as a genre was never legally banned, as it
was for a time in eighteenth-century France (G. May 1963, 78), it
was certainly stifled in its development by the moral climate of the
day.
    In the case of *Menaud, maître-draveur,* the conflict of codes is
more complicated, since both the literary and the social codes contain
a curious mix of indigenous and imported elements, especially when
we consider the ambiguous status of the novel's single most important
intertext, *Maria Chapdelaine.* I have argued in chapter 2 that
Menaud's madness and final defeat figure the novel's failure to
provide adequate compensation for the loss of history and that
Savard's text, published exactly one hundred years after French
Canada's first novel, marks a major, if involuntary, step towards an

autonomous literary institution in Quebec. Unable to sustain the literary form it has dreamed, the anachronistic vision cracks upon contact with contemporary reality, and the text it has generated is transformed into a monstrous monument to lost illusions.

In *Bonheur d'occasion,* on the other hand, we have a case of an author who selects a particular narrative code – third-person narration with shifting point of view, coupled with free indirect speech – and then finds herself incapable of living within the constraints which that code implies, not because her material is necessarily incompatible with the code but because she apparently does not trust her audience to get the "point" of the narrative without outside help. As a result of this lack of confidence in the communicative capacity of the code, Gabrielle Roy has recourse to a variety of strategies of intervention which, I have argued in chapter 3, represent the invasion of the literary form by a social consciousness which demands to be heard and, at the same time, reflect the outside observer's need to saturate the events she relates with what she considers to be the appropriate emotional colouring. In the terms of the "economic" analysis I have used to discuss the novel's thematic structure, one might surmise that, in the interests of communication within the symbolic community of feeling which she strives to create between author, characters, and reader, Roy is perfectly happy to renounce the sign value of a literary code which might be thought to conceal a certain fetishism of forms and the reification of social relations.

Belleau himself has made the case for seeing in *Poussière sur la ville* a clear example of the conflict of codes. According to the critic, Langevin's high-minded existentialism has a double function in the text; it generates an intellectual context for the treatment of the moral problems raised by Dubois's situation and also signals the novel's status as a "serious" work of literature as defined by the dominant French literary codes of the fifties. However, this tone of seriousness, which is intended to legitimate the text by indicating its literariness, is undermined by the novel's socio-cultural codes as manifested in Langevin's use of space: the mining town of Macklin reproduces the simplified topography of the western, with its single street, while the elevated existentialist discourse, with its echoes of Camus and Sartre, seems to call for a social stratification and an urban complexity which are entirely missing from the novel. Instead, the novel's spatial configurations reveal a more primitive worldview which undercuts the literary code and which Belleau assimilates to the dominant socio-cultural code of Quebec in the 1950s. In my own discussion of the novel in chapter 4, I have focused rather on the way in which transgressions of the chosen narrative code give rise to significant problems for the interpretation of Langevin's existentialist themes.

Prochain épisode, I would argue, is the only novel examined here that takes the conflict of codes and exploits it consciously and systematically as a structuring device, using intertextuality as a basis for parody. Weaving his text from an astonishing variety of competing literary and socio-cultural codes, both indigenous and imported, Aquin constantly pits discourse against discourse and rhetoric against rhetoric. European romanticism, Third World theories of decolonization, the *nouveau roman,* the James Bond novels, Sartrean existentialism, revolutionary separatism, the French-Canadian *mythos* of defeat – these are but some of the forms of discourse which vie with one another in an intertextual (and paradoxical) space which is not so much *constructed* by Aquin as *lived* by him. It is in this sense that one might speak of the conflict of codes, in its 1960s form, not simply as reflecting or representing Quebec's own difficulty of being, but as *being* that difficulty: the ontological problem becomes a problem of interdiscursivity.

Much of my discussion of *Kamouraska* in chapter 6 focused on the question of whether the novel should be considered modernist or postmodernist in inspiration. As I have argued, I believe this to be a bone of contention among the critics, with their strategic definitions, rather than a conflict of codes which is inscribed within the text itself. In fact I would suggest that, of the various novels studied here, Anne Hébert's is the least likely to produce interesting results when analysed from Belleau's point of view. This may seem paradoxical, given the apparent complexity of the novel's surface structure, but I think it can be explained by the fact that this narrative difficulty of being is generated according to a fairly simple set of transformational rules from the narrator's own relatively uncomplicated psychological difficulty of being. *Kamouraska* is a polished and sophisticated work of literature, but it would be a mistake to see in its elaborate techniques of fragmentation and dislocation evidence of a *lived* conflict of codes. In reality, the conflict is carefully contrived (and thematized in the novel) to reflect the psychological and sexual disorder underlying the smooth surface of Victorian society.

THIS BOOK is modest in scope. It deals with a handful of canonical texts, all written before 1970. Since that time much has happened in Quebec, including the election of a nationalist government and a referendum which denied that government the mandate it sought. The political upheavals of the seventies and eighties have wrought far-reaching changes in the fabric of Quebec society, transforming the socio-cultural codes we see at play in Langevin's or even Aquin's vision of Quebec and giving rise to new tendencies in the novel. In particular, the problems of national identity which dominated the literary production of the Quiet Revolution have given way, first, to feminist concerns and, more recently, to a recognition of the increasingly cosmopolitan nature of Quebec society which finds expression in what Sherry Simon has called "the language of difference" (Simon 1987). Although we have come a long way from the monolithic culture of the nineteenth century, the plurality of codes and discourses stemming from this shift of focus do not necessarily fall outside the framework of ontological and narrative uncertainty sketched in the pages of this book. However, the new literature is rich enough and different enough to warrant a separate study, and while the next episode, as Aquin knew only too well, is always problematic, it is where I should now like to turn, there where, in Régine Robin's words, there will be no story, just a plural voice.

Notes

FOREWORD

1 See, for example, Belleau 1983, 20–1.
2 For a pragmatics-oriented narratology, see in particular Chambers (1984) and Prince (1983). The literature on reader-response theory is well known and too vast to include here.
3 "Perhaps we would do best to speak of the *anticipation of retrospection* as our chief tool in making sense of narrative, the master trope of its strange logic" (Brooks 1984, 23).
4 One might cite, very selectively, the following contributions to narratological theories of end-determination: Sartre (1964), Kermode (1966), Grivel (1973), and, in a more critical perspective closer to my own approach, the recent works of Miller (1981) and Brooks (1984).
5 See, for example, the three conferences "Pour une thématique I, II, III" organized by the École des hautes études en sciences sociales and the Centre national de la recherche scientifique (CNRS) and held at the Canadian Cultural Centre in Paris in 1984, 1986, and 1988. Selected papers from the first two conferences have been published by Claude Bremond and Thomas Pavel in *Poétique* 64 (1985) and *Communications* 47 (1988), while Cesare Segre has collected papers from the third conference in *Strumenti Critici* 4.2 (1989). Other recent contributions of note to the theory of thematics are to be found in Zholkovsky (1984) and Shcheglov and Zholkovsky (1987).
6 For Walter Benjamin, the deathbed is a privileged site of narration, the storyteller's pulpit so to speak: "Death is the sanction of everything

the storyteller can tell. He has borrowed his authority from death"
(Benjamin 1969, 94). And of the many deathbed scenes in the nineteenth-century novel, Peter Brooks aptly comments that they "offer
the promise of a significant retrospect, a summing-up, the coming to
completion of a fully predicated, and readable, sentence" (Brooks
1984, 96).

7 One of which is the perhaps not unnatural, deep-seated suspicion of
expatriate Brits that one occasionally encounters in Canadian academic circles. I recall one SSHRCC assessor's report which concluded
its scathing evaluation of my competence and that of my collaborator to conduct our proposed research by pointing out that while it
was admirable for us to want to learn more about our adopted country and to expand our literary horizons, it should not be done at
SSHRCC's expense. (My collaborator had, long ago in a previous life,
been born and raised in the United States.) If I have been the object
of similar resentment in Quebec, I have never been made aware of it.

8 See Sutherland 1971, 1977. The best discussions of the Canadian
comparatist's dilemma are to be found in Blodgett 1982, 13–38, and
Stratford 1986, 1–11.

CHAPTER ONE

1 See, for example, Marion 1944, Hayne 1971, Dostaler 1977. It is tempting
to compare the sorry state of the novel in nineteenth-century Quebec with the crisis through which the genre went in eighteenth-century France and which has been amply documented by Georges May
in his excellent study of *Le Dilemme du roman au XVIIIe siècle.*
However, Yves Dostaler, while making the parallel, reminds us of
some important differences between the two situations (Dostaler 1977,
82, 96, 136–7, 142–3).

2 For a dissenting opinion, see Imbert 1987, who argues that the first
novel is in fact *Les Révélations du crime ou Cambray et ses com-
plices* by François-Réal Angers, published in July 1837.

3 Page references to *Jean Rivard, le défricheur* are to the 1874 edition,
reproduced in the margins of René Dionne's 1977 reprinting.

4 The *lecteur frivole* reappears in the body of the novel, where he
appears to be suffering from a form of *mal de siècle:* "O jeunes
gens pleins de force et d'intelligence, qui passez vos plus belles
années dans les bras de l'oisiveté, qui redoutez le travail comme
l'esclave redoute sa chaîne, vous ne savez pas de quel bonheur vous
êtes privés! Cette inquiétude vague, ces ennuis, ces dégoûts qui vous
obsèdent, cette tristesse insurmontable qui parfois vous accable, ces
désirs insatiables de changements et de nouveautés, ces passions

tyranniques qui vous rendent malheureux, tout cela disparaîtrait comme par enchantement sous l'influence salutaire du travail" (Gérin-Lajoie 1874, 119). In fact, the city-dwelling reader is figured in the text by the character Gustave Charmenil, who serves as a warning to the reader of what might befall him if he does not follow the example of Jean Rivard and leave the city for the land. At times, however, Gérin-Lajoie seems aware of the dangers of boring even his most benevolent readers to tears: "Mais il me faut entrer ici dans des détails tellement prosaïques que je désespère presque de me faire suivre par mes lecteurs même les plus bénévoles. En tous cas, je déclare loyalement que la suite de ce chapitre ne peut intéresser que les défricheurs et les économistes" (70).

5 Cf., for example, the third preface, dated 21 October 1836 and unpublished in Stendhal's lifetime, to his unfinished novel *Lucien Leuwen,* dedicated, as were a number of Stendhal's books, to the *happy few:* "À vrai dire, puisqu'on est forcé de faire un aveu si sérieux, crainte de pis, l'auteur serait au désespoir de vivre sous le gouvernement de New York. Il aime mieux faire la cour à M. Guizot que faire la cour à son bottier. Au dix-neuvième siècle, la démocratie amène nécessairement dans la littérature le règne des gens médiocres, raisonnables, bornés et plats, littérairement parlant" (Stendhal 1973, 1:54).

6 In their prefaces to, respectively, *Jeanne la fileuse* (1878), *Le Château de Beaumanoir* (1886), and *Jacques et Marie* (1866). The expression "re-establish the truth" ("rétablir la vérité") is Beaugrand's. It is Beaugrand, too, who explains how his choice of genre ("the popular form of the novel") is tailored to fit the interests of his readership, which is working-class and domiciled in the United States. (*Jeanne la fileuse,* published in Fall River, Massachussetts, in 1878, is subtitled *Épisode de l'émigration franco-canadienne aux États-Unis.*)

7 The most notable exception to this rule is, as in most things, Philippe Aubert de Gaspé Senior, who warns the reader: "J'entends bien avoir, aussi, mes coudées franches, et ne m'assujétir à aucunes règles prescrites, – que je connais d'ailleurs, – dans un ouvrage comme celui que je publie. Que les puristes, les littérateurs émérites, choqués de ces défauts, l'appellent roman, mémoire, chronique, salmigondis, pot-pourri: peu m'importe!" (Aubert de Gaspé 1899, 6).

8 Marmette, in the opening chapter of *François de Bienville,* while ostensibly allowing less latitude to his (female) reader's imagination concerning his hero's physical appearance, ultimately takes the strategy of narrative seduction even further than Gérin-Lajoie:

François Le Moyne, sieur de Bienville, compagnon de voyage de M. de Frontenac, avait vingt-quatre ans. Bien qu'il doive être un des principaux acteurs

dans ce récit des hauts faits d'un âge héroïque, veuillez bien, jolies lectrices,
ne le point orner d'avance de ces qualités extérieures dont beaucoup de
romanciers se plaisent à habiller leurs héros.

Bienville n'avait pas une de ces tailles élancées qui se dessinent si bien,
selon le goût moderne, sous la coupe plus ou moins élégante des habits de
nos tailleurs à la mode; bien au contraire, il était trapu, courtaud, robuste et
carré.

Sa main n'était ni effilée ni blanche, comme celle de ces héros de romans,
plutôt propres à chiffonner les dentelles d'une folle marquise dans une colla-
tion sur l'herbe, qu'à pourfendre un homme au champ d'honneur.

Le nôtre arrivait de la baie d'Hudson, où il avait guerroyé contre l'Anglais,
pendant plusieurs mois, avec ses frères d'Iberville, Sainte-Hélène et Maricourt.
Accoutumées, lors des fréquentes expéditions qu'il faisait à travers les bois, à
manier la hache autant que l'épée, ses mains étaient devenues épaisses, larges
et musculeuses.

Enfin, lectrices, dernière déception pour vous, M. de Bienville n'était pas
beau de figure. Cependant, pour rester dans le vrai, je dois me hâter d'ajouter
qu'il n'était certainement pas laid.

Si vous aviez examiné ses grands yeux bruns, où se lisaient l'intelligence, le
courage, ainsi qu'une aristocratique fierté, ses lèvres tant soit peu dédaigneuses
et si fines de contour, vous n'auriez pas remarqué, sans doute, qu'il avait la
figure osseuse et fort peu d'animation dans le teint. Si enfin, tenant vos doigts
mignons dans sa main nerveuse et dure, cet homme, frère de héros et héros
lui-même, vous eût dit: "Je vous aime," peut-être alors, mademoiselle, aurait-il
pris un extérieur plus séduisant à vos yeux, et n'auriez-vous pas retiré votre
main tremblante de celle du galant guerrier. (Marmette 1924, 22–3)

The recurring use of the negative in this description is in itself interesting and, as we can see from the last paragraph of the passage
just quoted, it is closely related to Prince's concept of the disnarrated, which I discuss below. Jean Sareil (1987) has pointed out
the importance of the reader's role in negative description. In the
case of Marmette, it is clear that the reader is called upon both to
reject the novel codes which generate a certain kind of romantic or
idealized description and, at the same time, to reinvest in the person
of the non-idealized, true-to-life hero of the non-novel, François de
Bienville, the desire which such descriptions are assumed to arouse.
As an illustration and amusing variant of Grivel's contention that the
novel is produced as a negation of its own narrative negativity
(Grivel 1973), Marmette's description is a narratologist's delight.
9 More recently still, Prince seems to be leaning toward the expression
"the alternarrated" or, in French, *l'alternarré* (Prince 1989). I retain

the term "disnarrated" here for convenience of quotation, though I shall come back to the notion of the "alternarrated" in chapter 5.

10 In this sense, there is some overlap between the disnarrated and the use of cliché or stereotype as described by Patrick Imbert, since both can be used to set up models within the text which are patently incongruent with the reader's experience and with the immediate social context (Imbert 1983, 10).

11 Carole Gerson, in charting the (conservative) range of opinion expressed by nineteenth-century English-Canadian commentators of the genre, cites Tardivel's condemnation of the novel as representative of the more extreme positions adopted in French Canada (Gerson 1989, 17).

12 Grivel 1973, passim. (See, in particular, pp. 239ff. of the companion volume.)

13 Cf. Guildo Rousseau's conclusion in the introduction to his useful anthology of nineteenth-century novel prefaces. Rousseau sees in the nineteenth-century Quebec novel a genre made of paradoxes. He points out that while the nineteenth-century Quebec novel is afraid of the French serial-novel, which it condemns as the work of the devil, it owes to the French serial-novel most of its literary-rhetorical techniques. (G. Rousseau 1970, 20).

14 The best introduction to current research on the literary institution in Quebec is to be found in Lemire 1986a, especially in the essays by Denis Saint-Jacques, David Hayne, and Benoît Melançon. For an institutional approach to comparative studies in Canadian literature, see Blodgett and Purdy 1988. Is there some irony in the fact that much of the research on the literary institution is being conducted by research institutes – IQRC, CRELIQ, and GRELQ in Quebec, and the HOLIC/HILAC project organized through the Research Institute for Comparative Literature at the University of Alberta?

15 According to Dostaler, the most widely read French authors were Lesage, Bernardin de Saint-Pierre, Chateaubriand, Hugo, Daudet, and Veuillot, along with a host of more popular novelists such as Dumas, Sue, and Scribe (Dostaler 1977, 15–33). For the fascinating history of the 1835–6 serialization of Balzac's *Le Père Goriot* in *L'Ami du peuple, de l'ordre et des lois,* see Imbert 1986.

16 In the modern period this distinction will take on a new relief, as Lucie Robert reminds us: "It is on this closure of aesthetic value that the modern paradigm of literature rests. A distinction can then be made between two bodies of works: domestic literature, which is of historic and sociological interest, and LITERATURE, which is of aesthetic interest. A few rare works of the Quebec corpus accede to the level of LITERATURE in capitals" (Robert 1988, 142).

CHAPTER TWO

1 Most recently, however, Clément Moisan has suggested that the problem
of genre is a smokescreen created by the literary handbooks to
avoid discussion of the political message of *Menaud.* According to
Moisan, it was probably of no interest to Savard whether he was
writing a novel, a novel-poem, a lyrical novel, a poetic story, an
epic poem, a poem *per se,* or an epic (Moisan 1987, 65).

2 A similar conclusion is expressed by Louise Vanhee-Nelson, who attributes the change to an attempt to come to terms with "a sometimes
ambiguous reality" (Vanhee-Nelson 1979, 94). The nature and source
of this ambiguity remain to be explained. On the different editions
of *Menaud, maître-draveur,* see Jules Tessier, who reminds us that
there are not, as is commonly believed, three versions of Savard's
novel but five: those of 1937, 1938, 1944, 1960, and 1964. He also
points out that there are major differences between the 1937 text and
the definitive edition of 1964, which nevertheless undoes a great deal
of the rewriting of 1944.

3 I use the term *diegesis* throughout this chapter, not in the Platonic or
Aristotelian sense, but to translate Genette's *diégèse* (and not *dié-
gésis,* which is opposed to *mimésis*) as he (re-)defines it in *Nouveau
discours du récit,* as a narrative's spatio-temporal context (Genette
1983, 13).

4 The ideological configuration associated with artisanal work in the
novel (continuity with the past, defending one's heritage and one's
freedom) is evident in the following image, which once again
evokes Menaud's state of mental excitement: "Patiemment, suivant le
rite hérité des ancêtres, il lace les nerfs de ses raquettes. Ainsi
apaise-t-il sa tête peuplée d'idées en marche par des gestes d'artisan
qui signifient volonté de conquête et passion de libre espace" (154).
The importance of the artisan class and of the travelling journeyman
in the historical development of storytelling has been admirably described by Walter Benjamin in his essay "The Storyteller" (Benjamin
1969, 83–109).

5 *Menaud* is so naïvely and overtly sexist and racist in its inspiration that
these aspects of the novel's ideology need not detain us here. As
Larry Shouldice remarks, "the contemporary reader risks finding in
Félix-Antoine Savard the expression of values which, today, would
be considered reactionary, ethnocentric, xenophobic, racist and sexist" (Shouldice 1987, 129).

6 Menaud's "country," which in reality is quite narrowly circumscribed –
"Le pays de Menaud est situé au nord-est de La Malbaie. Il comprend, dans la paroisse de Sainte-Agnès, les rangs de Mainsal, de

Cachette-Aubin, de Miscoutine, des Frênes et des Caribous; le Grand-Lac, le Petit-Lac, la mare à Josime; les montagnes à Philémon, du Friche et de la R'source, etc." (*Menaud,* 206) – functions as a synecdoche for Quebec, which is conceived atavistically as a racial (or tribal) homeland rather than as a political (or even geographic) entity. (For a dissenting view, see Lemieux 1987, 33.)

7 Marie-Andrée Beaudet makes a similar point concerning the voices heard by Maria and by Menaud: "Maria is tormented by the temptation of exile. The voices will ensure the victory of the group over the individual. In Savard, things are quite different: the voice of belonging echoes from the past to confirm the hero's isolation, his withdrawal from the community, and his final descent into madness" (Beaudet 1987, 60). For Clément Moisan, what separates the voices of *Maria Chapdelaine* from those of *Menaud* and gives them a meaning which is the opposite of the one they originally had, is the experience of the Depression: Savard's novel describes a community which has been radically destabilized and uprooted by such phenomena as urbanization and industrialization (Moisan 1987, 69).

8 Savard seems to acknowledge this impossibility in a radio talk given 10 December 1956, when he claims that it is not his fault if, at the end of the novel, Menaud is a broken man: "A hero that one carries within oneself is not, for all that, a puppet on a string. If he is genuine, he is born, suffers and dies according to the laws of his own necessity." (Quoted in P. Hébert 1987, 209–10.)

9 Cf. Lukács 1971: "Of madness the epic knows nothing, unless it be the generally incomprehensible language of a superworld that possesses no other means of expression ... For crime and madness are objectivations of transcendental homelessness – the homelessness of an action in the human order of social relations, the homelessness of a soul in the ideal order of a supra-personal system of values" (61–2).

10 Quoted in A. Major 1968, 11–12.

11 "The epic as a genre in its own right may, for our purposes, be characterized by three constitutive features: (1) a national epic past – in Goethe's and Schiller's terminology the "absolute past" – serves as the subject for the epic; (2) national tradition (not personal experience and the free thought that grows out of it) serves as the source for the epic; (3) an absolute epic distance separates the epic world from contemporary reality, that is, from the time in which the singer (the author and his audience) lives" (Bakhtin 1981, 13).

12 "Both the singer and the listener, immanent in the epic as a genre, are located in the same time and on the same evaluative (hierarchical) plane, but the represented world of the heroes stands on an utterly different and inaccessible time-and-value plane, separated by epic dis-

tance. The space between them is filled with national tradition. To portray an event on the same time-and-value plane as oneself and one's contemporaries (and an event that is therefore based on personal experience and thought) is to undertake a radical revolution, and to step out of the world of epic into the world of the novel" (Bakhtin 1981, 14).

13 Cf. Ricard 1972, 114.

14 Claude Filteau (1987) warns against the dangers of anachronism and reminds us of the profoundly religious nature of Menaud's commitment and of Savard's art.

CHAPTER THREE

1 On the theme of walking in *Bonheur d'occasion* (and associated themes such as imprisonment, immobility, and escape), see Le Grand (1965) and Blais (1970).

2 It is worth pointing out that the different characters do have a voice as well as a point of view, and that one of the things they frequently talk about, to the annoyance of at least one contemporary reviewer (Albert Alain, writing in *Le Devoir,* 15 September 1945, and quoted in *Bonheur d'occasion,* 390) is politics. The motif of narratorial eavesdropping is repeated in the 1947 address to the Royal Society: "I listened to people talk on the street corners, in the little shops, around the station and at the market" (Roy 1982, 158). And what they are talking about is still politics.

3 Guy Laflèche has some harsh words for what he calls "la rhétorique de la misère" in *Bonheur d'occasion,* arguing that Roy's treatment of poverty through the family (and especially through the children) does nothing more than exploit the facile sentimentality of the popular novel (Laflèche 1977, 110–11). Such a statement, of course, raises far more questions than it answers. Do we, for example, dismiss Dickens as a "serious" novelist because of his sentimental portrayal of poverty and sick or dying children? And what do we say about Orwellian *kitsch* which sentimentalizes the working-class family in a way Roy, for all her shortcomings as a writer, would surely find suspect? The following passage is particularly interesting, as it closes with an evocation of the outsider's uneasy awareness of his own invading presence: "I have often been struck by the peculiar easy completeness, the perfect symmetry as it were, of a working-class interior at its best. Especially on winter evenings after tea, when the fire glows in the open range and dances mirrored in the steel fender, when Father, in shirt-sleeves, sits in the rocking chair at one side of the fire reading the racing finals, and Mother sits on the

other with her sewing, and the children are happy with a pennorth
of mint humbugs, and the dog lolls roasting himself on the rag mat –
it is a good place to be in, provided that you can be not only in it
but sufficiently *of* it to be taken for granted" (Orwell 1962, 104).

4 In this limited sense, my approach is similar to that outlined by John
Vernon in his study *Money and Fiction* when he claims to be using
"the theme of money – perhaps the most common theme in nineteenth-century fiction – as a prism with which to separate and examine such elements as narrative time, plot, and the representation of
material objects, all of which are formal expressions of the novel's
social and economic context" (Vernon 1984, 7).

Surprisingly, "economic" readings of *Bonheur d'occasion* are not
common. See Lemire (1969), Shek (1977, 65–111), and Sirois (1982) on
the economic background of the novel, and Thorne (1968) and
Quigley (1980) on the inevitable parallel with Steinbeck's *Grapes of
Wrath*. A curiously shrill and dogmatic reading of Roy's "pro-imperialist comprador outlook" is to be found in Clark (1972). I shall make
no systematic attempt here to review the critical literature on the
novel, which is vast and of very uneven quality. There exist several
good and relatively recent bibliographical guides: Socken (1979),
Chadbourne (1984), C. Melançon (1984), Sirois (1984). For an amus-
ingly acerbic analysis of the clichés and myths which nourish much
of the secondary literature, see Laflèche (1977).

5 Resch (1978) is particularly useful on the function of space in the novel.
See also Shek (1971).

6 It is significant that Gilles Marcotte, on re-reading *Bonheur d'occasion*
as "la découverte de la misère," thinks not of Steinbeck or Zola, but
of Péguy (Marcotte 1950).

7 Roy returns to this theme in her address to the Royal Society, when
she has Sam Latour complain about an economic system which
makes poverty the inevitable correlative of abundance (Roy 1982, 166).

8 The act of looking in the novel has been studied by Brochu (1966b)
and more recently and systematically by Babby (1985) and Drummond (1986) from, respectively, thematic, structural, and existentialist
perspectives.

9 The official version is that Jean's parents had been killed in a car
accident. However, since at the time this was a common story told
to illegitimate children given up for adoption, it is quite possible that
Gabrielle Roy is trying to suggest that Jean is indeed a bastard. On
the respective roles of the "bastard" and the "foundling" in the Freudian family romance and in the development of the novel as a genre,
see Marthe Robert (1972).

10 It is not simply as a gesture toward grammatical gender equality that I

use the feminine to designate the proletarian. The true workers in *Bonheur d'occasion* are quite clearly Florentine and Rose-Anna, a point which Roy makes with some force in her address to the Royal Society: "I wondered why people talk about the bravery of women in the old days when they had to fight the Iroquois and do everything by hand. I don't see that they were more courageous than any girl today. The one who comes back from town in the streetcar, overloaded with parcels, standing up, weaving with fatigue, a long day's work behind her. The girls in the restaurants, the factories, the spinning mills, the textile works. The girl who helps out her family from a miserable salary usually less than that of a man doing the same work, only managing to keep even that job because she is docile and less demanding than he" (Roy 1982, 168). Patricia Smart has written eloquently on the feminine realism (at once feminist and maternal) of *Bonheur d'occasion* (Smart 1988, 197–233).

11 Baudrillard's critique draws not only on the classical analyses of Marx, Weber, and Veblen, but more immediately on the French tradition of Mauss (1923–24) and Bataille (1967). Closer to home and from different perspectives, Marcel Rioux has studied the social question of need and desire (Rioux 1984) and Anthony Wilden, in a series of books, has developed the Sartrean and Lacanian notion of the Imaginary in terms of communication and exchange. For an application of this concept to Canadian history, see Wilden (1980).

12 In a very different perspective from the one developed in this chapter, Charles Mauron's distinction between objects of communion (the teddy bear is a prime example) and objects of possession is helpful and illuminating (Mauron 1976, 24–7).

13 Such a statement requires immediate qualification of course. Orwell points out that "in a decade of unparalleled depression, the consumption of all cheap luxuries has increased" (Orwell 1962, 79). In explaining this phenomenon in terms of an *unconscious* social process (81), he is surprisingly close to Baudrillard.

14 Some years ago, André Brochu published an interesting study of the novel's semantic structure, which he analyses in terms of a Greimassian semiotic square based on the opposition dream/reality (Brochu 1979). While I have no particular use for semiotic squares as such, it seems to me that the method would generate an even more convincing and coherent reading of *Bonheur d'occasion* if it were to exploit the opposition need/desire; such a reading would enjoy the same advantages afforded by the generality of Brochu's opposition while at the same time anchoring the thematic analysis in an historically identifiable socio-economic context. Moreover, a glance at Paul Socken's useful concordance (Socken 1982) shows the relatively high

incidence in the novel of the terms *désir* and *besoin* and suggests the importance of the concepts for the novel's semantic structure, even on the lexical level.

15 Laflèche's own examples build on points made by Robidoux and Renaud (1966, 75–91) and on the excellent close readings of Bessette (1968, 217–308, especially 239–55).

16 The latest is Patricia Smart, who rises to the bait of Laflèche's provocations in arguing that what Laflèche and Bessette call respectively "confusion" and "brouillage" can be explained and ideologically valorized simply by accepting the fact that the narrator is not masculine but feminine and that her interventions are the maternal promptings of a creator who cannot stand idly by when her offspring are having trouble expressing themselves (Smart 1988, 205–7). Thus, what is seen by Bessette as inadvertent code-breaking and by Laflèche as excellent popular literature becomes, for Smart, a feminist transgression of the norms of masculine narrative.

CHAPTER FOUR

1 The indeterminate status of the narration is reflected in the hybrid term used by Réjean Robidoux and André Renaud when they describe Alain Dubois's narrative as "une espèce de journal parlé" – a kind of spoken diary (Robidoux and Renaud 1966, 135). I shall argue that the radical uncertainty implied by such a term is symptomatic of our uneasiness as readers.

2 There is an interesting exchange between Gilles Marcotte and Jacques Allard on the subject of socio-critical readings of *Poussière sur la ville,* particularly on possible allusions to the social and ideological confrontations of the 1949 Asbestos strike (Vigneault 1977, 81–96).

3 The novel, as critics have not been slow to point out, is full of screens of various kinds. Snow, rain, and frosted windows all function in much the same way as the ubiquitous dust of the title, preventing characters from seeing clearly or allowing them to see without being seen. In such cases, the external world constitutes an obstacle to true communication.

4 Early in the novel Dubois exclaims: "Hé, grands dieux! qu'est-ce que cela peut signifier être femme ou homme!" (36). The question, if a question it is, receives at least a partial answer: a man, like a husband, is someone who knows his rights and makes sure that he is not distracted by such trifling emotions as pity or compassion in the proper exercise of those rights. Cf. pp. 86, 172, 173.

5 Ronald Sutherland speaks of Dubois as suffering from the "failed priest syndrome," a legacy of Calvinist-Jansenist conditioning which the

critic sees as typically Canadian (Sutherland 1974). André Brochu, on
the other hand, recalls the criticisms formulated by Sartre and Jeanson in the early fifties following the publication of Camus's *L'Homme
révolté.* According to Jeanson, Camus's preoccupation with injustice
betrays a displaced transcendence, the result of a philosophy
haunted by the spectre of a malevolent deity. Brochu argues that
Jeanson's reproach ("You are infinitely more concerned with God
than with men") applies even more to the author of *Poussière sur la
ville* than to the author of *The Plague* (Brochu 1985, 170).

6 This is why I cannot accept Pierre Hébert's argument, formulated in several articles and reiterated in his book *Le Temps et la forme,* that
Poussière sur la ville is the story of a victory, which is realized in
Alain's final decision, namely his entry into the realm of action
(Hébert 1983, 68). As I have tried to show, Alain's decision is highly
problematic and scarcely supports a reading which seeks to characterize the novel's structure as a passage from "knowing" to "doing."

7 Gilles Marcotte is apparently the only critic to have grasped the importance of this fact: "The surprise," he writes, "that a re-reading of
Poussière sur la ville brings, is precisely that: we find out that Madeleine is murdered, murdered by the one who desires her the most,
by her husband" (Marcotte 1977, 85). Marcotte's reading is tantalizing:
Madeleine, whom the critic identifies with the people of Quebec,
dies because she is not ready to assume the liberty (and the responsibility) bestowed upon her by the democratic intellectual Alain.
While I cannot fully endorse this socio-critical interpretation, I can at
least concur that it is Alain's quest for knowledge, his "desire to
understand," that ultimately destroys Madeleine.

8 The absence of a concrete narrative situation leads André Brochu to
speak of "a degree zero narration": "In Langevin there is a pure convention of writing by which the narration is so to speak delegated
to a privileged character, *as if* he himself had to tell what happens
to him, but nothing more. The personalisation of the narration, its
attribution to a character, has no other function than the integral and
exclusive privileging of that character's point of view, an effect that
only a first-person narration can achieve sufficiently" (Brochu 1985,
112–13). I have problems with this reading, which I outline in notes
12 and 14 below.

9 Miller goes on: "The term is meant to cover the various incitements to
narrative, as well as the dynamic ensuing from such incitements, and
it is thus opposed to the 'nonnarratable' state of quiescence assumed
by a novel before the beginning and supposedly recovered by it at
the end" (Miller 1981, ix).

10 It is interesting to note that Prince's category of the *disnarrated* or

alternarrated here coincides, not with Miller's *narratable* as in the nineteenth-century novel, which uses it to identify and proscribe the imported story codes of blood and passion so distressing to the Church (see chapter 1 above), but with the *nonnarratable,* the logic of life, untellable and uninteresting.

11 Cf. Pierre Hébert: "*Poussière sur la ville* has long been seen as a story of failure" (Hébert 1983, 67). I have already indicated why I cannot accept Hébert's refutation of this reading. In this respect, my position is much closer to that of Jacques Allard, who argues that seeing leads neither to understanding nor to action and that this doctor-narrator fails in fact to heal himself (Allard 1977, 93).

12 Such a reading is suggested by André Brochu's notion of a "degree zero narration" using a "false" narrator: "The absolute focalization on Dubois is obtained at the price of an artifice which undermines the realist aesthetic, which is incompatible with the conception of a false narrator" (Brochu 1985, 113). According to Brochu, Dubois's immediate predecessor is Meursault, the "false" narrator of Camus's *The Outsider,* but the critic is quick to point out that, whereas Camus uses the past tense for his novel, *Poussière sur la ville* is narrated for the most part in the present. It is precisely this use of the narrative present that, on occasion, lays bare the convention of the "false" narrator, exposing the dissociation which exists, according to Brochu, between the "apparent" narrator (Dubois) and the "real" narrator (Langevin). To support his point, Brochu quotes a number of short passages in which there is an implicit contradiction between what is reported and the narrator's supposed state of knowledge at the time. He concludes that either the narrative present is a rhetorical device for recounting events after the fact or the first-person narrative is itself a rhetorical convention concealing an omniscient narrator (Langevin) who cannot resist filling in some of the blanks in Dubois's knowledge. The latter hypothesis would seem to point to what might be thought of as a kind of inverted metalepsis of the author and assign to the character actions accomplished in reality by the author.

13 Such a reading might be taken as evidence of the existence of an "implied author," conceived as "the governing consciousness of the work as a whole, the source of the norms embodied in the work" (Rimmon-Kenan 1983, 86). Rimmon-Kenan (86–8, 100–3) has a brief but useful discussion of this notion as it appears in writers like Booth, Iser, and Chatman. Genette, on the other hand, argues convincingly in *Nouveau discours du récit* that the notion of an "implied author" is superfluous, there being no room for a third narrative instance between narrator and (real) author (94–104). However, this

does not mean that the narrative confusion of *Poussière sur la ville* can be resolved by assimilating the "implied author" to the narrator in *all* first-person novels, as Agnès Whitfield tries to do (Whitfield 1987, 27); for while one can argue that this *ought* to be the case, in practice it is not. In this sense, it is unfortunate that Whitfield's study starts in 1960, thereby excluding Langevin's groundbreaking and problematic novel.

14 Brochu's analysis, while focusing on a different kind of narrative inconsistency and attacking the problem from another angle, uncovers essentially the same contradictions and ambiguities which I have tried to deal with in this chapter. However, his overall interpretation of Langevin's narrative project seems to be a synthesis of elements and possibilities which I have been at pains to distinguish and keep separate. Thus, as a narrator, Dubois is seen as the plaything of an omniscient Author just as, as a character, he is a pawn in the capricious games of an ultimately malevolent Providence: "To sum up, I will say that the narrative formula which makes the main character the narrator in name only is perfectly suited to a novelistic world in which the character refers to an I-other, in which his truth lies outside himself" (Brochu 1985, 118). Described in this way, the harmony or correspondence between form and content proposed by Brochu seems to pose more problems than it solves. The critic's tactic, and it is an interesting one, is to match the contradictions of form (the problem of the "false" or "apparent" narrator) with those of content (the paradox of a secular humanist obsessed with divine injustice). But does this matching do anything to allay the reader's sense that something is wrong? Far from finding resolution at a higher level, the inconsistencies of both form and content would seem, if anything, to be exacerbated by a reading which, with its invocation of narrative determinism, cuts off all debate, leaving us with the extraordinarily bleak and unsatisfying image of a Dubois condemned, as narrator and as character, to struggle in vain against an omniscient Author with, inevitably, another point of view.

15 Perhaps it was the sense of uneasiness generated by this kind of discontinuity or conflict between closure and the means of narrative production that led Langevin's translators, John Latrobe and Robert Gottlieb, to substitute the past for the present in their English version, a strategy which is questioned by Philip Stratford (1986, 42).

CHAPTER FIVE

1 Most of Aquin's essays first appeared in magazines and journals and have since been collected in *Point de fuite* and *Blocs erratiques*. Ref-

erences given here are to my English edition, *Writing Quebec: Selected Essays by Hubert Aquin* (Purdy 1988). Patricia Smart, in her excellent early study (Smart 1973), analyses *Prochain épisode* and *Trou de mémoire* in the context provided by the essays. On Aquin as essayist, see Purdy (1986a) and Smart (1985).

2 See, for example, Lapierre (1985), Bédard (1985), Allard (1988).

3 On the (frequently violent) exclusion of women from the discourse of revolutionary nationalism in the Quebec of the 1960s, see chapter 6 of Patricia Smart's *Écrire dans la maison du père*.

4 It is almost an unwritten law of narrative that epistemic dominance is a characteristic of the Villain rather than the Hero. In *Prochain épisode,* epistemic dominance translates not only into cultural superiority but also into narrative power, as will become clear later in this chapter.

5 Eco (1966): 86. My underlining.

6 For an interesting reading of the novel as semiotically produced object, see Allard (1987).

7 Cf. Faye 1972, 26: "A political ideology posits a founding narration in whose name it rises up against the Logos – and against its dialectic."

8 It would be hopelessly reductive to see the Other of French-Canadian history as simply English Canada. The Other, represented in *Prochain épisode* by the protean H. de Heutz, is a symbolic father-figure which has been internalized as a brother or double by the collective psyche and which is responsible for the "secret foundations of order" denounced by Aquin in the early essay "Dangerous Understanding": "We are dealing with a collective unconscious, the protean product of two centuries of repressed desire. It is high time that it saw the light of day" (*Writing Quebec,* 1). One of the best accounts of the French-Canadian's Other is to be found in Jean Bouthillette's *Le Canadien français et son double* (47–8).

9 The original French is "trou de mémoire," an expression which is not without a certain resonance in Aquin's work. (In fact it is the title of his second novel.) The principal source for the whole notion of cultural amnesia in Aquin's writing is probably Albert Memmi's *Portrait du colonisé,* though the idea is also present in Fanon's *Les Damnés de la terre.*

10 A similarly theatrical view of history runs through the essays collected in Harold Rosenberg's *Act and the Actor. Making the Self,* some of which appeared in French translation in Sartre's *Les Temps modernes* in the late forties and early fifties.

11 The expression "agent double de naissance," which can be found in act 1, scene 4 of the original, is lost in Kitty Black's English translation.

12 Cf. Bouthillette (1972, 70–1) on the internalization by French Canadians of the image of Wolfe and the story of the Plains of Abraham.

13 This is apparent in political terms as early as 1962, in "The Politics of Existence," where Aquin argues that the real opponents of independence are to be found not in Ottawa, but in Quebec City. In symbolic terms, this translates in *Prochain épisode* into the hero's paralysing identification with H. de Heutz, who is at once devil and brother, father and castrator, self and other.

14 I am using the terms *discourse* and *story* here as a kind of shorthand to designate two distinct narrative or diegetic levels, corresponding to the "I" of the narrator and the "I" of the hero, as well as to their respective worlds. Cf. the two levels of utterance (*discours* and *histoire*) distinguished by the linguist Émile Benveniste in the fifth part of his *Problèmes de linguistique générale*.

15 It is not possible, in the space of a single chapter, to deal adequately with the vast (and often excellent) secondary literature which *Prochain épisode* has attracted, or to situate in more than a cursory fashion my own argument in relation to the critical debates which surround the novel. An excellent annotated bibliography, prepared by Jacinthe Martel, is available in numbers 7 and 10 of the sadly defunct *Revue d'histoire littéraire du Québec et du Canada français*. As for the "naïve" readings of which I am complaining here, Léandre Bergeron's will serve as an example of one kind. Bergeron (1973) sees in *Prochain épisode* the uncritical portrait of a "cowboy-revolutionary," of a narcissistic individualist who, for metaphysical or psychological reasons, cultivates the image of a revolutionary. The problem with this reading is that it blithely ignores the critical tension that Aquin so carefully creates between the two basic levels of his text. Aquin's novels are all powerfully referential – indeed, this is what sets them apart from the French New Novel – but their referentiality is textualized according to complex structural strategies which cannot be grasped by grossly reductive ideological readings.

16 There is nothing to indicate that Fredric Jameson had read the early essays or was conversant with Aquin's positions on writing in a colonized society when he wrote of the "garish surface" and the ugliness of the language of *Prochain épisode*. An assumption of ignorance of the author's intentions would go some way to explaining Jameson's view of the novel's plot as "a clumsy, shoddy, homemade thing" and his initial hostility to its apparent self-indulgence: "I found it amateurish and repulsive, indulgent, narcissistic, and distressingly thin from any novelistic point of view" (Jameson 1983, 215–16).

17 There is a sense in which Aquin's future simple is reminiscent of Stendhal's future perfect, "a tense that allows for the infinite post-

ponement of accomplishment," "the tense of deferral, the tense that
denies retrospective satisfaction" (Brooks 1984, 78 and 88). As Brooks
points out, Stendhal's narrative mode gives "the impression of a per-
petual flight forward, a constant self-invention at the moment and of
the moment" (76). As is the case with Aquin, "Stendhalian time is
inorganic, momentary, characterized by abruptness and discontinuity,"
qualities which Brooks notes "may well appear paradoxical in a novelist so preoccupied with history" (77). Such a statement becomes all
the more intriguing when we recall that the July Revolution of 1830
is, in a very strong sense, the "next episode" of *Le Rouge et le Noir,*
an episode which the whole novel prepares and demands through
its chronology and its thematics, but which is replaced (or displaced)
in the text by Julien's execution.

18 Prince includes in the category of the disnarrated or alternarrated
"alethic expressions of impossibility or unrealized possibility, deontic
expressions of observed prohibition, epistemic expressions of ignorance, ontologic expressions of nonexistence, purely imagined
worlds, desired worlds, or intended worlds, unfulfilled expectations,
unwarranted beliefs, failed attempts, crushed hopes, suppositions and
false calculations, errors and lies, and so forth" (Prince 1988, 3).

19 Interestingly enough, in *Prochain épisode,* Aquin's "tangled hierarchies"
and "strange loops" contrive, thanks to the structure of the whole
work, to be dialectical. In his next novel, *Trou de mémoire,* all hierarchical distinction will be systematically negated and we shall be
left with several narratives whose ontological status remains hypothetical throughout. In such a case of non-dialectical, polyphonic dialo-
gism, we can think of the entire novel as being "disnarrated."

CHAPTER SIX

1 *Kamouraska* has no numbered chapters but is divided typographically
into narrative segments of varying length – "segments of thought" or
"movements of consciousness," as Grazia Merler calls them (Merler
1971, 60). If I refer here to chapter 49 (rather than to the forty-ninth
unnumbered narrative segment) it is simply as a matter of convenience.

2 Eva-Marie Kröller (1981) points out the use made by Claude Jutra of
the motif of the woman-at-the-window in his film of *Kamouraska.*
For further discussion of the motif, see Blodgett (1982) who relates it
to the process of self-reflection of character by house, Northey (1977)
who sees it as a variation of a common gothic image, and Émond
(1984) who discusses it in the context of Hébert's "poetics of the
look."

3 It does not seem to me very profitable to speculate, as some critics
have (see, for example, Hughes 1977), on *Kamouraska* as a sustained
historical allegory of the events surrounding the 1837–38 Rebellion,
especially in a chapter that follows hard on the heels of a reading
of *Prochain épisode*. The attempt to rehabilitate Anne Hébert as a
serious historical and political thinker is surely wrongheaded; which
is not to suggest in any way that the novel is devoid of social comment or criticism or that Hébert's work in general is not suffused
with a desire to give voice to aspects of a collective psyche
(Bouchard 1977).

4 For an interesting discussion of eavesdropping in the nineteenth-
century novel, see chapter 4 of John Vernon's *Money and Fiction*
(84–107).

5 It is interesting to note that the word "irréprochable" is repeated later
in the text in key passages. In chapter 14, it is used almost as a
reproach in the context of Madame Rolland's blameless "absence,"
i.e. the kind of absence or withdrawal I have tried to link with the
use of the third-person, simple past narrative mode. In chapter 8, the
word appears in a fragment of character testimony given by
Elisabeth's Aunt Adélaïde and is immediately characterized as a "petit
morceau de roman" (46). It takes on the same connotations of deceit
(but theatrical rather than fictional this time) in chapter 35, where
Elisabeth stages a brief "reconciliation" with Tassy to disguise her
pregnancy by George Nelson: "La vraie vie est en ordre. L'honneur
est sauf. L'épouse irréprochable pourra annoncer qu'elle est à nouveau enceinte de son mari" (146).

6 In his *Figures III,* Genette uses the term "récit intérieur" to describe
any personal narrative which is neither spoken nor written, whether
remembered or dreamed (Genette 1972, 241). Perhaps the most striking feature of *Kamouraska* in this respect is that we should have to
speak, not of an interior monologue, but of an interior polylogue, as
Elisabeth goes through the different grammatical persons in search of
a voice. Louis Francoeur seems to have recognized this peculiarity in
his discussion of phases of the ego in intrapersonal communication,
although he deals only with the first and second person forms of
address: "we shall speak here of intrapersonal communication, of
'interior dialogue' in which the two phases of the Ego are defined in
opposition to one another" (Francoeur 1976, 342).

7 The original French reads: "le Récit a un nom, il échappe à la terreur
d'une parole sans limite: la réalité s'amaigrit et se familiarise, elle
entre dans un style, elle ne déborde pas le langage" (Barthes 1968,
27). The sense of overflowing (*déborder*) is lost in the English translation.

8 The image of the overflowing breast is linked to the frame motif in a second, more literal way as an example of a reality which destroys a carefully contrived illusion, of a detail which gives the lie to an otherwise artfully posed portrait. Thus Elisabeth, as she brings order to the chaos of the nursery, sees herself in the role of Victoria:

Les enfants habillés, coiffés, calmés ont des poses charmantes autour de leur mère. Agathe joint les mains devant un aussi touchant tableau.

– On dirait la reine avec ses petits princes autour d'elle!

… Je ressemble à la reine d'Angleterre. Je me calque sur la reine d'Angleterre. Je suis fascinée par l'image de Victoria et de ses enfants. Mimétisme profond. Qui me convaincra de péché?

La voix flûtée de la petite Anne-Marie s'élève soudain.

– Mais maman est en robe de chambre! Ses cheveux sont en désordre. Et puis son visage a l'air tout rouge!

Quelle peste que cette petite fille sage et trop lucide. En un clin d'oeil le charme est rompu, la fausse représentation démasquée. Le désordre de la toilette de Mme Rolland jure comme une fausse note. Un si joli tableau d'enfants soignés et tirés à quatre épingles. Agathe semble honteuse de s'être laissée prendre par d'aussi pauvres apparences. (34)

Writing from another perspective, Françoise Maccabée Iqbal quotes this "fausse représentation démasquée" in a discussion of the theatre motif in *Kamouraska* (Iqbal 1979).

9 The distinction I am making here between story sequence and narrative sequence derives from Genette's discussion in *Figures III* of discrepancies occurring between "the time of the story" and "the time of the narrative" (77–182) and from Rimmon-Kenan's subsequent distinction between story-time and text-time (43–58). In an interesting disagreement with Eric S. Rabkin, W.J.T. Mitchell sees these two kinds of "time" as parallel spatial forms, "two distinct patterns in the virtual space-time of narrative" (Mitchell 1980, 552, n. 27). In this sense, it would certainly be possible to speak of a topography of plot.

10 The image of the root appears again in an archaeological context on page 62: "On dirait que je tire vers le jour avec effort un mot, un seul, lourd, lointain. Indispensable. Une sorte de poids enfoui sous terre. Une ancre rouillée. Au bout d'une longue corde souterraine. Une espèce de racine profonde, perdue." The word in question comes from the trial: "Désistement!" – "Charges withdrawn!"

11 Cf. Féral 1975, 282.

12 Hawthorne has a similar image in his tale "The Haunted Mind," in which he imagines someone starting from midnight slumber: "By unclosing your eyes so suddenly, you seem to have surprised the

personages of your dream in full convocation round your bed."
(*Twice Told Tales,* 304). He goes on to observe "that the glass is
ornamented with fanciful devices in frost work, and that each pane
presents something like a frozen dream. There will be time enough
to trace out the analogy, while waiting the summons to breakfast"
(305). Elisabeth, for her part, will spend long nights motionless at her
window: "Encore un peu de temps et je ne serai plus qu'une fleur
de givre parmi les arabesques du froid dessinées sur la vitre" (195).
Hébert's moral and psychological universe bears sufficient resemblance to Hawthorne's for us to speculate on a form of intertextuality which is not so much verbal – in the sense that the numerous
biblical echoes and quotations constitute a very visible verbal intertext in *Kamouraska* – as tonal and atmospheric: we feel as readers
that Elisabeth inhabits a world which is not so very different from
that of Hawthorne's novels and stories. As Gabrielle Pascal points
out, the jansenism of Quebec is at times very close to the puritanism
of New England (Pascal 1980, 75).

13 The speaker is Sarah Woodruff in John Fowles's *The French Lieutenant's
Woman* (176). Perhaps it is not entirely by accident that, as she
utters these words, Sarah reaches up and touches a branch of the
hawthorn. (See note 12 above and the first epigraph to this chapter.)

14 This is not to say that critics have neglected the referential aspects of
the novel, i.e., the story it tells and its historical setting. The best
account of the historical events which constitute the "true story" of
Elisabeth, Antoine Tassy, and George Nelson (or Joséphine, Achille
Taché, and Dr George Holmes, as they were in "real life") is in
Leblond 1972; Harvey (1982), Dufresne (1972) and Russell (1983) also
make useful points in this respect.

15 Jonathan Culler points out in *Structuralist Poetics* the dangers of using
Barthes's binary opposition as a principle of classification: "In *S/Z*
Barthes begins his discussion of Balzac with a distinction between
readable and unreadable texts – between those which are intelligible
in terms of traditional models and those which can be written (*le
scriptible*) but which we do not yet know how to read (p. 10). And
although Barthes's own analysis suggests that this distinction is not
itself a useful way of classifying texts – every 'traditional' novel of
any value will criticize or at least investigate models of intelligibility
and every radical text will be readable and intelligible from some
point of view – it does at least indicate the appropriateness and
fecundity of taking the play of intelligibility as the focal point of
one's analysis" (190). I shall argue that *Kamouraska* is a perfectly
readable or intelligible work in terms of what, in 1970, can be considered accepted models.

16 Cf. Whitfield 1987, 307.
17 Féral 1975, 278–80. A similar conclusion is suggested by Le Grand (1971, 132) and by Major (1982, 460). The most rigorous account of the narrative structure of *Kamouraska* is to be found in Whitfield 1987.

From a terminological point of view, it might be argued that Elisabeth should be seen as the focalizer rather than as the narrator of her story and that the narrator in fact remains heterodiegetic. (For a useful and concise discussion of the distinction, see Lintvelt 1981, 29–30.) While I understand the theoretical reasons for wanting to make such a distinction, I do not think it is particularly helpful in this particular instance, where it displaces rather than illuminates the problem and runs the risk of distracting the reader from what I consider to be the most important feature of the narration in *Kamouraska:* the fact that the polyphonic surface structure is generated by a single voice.

18 There is a tendency in recent Canadian theorizing to extend the category of the postmodern until it becomes indistinguishable from the modern. Linda Hutcheon (1988a, 1988b), for example, casts her net so wide that we are left wondering exactly what manner of fish it is that she has caught. It should, however, be pointed out that Paterson, in her excellent study, is far from dogmatic in her classification of *Kamouraska* as a postmodern work. See, in particular, the hesitations of her introduction and conclusion. A much more convincing analysis of an indisputably postmodern novel is to be found in her reading of Aquin's *Trou de mémoire,* a text which successfully resists all attempts at totalization (Paterson 1987). My own argument concerning modernism and postmodernism would find support in David Lodge's essays on the subject (Lodge 1977, 220–45, and 1981, 3–16). Similarly, Douwe Fokkema's distinction, although made from a somewhat different point of view, is by no means irreconcilable with my own: "Whereas the Modernist aimed at providing a valid, authentic, though strictly personal view of the world in which he lived, the Postmodernist appears to have abandoned the attempt towards a representation of the world that is justified by the convictions and sensibility of an individual" (Fokkema 1984, 40). However, the debate surrounding postmodernism frequently has an air of depressing academic futility, and I do not wish to labour the point here. Perhaps the most salutory statement in this context is Brian McHale's reminder that "all definitions in the field of literary history, all acts of categorization or boundary-drawing, are *strategic*" and that the best definitions are those which are most *productive,* most *interesting* and most *aware* of their own strategic nature (McHale 1986, 53–4). This perspective is maintained in McHale 1987.

19 The expression "stylisation de la réalité" comes from Grazia Merler, who situates the novel's "enigmatic beauty" in an extreme disjunction of form and content (Merler 1971, 55). It is strongly reminiscent of the kind of defamiliarization effect we have seen in *Menaud, maître-draveur*. My point is that the stylization in *Kamouraska* is motivated by the narrator's (i.e., Elisabeth's) own theatricality, whereas in Savard's novel such a possibility for motivation in terms of character does not exist. (It is worth pointing out that, for one reader at least, the stylistic devices which create such an impression can be irritating; in her review of *Les Fous de Bassan*, Suzanne Lamy complains of a particular kind of excess which has lost its power to subvert and degenerates into a series of stylistic tics (Lamy 1982, 3–2).)

20 A useful discussion of terms such as *motivation, recuperation,* and *readability* as I use them here is to be found in chapters 7 and 9 of Culler's *Structuralist Poetics*. Following the Russian formalists, Culler defines motivation as "the process of justifying items within the work itself by showing that they are not arbitrary or incoherent but quite comprehensible in terms of functions which we can name" (Culler 1975, 137–8).

Bibliography

Allard, Jacques. 1977. "À propos d'une lecture sociale de textes québécois." In Vigneault 1977, 90–6.

– 1987. "Avant-texte pour demain: *Prochain épisode* d'Hubert Aquin." *Littérature* 66: 78–90.

– 1988. "Pour un modèle génétique du récit aquinien." *Bulletin de l'ÉDAQ* 7: 81–91.

Amprimoz, Alexandre. 1977. "*Poussière sur la ville*: vers une sémiotique des gestes." *Présence Francophone* 14: 97–104.

Aquin, Hubert. 1961a. "Comprendre dangereusement." *Liberté* 3 (5): 679–80.

– 1961b. "Le bonheur d'expression." *Liberté* 3 (6): 741–3.

– 1962a. "L'existence politique." *Liberté* 21: 67–76.

– 1962b. "La fatigue culturelle du Canada français." *Liberté* 23: 299–325.

– 1964. "Profession: écrivain." *Parti pris* 1 (4): 23–31.

– 1965a. "L'art de la défaite: considérations stylistiques." *Liberté* 7 (1–2): 33–41.

– 1965b. *Prochain épisode*. Montréal: Le Cercle du Livre de France.

– 1968. *Trou de mémoire*. Montréal: Le Cercle du Livre de France.

– 1971. *Point de fuite*. Montréal: Le Cercle du Livre de France.

– 1977. *Blocs erratiques*. Textes (1948–1977) rassemblés et présentés par René Lapierre. Collection "Prose entière." Montréal: Quinze.

– 1988. *Writing Quebec. Selected Essays by Hubert Aquin*. Edited, with an introduction, by Anthony Purdy. Trans. Paul Gibson, Reva Joshee, Anthony Purdy, Larry Shouldice. Edmonton: The University of Alberta Press.

Aubert de Gaspé, Philippe-Ignace-François. 1837. *L'Influence d'un livre; roman historique*. Québec: William Cowan & fils.

Aubert de Gaspé, Philippe-Joseph. 1899. *Les Anciens Canadiens*. Montréal: C.O. Beauchemin & fils, Libraires-Imprimeurs. [First edition: Québec: Desbarats et Derbishire, Imprimeurs-Éditeurs, 1863.]

"L'Autonomisation de la littérature." 1987. *Études littéraires* 20 (1). [Numéro préparé par Clément Moisan et Denis Saint-Jacques.]

Babby, Ellen Reisman. 1985. *The Play of Language and Spectacle. A Structural Reading of Selected Texts by Gabrielle Roy*. Toronto: ECW Press.

Bakhtin, M.M. 1981. *The Dialogic Imagination. Four Essays*. Ed. Michael Holquist. Trans. Caryl Emerson and Michael Holquist. University of Texas Press Slavic Series 1. Austin: University of Texas Press.

Barthes, Roland. 1953. *Le Degré zéro de l'écriture*. Paris: Éditions du Seuil.

– 1968. *Writing Degree Zero*. Trans. Annette Lavers and Colin Smith. Preface by Susan Sontag. New York: Hill & Wang.

– 1974. *S/Z*. Trans. Richard Miller. Preface by Richard Howard. New York: Hill & Wang.

– 1975. *The Pleasure of the Text*. Trans. Richard Miller. With a note on the text by Richard Howard. New York: Hill & Wang.

Bataille, Georges. 1967. *La Part maudite, précédé de La Notion de dépense*. Paris: Les Éditions de Minuit.

Baudrillard, Jean. 1981. *For a Critique of the Political Economy of the Sign*. Translated with an introduction by Charles Levin. St. Louis, Mo.: Telos Press.

Beaudet, Marie-Andrée. 1987. "Le procédé de la citation dans *Menaud, maître-draveur*." *Revue de l'histoire littéraire du Québec et du Canada français* 13: 59–64.

Beaugrand, Marie-Louis-Honoré. 1878. *Jeanne la fileuse; épisode de l'émigration franco-canadienne aux États-Unis*. Fall-River, Mass.: H. Beaugrand. [First published in serial form in *La République*, 1875.]

Beaver, John. 1973. "La métaphore théâtrale dans l'oeuvre romanesque d'André Langevin." *Études littéraires* 6 (2): 169–97.

Bédard, Nicole. 1985. "L'apport d'un inédit: *L'Invention de la mort*." *Revue d'histoire littéraire du Québec et du Canada français* 10: 51–5.

Belleau, André. 1981. "Le conflit des codes dans l'institution littéraire québécoise." *Liberté* 134: 15–20. Rpt. in Belleau 1984, 154–7.

– 1983. "Code social et code littéraire dans le roman québécois." *L'Esprit créateur* 23 (3): 19–31.

– 1984. *Y a-t-il un intellectuel dans la salle?* Montréal: Primeur.

Benjamin, Walter. 1969. *Illuminations*. Edited and with an introduction by Hannah Arendt. Trans. Harry Zohn. New York: Schocken Books.

Benveniste, Émile. 1966. *Problèmes de linguistique générale*. Paris: Gallimard.

Bergeron, Léandre. 1973. "*Prochain épisode* et la révolution." *Voix et images du pays* 6: 123–9. Montréal: Presses de l'Université du Québec.

Berthiaume, André. 1973. "Le thème de l'hésitation dans *Prochain épisode*." *Liberté* 85: 135–48.

Bérubé, Renald. 1969. Introduction, *Poussière sur la ville,* 9–22. Ottawa: Éditions du Renouveau Pédagogique.

Bessette, Gérard. 1968. *Une Littérature en ébullition.* Montréal: Éditions du Jour.

Blais, Jacques. 1970. "L'unité organique de *Bonheur d'occasion*." *Études françaises* 6 (1): 25–50.

Blodgett, E.D. 1982. *Configuration: Essays on the Canadian Literatures.* Downsview, Ont.: ECW Press.

–, and A.G. Purdy, eds. 1988. *Problems of Literary Reception/Problèmes de réception littéraire.* Proceedings of a conference "Towards a History of the Literary Institution in Canada 1/Vers une histoire de l'institution littéraire au Canada 1" organized by the Research Institute for Comparative Literature at the University of Alberta, 16–18 October 1986. Edmonton: Research Institute for Comparative Literature.

Bouchard, Denis. 1977. *Une Lecture d'Anne Hébert: la recherche d'une mythologie.* Cahiers du Québec 34. Collection Littérature. Montréal: Hurtubise HMH.

Bourassa, Napoléon. 1866. *Jacques et Marie, souvenir d'un peuple dispersé.* Montréal: Eusèbe Sénécal, Imprimeur-Éditeur.

Bourdieu, Pierre. 1971. "Le marché des biens symboliques." *L'Année sociologique* 22: 49–126.

Bouthillette, Jean. 1967. "Écrivain faute d'être banquier." *Perspectives* 41: 64–7. Rpt. in Aquin 1971, 13–20.

– 1972. *Le Canadien français et son double.* Montréal: Les Éditions de l'Hexagone.

Bowlby, Rachel. 1985. *Just Looking: Consumer Culture in Dreiser, Gissing and Zola.* University Paperbacks 889. New York & London: Methuen.

Brochu, André. 1966a. "*Menaud* ou l'impossible fête." *L'Action nationale* 56 (3): 266–91. Rpt. in Brochu 1974, 247–74.

– 1966b. "Thèmes et structures de *Bonheur d'occasion*." *Écrits du Canada français* 22: 163–208. Rpt. in Brochu 1974, 206–46.

– 1974. *L'Instance critique 1961–1973.* Montréal: Leméac.

– 1979. "La structure sémantique de *Bonheur d'occasion*." *Revue des sciences humaines* 45: 37–47.

– 1985. *L'Évasion tragique: Essai sur les romans d'André Langevin.* Cahiers du Québec 81. Collection Littérature. Montréal: Hurtubise HMH.

Brooks, Peter. 1984. *Reading for the Plot. Design and Intention in Narrative.* New York: A.A. Knopf.

Campbell, Beatrix. 1984. *Wigan Pier Revisited. Poverty and Politics in the Eighties.* London: Virago Press.

Camus, Albert. 1948. *The Plague.* Trans. Stuart Gilbert. London: Hamish Hamilton.

– 1955. *The Myth of Sisyphus and Other Essays.* Trans. Justin O'Brien. New York: Vintage Books.

Chadbourne, Richard. 1984. "Essai bibliographique: cinq ans d'études sur Gabrielle Roy, 1979–1984." *Études littéraires* 17: 597–609.

Chambers, Ross. 1984. *Story and Situation. Narrative Seduction and the Power of Fiction.* Theory and History of Literature 12. Minneapolis: University of Minnesota Press.

Chauveau, Pierre-J.-Olivier. 1978. *Charles Guérin, roman de moeurs canadiennes.* Édition présentée et annotée par Maurice Lemire. Bibliographie de Aurélien Boivin. Collection du Nénuphar. Montréal: Fides. [First edition: Montréal: G.H. Cherrier, 1853.]

Clark, J. Wilson. 1972. "Pro-imperialist ideas in Gabrielle Roy's *Tin Flute.*" *Literature and Ideology* 13: 31–40.

Conan, Laure [Félicité Angers]. 1884. *Angéline de Montbrun.* Québec: Imprimerie Léger Brousseau. [First published in serial form in *La Revue canadienne,* 1881–82.]

Culler, Jonathan. 1975. *Structuralist Poetics. Structuralism, Linguistics and the Study of Literature.* London & Henley: Routledge Kegan Paul.

Dällenbach, Lucien. 1977. *Le Récit spéculaire. Essai sur la mise en abyme.* Paris: Éditions du Seuil.

de Grandpré, Chantal. 1985. "La canadianisation de la littérature québécoise: le cas Aquin." *Liberté* 27 (3): 50–9.

Derrida, Jacques. 1972. *La Dissémination.* Collection "Tel Quel." Paris: Éditions du Seuil.

Diderot, Denis. 1964. *Quatre contes.* Édition critique avec notes et lexique par Jacques Proust. Textes littéraires français. Genève: Librairie Droz.

Dostaler, Yves. 1977. *Les Infortunes du roman dans le Québec du XIXe siècle.* Cahiers du Québec. Collection Littérature. Montréal: Hurtubise HMH.

Doutre, Joseph. 1844. *Les Fiancés de 1812.* Essai de littérature canadienne. Montréal: Louis Perreault, Imprimeur.

Drummond, D. 1986. "Identité d'occasion dans *Bonheur d'occasion.*" *Solitude rompue.* Textes réunis par Cécile Cloutier-Wojciechowska et Réjean Robidoux en hommage à David M. Hayne, 85–102. Cahiers du CRCCF 23. Ottawa: Éditions de l'Université d'Ottawa.

"Du thème en littérature." 1985. *Poétique* 64. [Conference papers collected by Viviane Alleton, Claude Bremond, and Thomas Pavel.]

Dubois, Jacques. 1978. *L'Institution de la littérature. Introduction à une sociologie.* Collection Dossiers Media. Bruxelles: Fernand Nathan/Éditions Labor.

Ducrocq-Poirier, Madeleine. 1978. *Le Roman canadien de langue française de 1860 à 1958. Recherche d'un esprit romanesque.* Paris: A.G. Nizet.

Dufresne, Françoise M. 1972. "Le drame de Kamouraska." *Québec histoire* 1 (5–6): 72–7.

Dvorak, Martha. 1975. "Une analyse structurale des personnages dans *Prochain épisode* de Hubert Aquin." *Revue de l'Université d'Ottawa* 45 (3): 371–81.

Eco, Umberto. 1966. "James Bond: une combinatoire narrative." *Communications* 8: 77–93.

– 1984. *The Role of the Reader. Explorations in the Semiotics of Texts.* Bloomington: Indiana University Press.

Émond, Maurice. 1984. *La Femme à la fenêtre. L'univers symbolique d'Anne Hébert dans "les Chambres de bois," "Kamouraska" et "les Enfants du sabbat."* Vie des Lettres québécoises 22. Québec: Les Presses de l'Université Laval.

Fanon, Frantz. 1961. *Les Damnés de la terre.* Paris: F. Maspero.

Faye, Jean Pierre. 1972. *Théorie du récit.* Paris: Hermann.

Féral, Josette. 1975. "Clôture du moi, clôture du texte dans l'oeuvre d'Anne Hébert." *Voix et images* 1 (2): 265–83.

Filteau, Claude. 1987. "La mystique du corps social dans *Menaud, maître-draveur.*" *Revue d'histoire littéraire du Québec et du Canada français* 13: 39–57.

Fokkema, Douwe W. 1984. *Literary History, Modernism, and Postmodernism.* Utrecht Publications in General and Comparative Literature 19. Amsterdam/Philadelphia: John Benjamins Publishing Company.

Fowles, John. 1969. *The French Lieutenant's Woman.* London: Jonathan Cape.

Francoeur, Louis. 1976. "Le monologue intérieur narratif (sa syntaxe, sa sémantique et sa pragmatique)." *Études littéraires* 9: 341–65.

Frank, Joseph. 1981. "Spatial Form: Thirty Years After." *Spatial Form in Narrative,* ed. Jeffrey R. Smitten and Ann Daghistany, 202–43. Ithaca & London: Cornell University Press.

Garcia-Mendez, Javier. 1983. "Les romanciers du XIXᵉ siècle face à leurs romans: Notes pour la reconstitution d'une argumentation." *Voix et images* 8 (2): 331–43.

Genette, Gérard. 1972. *Figures III.* Collection Poétique. Paris: Éditions du Seuil.

– 1983. *Nouveau discours du récit.* Collection Poétique. Paris: Éditions du Seuil.

– 1987. *Seuils.* Collection Poétique. Paris: Éditions du Seuil.

Gérin-Lajoie, Antoine. 1977. *Jean Rivard, le défricheur, récit de la vie réelle suivi de Jean Rivard, économiste.* Postface de René Dionne. Cahiers du Québec. Collection Textes et documents littéraires. Montréal: Hurtubise HMH. [Reproduces the text of the original editions published in Montreal by J.B. Rolland & fils, Libraires-Éditeurs, in 1874 and 1876 respectively. *Jean*

Rivard, le défricheur was first published in serial form in *Les Soirées canadiennes,* 1862.]

Gerson, Carole. 1989. *A Purer Taste: The Writing and Reading of Fiction in English in Nineteenth-Century Canada.* Toronto: University of Toronto Press.

Grivel, Charles. 1973. *Production de l'intérêt romanesque. Un état du texte (1870–1880), un essai de constitution de sa théorie.* The Hague, Paris: Mouton. Companion volume of examples and illustrations published simultaneously under the same title with Hoekstra Offset (Amstelveen, Holland).

Harvey, Robert. 1982. *"Kamouraska" d'Anne Hébert: Une écriture de La Passion, suivi de Pour un nouveau "Torrent."* Cahiers du Québec 69. Collection Littérature. Ville LaSalle, Québec: Hurtubise HMH.

Hawthorne, Nathaniel. 1974. *Twice-Told Tales.* 1837. Volume XIX of the Centenary Edition of the Works of Nathaniel Hawthorne. Ohio State University Press.

Hayles, N. Katherine. 1984. *The Cosmic Web. Scientific Field Models and Literary Strategies in the Twentieth Century.* Ithaca & London: Cornell University Press.

Hayne, David M. 1971. "Les origines du roman canadien-français." *Le Roman canadien-français,* Archives des lettres canadiennes, tome 3, 37–67. Montréal: Fides.

– 1986. "Institution québécoise et institution française au XIXe siècle." In Lemire 1986, 51–60.

Hébert, Anne. 1970. *Kamouraska.* Paris: Éditions du Seuil.

Hébert, Maurice. 1937. *"Menaud, maître-draveur."* Le Canada français 25 (2/3): 225–32, 320–35.

Hébert, Pierre. 1983. *Le Temps et la forme: Essai de modèle et lecture de trois récits québécois.* Sherbrooke: Éditions Naaman.

– 1987. "Quand Félix-Antoine Savard parlait de son *Menaud...*" *Revue d'histoire littéraire du Québec et du Canada français* 13: 207–10.

Hofstadter, Douglas R. 1980. *Gödel, Escher, Bach: An Eternal Golden Braid.* New York: Vintage Books.

Holdheim, Wolfgang W. 1984. *The Hermeneutic Mode. Essays on Time in Literature and Literary Theory.* Ithaca & London: Cornell University Press.

Hughes, Kenneth J. 1977. "Le vrai visage du [sic] *Antoinette de Mirecourt* et *Kamouraska.*" *The Sphinx* 2 (3): 33–9. [English text.]

Hutcheon, Linda. 1988a. *A Poetics of Postmodernism. History, Theory, Fiction.* University Paperbacks 986. New York & London: Routledge.

– 1988b. *The Canadian Postmodern. A Study of Contemporary English-Canadian Fiction.* Studies in Canadian Literature. Toronto, New York, Oxford: Oxford University Press.

Imbert, Patrick. 1983. *Roman québécois contemporain et clichés.* Cahiers du CRCCF 21. Ottawa: Éditions de l'Université d'Ottawa.

– 1986. "*Le Père Goriot* au Canada: feuilleton et censure." *Année Balzacienne:* 237–46.

– 1987. "Tout texte fondateur en cache un autre!" *Lettres québécoises* 47: 58–60.

Iqbal, Françoise Maccabée. 1979. "*Kamouraska,* 'la fausse représentation démasquée'." *Voix et images* 4 (3): 460–78.

Jakobson, Roman. 1956. "Two Aspects of Language and Two Types of Aphasic Disturbances." In Roman Jakobson and Morris Halle, *Fundamentals of Language,* 53–82. Janua Linguarum 1. 'S-Gravenhage: Mouton & Co.

Jameson, Fredric. 1983. "Euphorias of substitution: Hubert Aquin and the Political Novel in Quebec." *Yale French Studies* 65: 214–23.

Kermode, Frank. 1966. *The Sense of an Ending. Studies in the Theory of Fiction.* Oxford: Oxford University Press.

Kröller, Eva-Marie. 1981. "La lampe dans la fenêtre. The visualization of Quebec fiction." *Canadian Literature* 88: 74–82.

Lacombe, Patrice. 1972. *La Terre paternelle.* Présentation par André Vanasse. Cahiers du Québec. Collection Textes et documents littéraires. Montréal: Hurtubise HMH. [First published anonymously in the *Album littéraire et musical de la Revue canadienne,* 1 (1846): 14–25.]

Laflèche, Guy. 1977. "Les Bonheurs d'occasion du roman québécois." *Voix et images* 3 (1): 96–115.

Lamy, Suzanne. 1982. "Le roman de l'irresponsabilité. *Les Fous de Bassan* d'Anne Hébert." *Spirale* (novembre): 3–2.

Langevin, André. 1953. *Poussière sur la ville.* Montréal: Le Cercle du Livre de France.

Lapierre, René. 1985. "Aquin, lecteurs cachés: une poétique de la prédiction." *Revue d'histoire littéraire du Québec et du Canada français* 10: 65–9.

Leblond, Sylvio. 1972. "Le drame de Kamouraska d'après les documents de l'époque." *Cahiers des dix* 37: 239–73.

Le Grand, Albert. 1965. "Gabrielle Roy ou l'être partagé." *Études françaises* 1 (2): 39–65.

– 1971. "*Kamouraska* ou l'Ange et la Bête." *Études françaises* 7: 119–43.

Lemieux, Pierre-H. 1987. "L'architecture de *Menaud, maître-draveur.*" *Revue d'histoire littéraire du Québec et du Canada français* 13: 29–38.

Lemire, Maurice. 1969. "*Bonheur d'occasion* ou le salut par la guerre." *Recherches sociographiques* 10 (1): 23–35.

–, ed. 1986a. *L'Institution littéraire.* Actes du colloque organisé conjointement par l'Institut québécois de recherche sur la culture et le Centre de recherche en littérature québécoise. Québec: IQRC & CRELIQ.

– 1986b. "La valorisation du champ littéraire canadien à partir de 1840." In Lemire 1986a, 61–73.

– 1987. "L'autonomisation de la 'littérature nationale' au XIXᵉ siècle." *Études littéraires* 20 (1): 75–98.

Lintvelt, Jaap. 1981. *Essai de typologie narrative: Le "point de vue." Théorie et analyse.* Paris: José Corti.

Lodge, David. 1976. "The language of modernist fiction: metaphor and metonymy." *Modernism, 1890–1930,* eds. Malcolm Bradbury and James McFarlane, 481–96. Pelican Guides to European Literature. Harmondsworth, Middlesex: Penguin Books.

– 1977. *The Modes of Modern Writing. Metaphor, Metonymy, and the Typology of Modern Literature.* Ithaca, N.Y.: Cornell University Press.

– 1981. *Working With Structuralism. Essays and Reviews on Nineteenth- and Twentieth-century Literature.* Boston, London & Henley: Routledge Kegan Paul.

Lukács, Georg. 1971. *The Theory of the Novel. A historico-philosophical essay on the forms of great epic literature.* Trans. Anna Bostock. London: Merlin Press.

Major, André. 1968. *Félix-Antoine Savard.* Collection "Écrivains canadiens d'aujourd'hui." Montréal: Fides.

Major, Robert. 1983. "*Prochain épisode* et *Menaud, maître-draveur:* le décalque romanesque." *Canadian Literature* 99: 55–65.

Major, Ruth. 1982. "*Kamouraska* et *Les Enfants du sabbat:* faire jouer la transparence." *Voix et images* 7 (3): 459–70.

Malette, Yvon. 1968. "*Menaud, maître-draveur* et *Maria Chapdelaine.*" *Incidences* 13: 20–8.

Marcotte, Gilles. 1950. "En relisant *Bonheur d'occasion.*" *L'Action nationale* 35 (3): 197–206.

– 1971. *Une littérature qui se fait. Essais critiques sur la littérature canadienne-française.* Nouvelle édition augmentée. Montréal: Hurtubise HMH.

– 1977. "Alain et Abel." In Vigneault 1977, 81–9.

– 1981. "Institution et courants d'air." *Liberté* 134: 5–14.

Marion, Séraphin. 1944. "Le roman et le Canada français." *Les Lettres canadiennes d'autrefois,* tome IV, 13–45. Ottawa: Éditions de l'Université d'Ottawa.

Marmette, Joseph. 1924. *François de Bienville; scènes de la vie canadienne au XVIIᵉ siècle.* Quatrième édition. Bibliothèque canadienne, collection Champlain. Montréal: Librairie Beauchemin. [First edition: Québec: Léger Brousseau, Imprimeur-Éditeur, 1870.]

Martineau, François. 1972. "Le sens originel des extraits de *Maria Chapdelaine* et leur interprétation dans *Menaud, maître-draveur.*" *Co-incidences* 2 (3): 12–21.

Mauron, Charles. 1976. *Van Gogh: études psychocritiques.* Paris: José Corti.

Mauss, Marcel. 1923–24. "Essai sur le don. Forme et raison de l'échange dans les sociétés archaïques." *Année sociologique,* seconde série, tome I.

May, Georges. 1963. *Le Dilemme du roman au XVIIIᵉ siècle. Étude sur les rapports du roman et de la critique (1715–1761)*. Paris: Presses Universitaires de France.

McHale, Brian. 1986. "Change of dominant from modernist to postmodernist writing." *Approaching Postmodernism,* eds. Douwe Fokkema and Hans Bertens, 53–79. Amsterdam/Philadelphia: John Benjamins Publishing Company.

– 1987. *Postmodernist Fiction*. University Paperbacks 949. New York & London: Methuen.

Melançon, Benoît. 1986. "Théorie institutionnelle et littérature québécoise." In Lemire 1986, 27–42.

Melançon, Carole. 1984. "Évolution de la réception de *Bonheur d'occasion* de 1945 à 1983 au Canada français." *Études littéraires* 17: 457–68.

Memmi, Albert. 1966. *Portrait du colonisé*. Paris: Jean-Jacques Pauvert.

Merler, Grazia. 1971. "La réalité dans la prose d'Anne Hébert." *Écrits du Canada français* 33: 45–83.

Miller, D.A. 1981. *Narrative and its Discontents. Problems of Closure in the Traditional Novel*. Princeton, N.J.: Princeton University Press.

Mitchell, W.J.T. 1980. "Spatial Form in Literature: Toward a General Theory." *Critical Inquiry* 6 (3): 539–67.

– 1986. *Iconology. Image, Text, Ideology*. Chicago & London: The University of Chicago Press.

Mitterand, Henri. 1980. *Le Discours du roman*. Collection Écriture. Paris: Presses Universitaires de France.

Moisan, Clément. 1987. "*Menaud, maître-draveur* dans l'histoire littéraire." *Revue d'histoire littéraire du Québec et du Canada français* 13: 65–74.

Northey, Margot. 1977. *The Haunted Wilderness: The Gothic and Grotesque in Canadian Fiction*. Toronto: University of Toronto Press.

O'Connor, John. 1981. "Letters in Canada 1980. Translations." *University of Toronto Quarterly* 50 (4): 92–4.

Orwell, George. 1962. *The Road to Wigan Pier*. 1937. Harmondsworth, Middlesex: Penguin Books.

Pascal, Gabrielle. 1980. "Soumission et révolte dans les romans d'Anne Hébert." *Incidences* 4 (2–3): 59–75.

Paterson, Janet M. 1980. "L'écriture de la jouissance dans l'oeuvre romanesque d'Anne Hébert." *Revue de l'Université d'Ottawa* 50: 69–73.

– 1985. *Anne Hébert: Architexture romanesque*. Ottawa: Éditions de l'Université d'Ottawa.

– 1987. "Écriture postmoderne, écriture subversive: *Trou de mémoire* d'Hubert Aquin." *Québec-Acadie. Modernité/Postmodernité du roman contemporain,* 87–100. Sous la responsabilité de Madeleine Frédéric et Jacques Allard. Actes du Colloque international de Bruxelles (27–9 novembre 1985). Les Cahiers du département d'études littéraires 11. Montréal: Université du Québec à Montréal.

Prince, Gerald. 1983. "Narrative Pragmatics, Message, and Point." *Poetics* 12: 527–36.

– 1988. "The Disnarrated." *Style* 22 (1): 1–8.

– 1989. "L'alternarré." *Strumenti critici* 4 (2): 223–31.

Purdy, Anthony. 1985a. "De 'L'art de la défaite' à *Prochain épisode*." *Voix et images* 10 (3): 113–25.

– 1985b. "Stopping the Kaleidoscope. The Logic of Life and the Logic of Story in André Langevin's *Poussière sur la ville*." *Dalhousie French Studies* 8: 78–102.

– 1986a. "Form and (Dis-)content. The Writer, Language, and Society in the Essays of Hubert Aquin." *French Review* 59 (6): 885–93.

– 1986b. "Métaphore et métonymie dans *Menaud, maître-draveur*." *Voix et images* 12 (1): 68–85.

– ed. 1988. *Writing Quebec. Selected Essays by Hubert Aquin*. Trans. Paul Gibson, Reva Joshee, Anthony Purdy, Larry Shouldice. Edmonton: University of Alberta Press.

Quigley, Theresa. 1980. "Two great novels of social concern: John Steinbeck's *The Grapes of Wrath* and Gabrielle Roy's *Bonheur d'occasion*." *Humanists in Canada* 13 (2): 36–8.

Resch, Yannick. 1978. "La ville et son expression romanesque dans *Bonheur d'occasion* de Gabrielle Roy." *Voix et images* 4 (2): 244–57.

Ricard, François. 1972. *L'Art de Félix-Antoine Savard dans "Menaud, maître-draveur."* Montréal: Fides.

– 1980. "*Menaud, maître-draveur*, roman de l'abbé Félix-Antoine Savard." *Dictionnaire des oeuvres littéraires du Québec, tome II, 1900–1939*, 691–700. Montréal: Fides.

Rimmon-Kenan, Shlomith. 1983. *Narrative Fiction: Contemporary Poetics*. New Accents. London & New York: Methuen.

Rioux, Marcel. 1984. *Le Besoin et le désir, ou le code et le symbole*. Montréal: Éditions de l'Hexagone.

Robert, Lucie. 1988. "L'émergence de la notion de 'littérature canadienne-française' dans la presse québécoise (1870–1948)." In Blodgett and Purdy 1988, 136–43.

Robert, Marthe. 1972. *Roman des origines et origines du roman*. Paris: Grasset.

Robidoux, Réjean, et André Renaud. 1966. *Le Roman canadien-français du vingtième siècle*. Ottawa: Éditions de l'Université d'Ottawa.

Robin, Régine. 1983. *La Québécoite*. Montréal: Québec/Amérique.

Rosenberg, Harold. 1959. *The Tradition of the New*. New York: Horizon Press.

– 1970. *Act and the Actor. Making the Self*. Perspectives in Humanism. New York & Cleveland: New American Library/World Publishing Company.

Rousseau, Edmond. 1886. *Le Château de Beaumanoir; roman canadien*. Lévis: Mercier & cie, Éditeurs.

– 1888. *Les Exploits d'Iberville*. Québec: C. Darveau.

Rousseau, Guildo, ed. 1970. *Préfaces des romans québécois du XIXᵉ siècle.* Sherbrooke: Éditions Cosmos.

Roy, Gabrielle. 1977. *Bonheur d'occasion.* 1945. Québec 10/10. Montréal: Alain Stanké.

– 1982. *The Fragile Lights of Earth. Articles and Memories, 1942–1970.* Trans. Alan Brown. Toronto: McClelland & Stewart.

Russell, Delbert W. 1983. *Anne Hébert.* Twayne's World Authors Series 684. Boston: Twayne Publishers.

Saint-Jacques, Denis. 1986. "L'envers de l'institution." In Lemire 1986, 43–8.

Sareil, Jean. 1987. "La description négative." *Romanic Review* 78: 1–9.

Sartre, Jean-Paul. 1948. *Situations II.* Paris: Gallimard.

– 1952. *Lucifer and the Lord.* Trans. Kitty Black. London: Hamish Hamilton.

– 1964. *Nausea.* Trans. Lloyd Alexander. New York: New Directions.

– 1967. *No Exit and The Flies.* Trans. Stuart Gilbert. New York: Alfred A. Knopf.

Savard, Félix-Antoine. 1982. *Menaud, maître-draveur.* 1937. Présentation d'André Renaud, chronologie, bibliographie et jugements critiques d'Aurélien Boivin. Montréal: Fides.

Shcheglov, Yuri, and Alexander Zholkovsky. 1987. *Poetics of Expressiveness. A Theory and Applications.* Linguistic & Literary Studies in Eastern Europe (LLSEE) 18. Amsterdam/Philadelphia: John Benjamins Publishing Company.

Shek, Ben-Z. 1971. "L'espace et la description symbolique dans les romans 'montréalais' de Gabrielle Roy." *Liberté* 13 (1): 78–96.

– 1977. *Social Realism in the French-Canadian Novel.* Montreal: Harvest House.

Shouldice, Larry. 1987. "*Menaud* en anglais." *Revue d'histoire littéraire du Québec et du Canada français* 13: 129–36.

Simon, Sherry. 1987. "The Language of Difference: Minority Writers in Quebec." *A/Part.* Papers from the 1984 Ottawa Conference on Language, Culture and Literary Identity in Canada. Ed. J.M. Bumsted. *Canadian Literature,* Supplement no. 1: 119–28.

Singer, François-Benjamin. 1871. *Souvenirs d'un exilé canadien.* Montréal: John Lovell.

Sirois, Antoine. 1982. "*Bonheur d'occasion,* roman de Gabrielle Roy." *Le Dictionnaire des oeuvres littéraires du Québec, tome III (1940–1959).* Montréal: Fides. 127–36.

– 1984. "Gabrielle Roy et le Canada anglais." *Études littéraires* 17: 469–79.

Smart, Patricia. 1973. *Hubert Aquin, agent double. La dialectique de l'art et du pays dans "Prochain épisode" et "Trou de mémoire."* Collection Lignes québécoises. Montréal: Les Presses de l'Université de Montréal.

– 1985. "Hubert Aquin, essayiste." *L'Essai et la prose d'idées au Québec,* Archives des lettres canadiennes, tome 6, 513–25. Montréal: Fides.

– 1988. *Écrire dans la maison du père. L'émergence du féminin dans la tradition littéraire du Québec*. Collection Littérature d'Amérique. Montréal: Québec/Amérique.

Socken, Paul. 1979. "Gabrielle Roy, an annotated bibliography." *The Annotated Bibliography of Canada's Major Authors* I, eds. R. Lecker and J. David, 213–61. Downsview, Ont.: ECW Press.

– 1982. *Concordance de "Bonheur d'occasion" de Gabrielle Roy*. Waterloo: University of Waterloo Press.

Stendhal. 1973. *Lucien Leuwen*. Édition éditée et annotée par Henri Martineau. Préface de Paul Valéry. 2 vols. Collection Folio. Paris: Gallimard.

Stratford, Philip. 1986. *All the Polarities. Comparative Studies in Contemporary Canadian Novels in French and English*. Toronto: ECW Press.

Sutherland, Ronald. 1971. *Second Image: Comparative Studies in Quebec/Canadian Literature*. Toronto: New Press.

– 1974. Introduction, *Dust Over the City*. Trans. John Latrobe and Robert Gottlieb. New Canadian Library 113. Toronto: McClelland & Stewart. no p.

– 1977. *The New Hero: Essays in Comparative Quebec/Canadian Literature*. Toronto: Macmillan.

Tardivel, Jules-Paul. 1975. *Pour la patrie; roman du XXᵉ siècle*. Présentation par John Hare. Collection Textes et Documents littéraires. Les Cahiers du Québec. Montréal: Hurtubise HMH. [First edition: Montréal: Cadieux et Derome, 1895.]

Tessier, Jules. 1982. "Le mythe des trois versions de *Menaud, maître-draveur*." *Revue d'histoire littéraire du Québec et du Canada français* 4: 83–90.

Thorne, W.B. 1968. "Poverty and wrath: a study of *The Tin Flute*." *Journal of Canadian Studies* 3 (3): 3–10.

Ullmann, Stephen. 1957. *Style in the French Novel*. Cambridge: Cambridge University Press.

Vanhee-Nelson, Louise. 1979. "Trois versions de *Menaud, maître-draveur*." *Essays on Canadian Writing* 15: 86–110.

"Variations sur le thème." 1988. *Communications* 47. [Conference papers collected by Claude Bremond and Thomas Pavel.]

Vernon, John. 1984. *Money and Fiction. Literary Realism in the Nineteenth and Early Twentieth Centuries*. Ithaca & London: Cornell University Press.

Vigneault, Robert, ed. 1977. *Langue, littérature, culture au Canada français*. Cahiers du CRCCF 12. Ottawa: Les Éditions de l'Université d'Ottawa.

Wadhams, Stephen, ed. 1984. *Remembering Orwell*. Introduction by George Woodcock. Markham, Ont.: Penguin Books Canada.

Whitfield, Agnès. 1987. *Le Je(u) illocutoire. Forme et contestation dans le nouveau roman québécois*. Centre de recherche en littérature québécoise. Vie des lettres québécoises 25. Québec: Les Presses de l'Université Laval.

Wilden, Anthony. 1980. *The Imaginary Canadian*. Vancouver: Pulp Press.

Williams, Raymond. 1984. *Orwell*. Flamingo. London: Fontana Paperbacks.

Zholkovsky, Alexander. 1984. *Themes and Texts. Toward a Poetics of Expressiveness*. Ithaca, N.Y.: Cornell University Press.

Index

Alternarrated. *See* Disnarrated
Amnesia, cultural, 96, 99, 153n9
Amprimoz, Alexandre, 78
Aphasia, 30–1
Aquin, Hubert: and Camus, 94; and compensatory function of literature, 88, 92–3, 95, 101, 103; and criticism in the 1980s, 84; and cultural amnesia, 96, 99, 153n9; and *enracinement,* 103–5; and fatigue (cultural and dialectic), xiii, 86–8, 92, 97, 100, 104; and Faye (history as narrative), 85; and Fontenelle, xv, 2, 104; and history, 83–6, 96–7, 105–6; and Langevin, 84; and Lord Durham, 84–5, 96; and Pascal, 86; and Rosenberg, 95–6; and Sartre, 98–9, 105–6, 137; and style, 103–6; and Trudeau, 85–7 passim. *See also Prochain épisode.*
Aubert de Gaspé, Philippe-Ignace-François, *L'Influence d'un livre,* 5, 9
Aubert de Gaspé, Philippe-Joseph, *Les Anciens Canadiens,* 5, 6, 141n7

Bachelard, Gaston, xiv
Bakhtin, M.M.: on epic distance, 19, 38, 145–6n12; on epic as genre, 145n11
Barth, John, *The Sot-Weed Factor,* 62
Barthes, Roland: on end-determination, xii; on French simple past, 113–14, 118; on literary institution, 15; on pleasure/bliss, 129–30; on readerly/writerly, 158n15
Baudrillard, Jean, 56–7
Beaudet, Marie-Andrée, 39
Beaugrand, Marie-Louise-Honoré, *Jeanne la fileuse,* 7, 141n6
Beaver, John, 76
Belleau, André: on conflict of codes, xi, 16, 82, 134, 136, 137; on literary institution, 15–16; on *Poussière sur la ville,* 82, 136
Benjamin, Walter: on storytelling and artisan class, 144n4; on storytelling and death, 78, 139–40n6
Berger, John, *G.,* 83, 108
Berthiaume, André, 105
Bérubé, Renald, 76
Bonheur d'occasion, xiii; and *Menaud,*